THE FORGOTTEN INSTRUCTION: THE ROMAN LITURGY, INCULTURATION, AND LEGITIMATE ADAPTATIONS

KENNETH J. MARTIN

LITURGY
TRAINING
PUBLICATIONS

The officially approved English translation of the Fourth Instruction, *Varietates legitimae,* appears with the kind permission of the Vatican in Rome, by the Congregation for Divine Worship and the Discipline of the Sacraments. This official Vatican translation is an updated version of the Vatican English text initially published in *Origins* 23 (1994): 745–56, from which the author cites in his analysis throughout this work.

THE FORGOTTEN INSTRUCTION: THE ROMAN LITURGY, INCULTURATION, AND LEGITIMATE ADAPTATIONS © 2007 Archdiocese of Chicago: Liturgy Training Publications, 1800 North Hermitage Avenue, Chicago IL 60622; 1-800-933-1800, fax 1-800-933-7094, e-mail orders@ltp.org. All rights reserved. See our Web site at www.LTP.org.

Printed in the United States of America.

Library of Congress Control Number: 2007920569

ISBN 978-1-56854-505-9
FORINS

To my grandparents and parents, whose love for
the Sacred Liturgy inspired me to write this book.

CONTENTS

TABLES

PREFACE

On Holy Thursday April 10, 2000, Pope John Paul II formally approved the *Missale Romanum* that contained a revised and enlarged *Institutio Generalis Missalis Romani*, or, as it is commonly know in English, *General Instruction of the Roman Missal.*[1] This third typical edition replaced both the *Second Typical Edition of the Roman Missal* (1974, Latin; 1975, English) and its accompanying instruction included at the beginning of what publishers in the United States (and elsewhere) labeled the *Sacramentary.* With the publication of the *Missale Romanum, editio typica tertia*, in 2002, the *Institutio Generalis* (with some corrections and revisions from the version that appeared in 2000) became the universal law of the Church to govern the correct and proper manner for celebrating the Eucharistic liturgy of the Roman rite.

The publication of the new instruction occasioned much speculation on the part of pastors, professors, and people involved with "liturgy." Questions about the document generally oscillated between two poles: Is this new general instruction an attempt to "roll back" some of the liturgical reforms of the Second Vatican Council? Or, is the publication of a new instruction on the proper way to celebrate Mass an attempt to correct some minor oversights that were not included in the 1975 General Instruction? Whatever the answer (and there is no dearth of them!), Roman Catholic liturgy will undoubtedly be affected by the most recent *Institutio Generalis* which, one can readily perceive, is much longer and more detailed than its predecessor.

In the pages that follow, however, it is not my intention to enter into a discussion of the merits or deficiencies of the new *Institutio Generalis*. Rather, I hope to offer a *point de départ* for those who struggle with the multicultural makeup of many Roman Catholic parishes under the heading of "inculturation." Any consideration of liturgical inculturation will necessarily

---

1. Congregatio de Cultu Divino et Disciplina Sacramentorum, Prot. N. 143/00/L, *Decretum de Editione Typica Tertia, in Missale Romanum, editio typica tertia* (Città del Vaticano: Typis Vaticanis, 2002). "Hanc editionem tertiam Missalis Romani Summus Pontifex IOANNES PAULUS II die 10 mensis aprilis 2000 auctoritate sua approbavit et Congregatio de Cultu Divino et Disciplina Sacramentorum nunc edit et typicam declarat."

require a thorough reading and comprehensive understanding of the prescriptions of the revised *Institutio Generalis* and, more importantly, of its completely new ninth chapter at the end of the document. The title of chapter nine reveals both the motivation for its inclusion as well as its intent: "Adaptations Within the Competence of Bishops and Bishops' Conferences" [*De Aptationibus Quae Episcopis Eorumque Conferentiis Competunt*]. The detailed explanation of the adaptations to be made by Conferences of Bishops in numbers 388–97 is recalled early on in the revised *Institutio Generalis* in numbers 25 and 26, replacing a seemingly broader mandate found in the 1975 version. These are compared below:

Institutio Generalis, *editio typica altera*	*Institutio Generalis,* *editio typica tertia*
Chapter I, "Importance and Dignity of the Eucharistic Celebration":	Chapter I, "The Importance and Dignity of the Eucharistic Celebration":
No. 6: "The purpose of this Instruction is to give the general guidelines for planning the eucharistic celebration properly and to set forth the rules for arranging the individual forms of celebration. In accord with the Constitution on the Liturgy, each conference of bishops has the power to lay down norms for its own territory that are suited to the traditions and character of peoples, regions, and various communities" [original capitalization maintained throughout].[2]	No. 25: "In addition, certain adaptations are indicated in the proper place in the Missal and pertain respectively to the diocesan Bishop or to the Conference of Bishops, in accord with the *Constitution on the Sacred Liturgy* (cf. nos. 387, 388–393)."
	No. 26: "As for variations and the more substantial adaptations in view of the traditions and culture of peoples and regions, to be introduced in accordance with article 40 of the *Constitution on the Sacred Liturgy* because of benefit or need, the norms set forth in the Instruction *On the Roman Liturgy and Inculturation* and in nos. 395–399 are to be observed."[3]

2. International Commission on English in the Liturgy, trans., *General Instruction of the Roman Missal, Fourth Edition*, 27 March 1975 (New York: Catholic Book Publishing Company, 1975), Chapter I, "Importance and Dignity of the Eucharistic Celebration," no. 6. [*Missale Romanum*, "Institutio Generalis Missalis Romani," *editio typica altera* (Città del Vaticano: Typis Polyglottis Vaticanis, 1975), Caput I: De Celebratione Eucharisticae Momento et Dignitate, no. 6: "Haec itaque Institutio eo spectat ut tum lineamenta

Where the 1975 *Institutio Generalis* ascribed to a Bishops' Conference a broad and ambiguous power to lay down norms for its own territory that are suited to the traditions and character of people, regions, and various communities, the revised and enlarged instruction is more specific, enumerating the particular and respective adaptations belonging to Bishops' Conferences and to the diocesan Bishop. These enumerations are followed by a reference to the more profound adaptations made in the light of the distinctive culture of the Church served by a particular episcopal conference. It is most noteworthy that number 26 of the new *Institutio Generalis* refers the readers to the "Fourth Instruction on the Correct Implementation of *Sacrosanctum Concilium* (nos. 37–40)," *On the Roman Liturgy and Inculturation*, the subject of our study in this book.

Furthermore, this ninth chapter of the new *Institutio Generalis* recalls that it falls to the diocesan Bishop to foster, govern, and watch over the liturgical life of his diocese, including the establishment of rules for concelebration, for assisting the priest at the altar, for the distribution of Holy Communion under both kinds, and for the construction and ordering of church building.[4] We are also reminded that the primary task of the diocesan Bishop remains to nourish priests, deacons, and the faithful with the spirit of the Sacred Liturgy.[5]

---

generalia praebeat, quibus Eucharistiae celebratio apte ordinetur, tum regulas exponat, quibus singulae celebrationis formae disponantur. Conferentiae autem Episcopales, iuxta Constitutionem de sacra Liturgia, normas pro sua dicione statuere possunt, quae ad traditiones et ingenium populorum, regionum et diversorum coetuum attendant."]

3. International Commission on English in the Liturgy, trans., *General Instruction of the Roman Missal*, in Liturgy Documentary Series 2 (Washington, DC: United States Conference of Catholic Bishops, 2003), Chapter I: "The Importance and Dignity of the Eucharistic Celebration," no. 25. Official Latin text in *Missale Romanum, editio typical tertia, "Institutio Generalis Missalis Romani"* (Città del Vaticano:Typis Vaticanis, 2002) ["Insuper in Missali suo loco aptationes quaedam innuuntur quae, iuxta Constitutionem de sacra Liturgia, respective competunt aut Episcopo dioecesano aut Conferentiae Episcoporum (cf. infra nn. 387, 388–393)." No. 26: "Quod autem ad varietates et adaptationes profundiores attinet, quae ad traditiones et ingenium populorum et regionum attendant, ad mentem art. 40 Constitutionis de sacra Liturgia pro utilitate vel necessitate introducendas, ea serventur quae in Instructione 'De Liturgia romana et inculturatione,' et infra (nn. 396–399) exponuntur."]

4. Cf. ibid., no. 387. ["Episcopus dioecesanus, qui ut sacerdos magnus sui gregis habendus est, a quo vita suorum fidelium in Christo quodammodo derivatur et pendet, vitam liturgicam fovere, moderari eique invigilare debet in sua diocesi. Ipsi, in hac Institutione, committitur concelebrationis disciplinam moderari (cf. nn. 202, 374), normas statuere circa munus inserviendi sacerdoti ad altare (cf. n. 107), circa sacram Communionem sub utraque specie distribuendam (cf. n. 238), circa domos ecclesiae exstruendas et ordinandas (cf. nn. 291, 315).]

5. Ibid. "Sed ad ipsum primarie spectat spiritum sacrae Liturgiae in presbyteris, diaconis et fidelibus alere."

The duties and responsibilities of the Conferences of Bishops ensue in numbers 389–93. First among these responsibilities is the preparation and approval of a vernacular edition of the *Roman Missal* so that once the *acta* have been given the *recognitio* of the Apostolic See, it may be used in the regions to which it is proper (no. 389).[6]

Other specific tasks for adaptation that are assigned to the Conferences of Bishops by the *Institutio Generalis* itself are then listed in number 390.[7] In the dioceses of the United States of America these items—which call specifically for adaptations on the part of a Conference of Bishops—had been incorporated traditionally into an *Appendix* to the *Institutio Generalis* of previous English language typical editions of the *Roman Missal*. However, number 390 allows the incorporation of approved adaptations directly into the text of the vernacular language version of the third typical edition of the *Institutio Generalis*.[8] The locations of these adaptations in the current typical edition of the *General Instruction of the Roman Missal* (English language version for use in the dioceses of the United States) are listed below for the convenience of the reader:

1. the posture of the faithful during the Eucharistic Prayer: no. 43;
2. the options for the Entrance Chant: no 48;
3. the options for the Responsorial Psalm: no. 61;
4. the options for the Communion Chant: no. 87;
5. the Sign of Peace: no. 154;
6. the posture and gesture of the faithful when receiving Holy Communion: no. 160;

---

6. Ibid., no. 390: "Ad Conferentias Episcoporum competit imprimis huius Missalis Romani editionem in probatis linguis vernaculis apparare atque approbare, ut actis ab Apostolica Sede recognitis, in regionibus ad quas pertinet adhibeatur."

7. Ibid. "fidelium gestus et corporis habitus (nn. 24, 25, 43, 160) [text corrected to include number 24]; gestus vererationis erga altare et Evangeliarium (n. 273); textus cantuum ad introitum, ad offertorium et ad communionem (nn. 48, 74, 87); lectiones e Sacra Scriptura peculiaribus in adiunctis desumendae (n. 362); forma pro pace tradenda (n. 82); modus sacrae communionis recipiendae (n. 160); materia altaris et sacrae supellectilis, praesertim sacrorum vasorum, necnon materia, forma et color vestium liturgicarum (nn. 301, 326, 329, 339, 342–343)."

8. Ibid, 390. "Directoria vero aut Instructiones pastorales, quas Conferentiae Episcoporum utiles iudicaverint, praevia Apostolicae Sedis recognitiae, in Missale Romanum, loco opportuno, induci poterunt." [Directories or pastoral instructions which the Conferences of Bishops judge useful may, with the prior *recognitio* of the Apostolic See, be introduced into the *Roman Missal* in a suitable location.]

7. the norms for the reception of Holy Communion under both kinds: no. 283;
8. the materials for fixed altars: no. 301;
9. the color of altar cloths: no. 304;
10. the materials for sacred furnishings: no. 326;
11. the materials for sacred vessels: no. 329;
12. the vesture for lay ministers: no. 339;
13. the color of sacred vestments: no. 346;
14. the readings for Mass: no. 362;
15. special days of prayer: no. 373;
16. musical instruments and the approval of musical settings: no. 393.

These same Conferences of Bishops are next exhorted (no. 391) to exercise special care regarding the translation of biblical texts in language that responds to the capacity for the faithful and is suitable for public proclamation—all the while maintaining those characteristics that are proper to the different manners of speaking employed in the biblical books.[9] Additionally, the Conferences of Bishops are charged with the careful preparation of a translation of other texts, in such a way that while respecting the nature of each language, the sense of the original Latin text is fully and faithfully rendered.[10]

Number 393 in this ninth chapter outlines a further duty of the Conferences of Bishops that was not included in the 1975 instruction; namely, that they are responsible for approving appropriate melodies, especially for the *Order of Mass*, for the people's responses and acclamations, and for the special rites that occur in the course of the liturgical year. Likewise, they may judge which musical forms, melodies, and musical instruments may be admitted into divine worship, provided that they are truly apt for sacred

---

9. Ibid., no. 391: "Iisdem Conferentiis spectat versionibus textuum biblicorum qui in Missae celebratione adhibentur, peculari cura attendere. . . . Sermo adhibeatur qui captui fidelium respondeat et publicae proclamationis aptus sit, notis tamen servatis quae propriae sunt diversis modis loquendi in libris biblicis adhibitis." In this regard, see also the *Fifth Instruction For the Right Implementation of the Constitution on the Sacred Liturgy, (Sacrosanctum Concilium, art. 36)," Liturgiam authenticam. [Instructio quinta ad exsecutionem Constitutionis Concilii Vaticani Secundi de sacra Liturgia recte ordinandam (ad. Const. Art. 36), "De usu linguarum popularium in libris liturgiae Romanae edendis."]* Available from http://www.vatican.va/roman_curia/congregations/ccdds/documents/rc_con_ccdds_doc_20010507_liturgiam-authenticam_lt.html.

10. Ibid., no. 392: "Item Conferertiarum Episcoporum erit versionem aliorum textuum assiduo studio apparare, ut, etiam servata indole cuisque linguae, sensus textus primigenii latini plene et fideliter reddatur."

use or can be rendered apt.[11] Number 394 reminds the Conferences of Bishops that they should collaborate, where possible, on the formation of a proper calendar for Mass, approved by the Holy See, and that in these same calendars, Rogation days and Ember days should also be indicated.[12]

Finally, numbers 395–99 of the new *Institutio* take up the question of more profound adaptations that fall under the competence of the Conferences of Bishops in order that the sacred celebration respond to the customs and traditions of different peoples. Within the short space of these four prescriptions in this document, the *Fourth Instruction*, i.e., *On the Roman Liturgy and Inculturation*, is cited seven times, regarding the principles and practical norms for inculturation of the Roman rite and the areas of adaptation in the Roman rite.[13]

Moreover, as this book goes to the printer, the "Post Synodal Apostolic Exhortation, *Sacramentum Caritatis*, Of The Holy Father Benedict XVI To The Bishops, Clergy, Consecrated Persons And The Lay Faithful On The Eucharist As The Source And Summit Of The Church's Life And Mission" has recently been made available by the Vatican on the Internet.[14] In the Second Part of his exhortation, under the heading of "The Structure of the Eucharistic Celebration," more particularly in

---

11. Ibid., no. 393. ". . . Conferentiarom Episcoporum est melodias aptas approbare, praesertim pro textibus Ordinarii Missae pro populi responsionibus et acclamationibus, et pro peculiaribus ritibus per annum liturgicum occurrentibus. Item iudicare quasnam formas musicales, melodias, instrumenta musica in cultum divinum admittere liceat, quatenus usui sacro vere apta sin vel aptari possint."

12. Ibid., no. 394: "Conferentia vero episcoporum, pro sua parte, conficiat calendarium proprium nationis, vel una cum aliis Conferentiis, calendarium amplioris dicionis, ab Apostolica Sede approbandum. . . . In calendario nationis conficiendo, dies indicentur Rogationum e Quattuor anni Temporum et formae et textus ad illas celebrandas. . . ."

13. Ibid. The *Fourth Instruction* is cited in the *Institutio Generalis* as follows: Number 395: *Fourth Instruction*, nos. 54, 62–69; 66–68; number 397: *Fourth Instruction*, nos. 26–27; 2, 36; number 398: *Fourth Instruction*, nos. 46 and 36, respectively; number 399: *Fourth Instruction*, no. 54.

14. Benedicti PP XVI, Summi Pontificis, "Adhortatio Apostolica Postsynodalis *Sacramentum Caritatis* Ad Episcopos Sacerdotes Consacratos Consacratasque Necnon Cristifideles Laicos De Eucharistia Missionisque Ecclesiae Fonte et Culmine," die XXII mensis Februarii, in festo Cathedrae Sancti Petri Apostoli, anno MMVII: http://www.vatican.va/holy_father/benedict_xvi/apost_exhortations/documents/hf_ben-xvi_exh_20070222_sacramentum-caritatis_lt.html. [Benedict XVI, Supreme Pontiff, "Post Synodal Apostolic Exhortation, *Sacramentum Caritatis*, Of The Holy Father Benedict XVI To The Bishops, Clergy, Consecrated Persons And The Lay Faithful On The Eucharist As The Source And Summit Of The Church's Life And Mission," 22 February on the feast of The Chair of Saint Peter, Apostle, 2007: http://www.vatican.va/holy_father/benedict_xvi/apost_exhortations/documents/hf_ben-xvi_exh_20070222_sacramentum-caritatis_en.html].

a section devoted to "Authentic Participation," and specifically, "The Eucharistic Celebration and Inculturation,"[15] His Holiness Pope Benedict XVI made the following observation about the importance of the *Fourth Instruction* and inculturation as it is related to the celebration of the eucharistic liturgy:

> A more effective participation of the faithful in the holy mysteries will thus benefit from the continued inculturation of the eucharistic celebration, with due regard for the possibilities for adaptation provided in the *General Instruction of the Roman Missal*, interpreted in the light of the criteria laid down by the Fourth Instruction of the Congregation for Divine Worship and the Discipline of the Sacraments *Varietates Legitimae* of 25 January 1994.[16]

It is, therefore, of the utmost importance that the *Fourth Instruction* be studied thoroughly so that the new *Institutio* and the most recent Apostolic Exhortation be seen not as a "bolts out of the blue" but rather as consistent, logical developments of the Church's official teaching on inculturation and liturgical adaptation. It is with this purpose in mind that this book is presented.

---

15. Ibid. Pars Altera Eucharistia, Mysterium Celebrandum: Celebrationis eucharisticae structura: "Acutosa Participatio," Celebratio Eucharistica et inculturatio.

16. Ibid., no. 53: "Quapropter ad efficaciorem fidelium in sacris Mysteriis participationem utile est provehere inculturationis processum in ambitu Celebrationis eucharisticae, prae oculis habitis accommodationis facultatibus in *Institutione Generali Missalis Romani* contentis, quas interpretari oportet secundum praescripta, quae IV Instructio *Varietates legitimae,* die XXV mensis Ianuarii anno MCMXCIV evulgata, Congregationis de Cultu Divino et Disciplina Sacramentorum."

ABBREVIATIONS

AAS	*Acta Apostolicae Sedis*
BCL	Bishops' Committee on the Liturgy
CIC	*Codex Iuris Canonici*
CDWDS	Congregation for Divine Worship and the Discipline of the Sacraments
DOL	*Documents on the Liturgy 1963–1979: Conciliar, Papal, and Curial Text*
GS	*Gaudium et Spes*
ICEL	International Commission on English in the Liturgy
OCM, 1969	*Ordo celebrandi Matrimonium,* editio typica, 1969[1]
OCM, 1991	*Ordo celebrandi Matrimonium,* editio typica altera, 1991
OI	*Ordo Unctionis infirmorum eorumque pastoralis curae*
OE	*Ordo exsequiarum*
SC	*Sacrosanctum Concilium*
SCCD	Sacra Congregatio pro Cultu Divino
SRC	Sacra Rituum Congregatio
USCC	United States Catholic Conference

---

1. In this work, the capitalization of the Latin titles of the rites follows the capitalization of same in the decree of promulgation of the *editiones typicae.* The capitalization of the Latin titles of other documents and writings follows the capitalization of same in the AAS. All other titles follow the rules for capitalization found in Kate L. Turabian, *A Manual for Writers of Term Papers, Theses, and Dissertations* 6th edition, rev. and ed. by John Grossman and Alice Bennett (Chicago: The University of Chicago Press, 1996), 64–68. Finally, although some of the abbreviations above appear in italics in the second column, during the past few decades abbreviations have been used increasingly in the literature of this field of study both in the text and footnotes without italics. I will follow the more recent practice in this work.

CHAPTER I

THE CHURCH, MODERN CULTURE, AND LITURGY: *SACROSANCTUM CONCILIUM* AND LITURGICAL INCULTURATION

PRELIMINARY OBSERVATIONS

With the publication of *Sacrosanctum Concilium* on December 4, 1963, the Roman Catholic Church ushered in a new era of liturgical reform and renewal. Ritual conformity to language, postures, and gestures in liturgical celebrations, mainstays of worldwide Roman Catholic worship since the time of Pius V in the latter part of the sixteenth century, yielded to a new way of commemorating the mysteries of salvation history. Latin gave way to the vernacular; altars were turned around, and priest celebrants faced their congregations. The congregation that attended Mass in a passive and generally silent manner was transformed into the fully active and conscious assembly which celebrated the liturgy. In short, the content and form of ritual worship in the Roman Catholic Church were considerably modified and corrected.

Beginning with a brief presentation of the opinions of some *periti* regarding the encounter between the Church and the modern world occasioned by the Second Vatican Council, the first chapter will examine *Sacrosanctum Concilium* as the backdrop for the 1994 document from the Vatican Congregation for Divine Worship and the Discipline of the Sacraments: *On The Roman Liturgy and Inculturation: Fourth Instruction for the Right Application of the Conciliar Constitution on the Liturgy (Nos. 37–40).*[1]

---

1. Congregatio de Cultu Divino et Disciplina Sacramentorum (hereafter CDWDS), *De Liturgia Romana et inculturatione: Instructio quarta "Ad exsecutionem Constitutionis Concilii Vaticani Secundi de sacra Liturgia recte ordinandam," (ad. Const. art 37–40)*, [also referred to as *De Liturgia Romana et inculturatione* and *Varietates Legitimae*] *Notitiae* 30 (1994): 80–115. [Congregation for Divine Worship and the Discipline of the Sacraments, *On The Roman Liturgy and Inculturation: "Fourth Instruction for the Right Application of the Conciliar Constitution on the Liturgy" (Nos. 37–40) Origins* 23 (1994): 745–56.] The official Latin text was published in 1995 in *Acta Apostolicae Sedis* (hereafter AAS) 87 (1995): 288–314. In subsequent citations of textual references from the first three instructions on the proper implementation of *Sacrosanctum Concilium*, the Latin title of the respective instruction will be mentioned. Since the *Fourth Instruction* (unlike the three previous instructions) has its own title; namely, "On The Roman Liturgy and Inculturation," in order to focus on

After considering, albeit briefly, the necessary link between the universal Church and the local church, we will then present pertinent quotations from *Sacrosanctum Concilium*[2] as the basis for liturgical inculturation. Numbers 37–40 of the liturgical constitution present the norms for adapting the liturgy to the customs, native character, and traditions of the people. After examining the prescriptions contained in the numbers mentioned above, we will conclude with a review of important Latin vocabulary terms dealing with adaptation of the liturgy.

THE CHURCH AND MODERN CULTURE

In the years immediately following the end of the Second Vatican Council and continuing into more recent times, several prominent *periti*, most of whom were present as advisers at many of the sessions of Vatican II, commented on various aspects of *Sacrosanctum Concilium* and on the renewed dialog between the Church and modern culture which this document occasioned.[3] French liturgist P.-M. Gy, for example, noted that the publication of *Sacrosanctum Concilium* occasioned a renewed tension between liturgy and culture. Gy proposed that the liturgical constitution

---

similarities and differences between the three earlier instructions and the most recent instruction, the latter will usually be referred to as the *Fourth Instruction* in the body of this work and as *De Liturgia Romana et inculturatione* in the footnotes. The actual date for the issuance of this instruction appears at the end of the document (in the Appendix) and is January 25, 1994, the feast of the Conversion of Saint Paul, Apostle. The instruction appeared in print in several languages on March 24, 1994.

2. Vatican Council II, *Constitution on the Sacred Liturgy, Sacrosanctum Concilium,* [hereafter SC] in Norman P. Tanner, SJ, English ed., *Decrees of the Ecumenical Councils,* vol. 2, *Trent to Vatican II* (London: Sheed and Ward, 1990), 820–49. Subsequent quotations in Latin from conciliar documents are from the Tanner edition. English citations are from Tanner unless a more familiar translation appears in *Documents on the Liturgy 1963–1979: Conciliar, Papal, and Curial Texts,* trans. and ed. Thomas C. O'Brien of the International Commission on English in the Liturgy [hereafter ICEL] Secretariat (Collegeville, MN: The Liturgical Press, 1982). In these instances, the abbreviation DOL will indicate the use of this volume.

3. See, for example, Josef Jungmann in *Commentary on the Documents of Vatican II,* ed. Herbert Vorgrimler (New York: Herder and Herder, 1967), 1:1–87; Yves Congar, OP, "The Role of the Church in the Modern World," in ibid., 5:202–223; Annibale Bugnini, *The Reform of the Liturgy 1948–1975,* trans. Matthew J. O'Connell (Collegeville, MN: The Liturgical Press, 1990), 29–53; Y. Congar, OP, "L' 'Ecclesia' ou communauté chrétienne, sujet intégral de l'action liturgique," in *La liturgie après Vatican II: Bilans, Études, prospective,* ed. J.-P. Jossua and Y. Congar, Unam Sanctam 66 (Paris: Les Éditions du Cerf, 1967), P.-M. Gy, OP, "Situation historique de la Constitution," in ibid., 111–26; J.-P. Jossua, OP, "La Constitution *Sacrosanctum Concilium* dans l'ensemble de l'oeuvre conciliaire," in ibid., 127–56; and Karl Rahner, "Towards A Fundamental Theological Interpretation of Vatican II," *Theological Studies* 40 (1979): 716–27.

contained within itself a dual intentionality: a) on the one hand, to conserve and honor the spiritual and cultural heritage of the West which, up to now, had been preserved in the Roman liturgy; and b) to make the liturgy an expression of the active, contemporary relationship between the God being worshipped and the people of God doing the worshipping.[4]

J.-P. Jossua, another distinguished French liturgical scholar, saw an expression of a similar tension between the classic vision of Christian experience expressed in *Sacrosanctum Concilium* and the new aspirations and larger perspectives contained in a related conciliar document, *Gaudium et Spes (Pastoral Constitution on the Church in the Modern World)*.[5]

An important statement about the interaction among Church, culture, and liturgy occurs in *Gaudium et Spes*, article 58:

> Thus, in fulfilling its particular charge [i.e., evangelization], the church thereby encourages and contributes to human and social culture, and by its activity, *including the liturgy* (emphasis added), it educates people to inner freedom.[6]

It is indeed to be expected that subsequent intercourse between the modern world, its culture, and the Church occur in the ritual celebrations of the liturgical life of the Church.

THE LOCAL CHURCH, LITURGY, AND CULTURE

In more recent years, some theologians, focusing especially on the cultural diversity that exists within the Roman Catholic communion, have turned their attention to this interaction between

---

4. Cf. P.-M. Gy, "Situation historique de la Constitution," 124: "La Constitution conciliaire affirme à plusieurs reprises à la fois la volonté de rendre à nouveau la liturgie capable d'exprimer l'un à l'autre le Seigneur et l'homme de notre temps, et la volonté de conserver et d'honorer la part de l'héritage spirituel et culturel de l'Occident dont la liturgie romaine est dépositaire. Ces deux volontés ou ces deux intentions, sont-elles compatibles, et la fidélité à la deuxième (fidélité qui est quasi une composante du rôle historique du Siège romain) risque-t-elle de faire échec à la première?"

5. Cf. J.-P. Jossua, "La Constitution dans l'oeuvre conciliaire," 149: "Une tension plus sensible encore et plus générale nous semble se manifester entre la classique vision de l'expérience chrétienne qui s'exprime dans la Constitution liturgique, et les aspiration nouvelles, les perspectives plus larges dont *Gaudium et Spes* en particulier s'est fait l'écho."

6. Vatican Council II, *Pastoral Constitution on the Church in the World of Today, Gaudium et Spes* (hereafter GS), in Tanner, 1069–1135, no. 58: "Sic ecclesia, proprium implendo munus, iam eo ipso ad humanum civilemque cultum impellit atque confert, et actione sua, *etiam liturgica* (emphasis added) hominem ad interiorem libertatem educat."

liturgy and culture.[7] Other contemporary Roman Catholic theologians, such as David N. Power, OMI, Patrick Granfield, OSB, and Joseph Komonchak, have examined the relationship between the universal Church and the local church and the subsequent implications for ecclesiology and liturgy.[8] In an essay that appeared first in *East Asian Pastoral Review* in 1984,[9] later published in his 1990 collection of essays entitled *Worship: Culture and Theology,* David Power observed that while a traveler might venture to a number of countries and experience a wide a variety of local

---

7. A comprehensive bibliography on this topic is beyond the scope of the present work. Suffice it to mention here, several contemporary scholars and some selected works in English: Aylward Shorter, *Toward a Theology of Inculturation* (Maryknoll, NY: Orbis Books, 1988); Peter Schineller, *A Handbook on Inculturation* (New York: Paulist Press, 1990); Stephen Bevans, SVD, *Models of Contextual Theology,* Faith and Culture Series (New York: Orbis Books, 1992), especially 42–46; 60–62; and 92–96; Chris Nwaka Egbulem, OP, "An African Interpretation of Liturgical Inculturation: The *Rite Zaïrois,*" in *A Promise of Presence: Studies In Honor Of David N. Power, OMI,* ed. Michael Downey and Richard Fragomeni (Washington, DC: The Pastoral Press, 1992), 227–50; Anthony Kain, "My Son's Bread": About Culture, Language and Liturgy," in ibid., 251–67; the bibliography on Power's writings pertaining to "Worship and Culture," in ibid., 317–19; Anscar Chupungco, OSB, *Cultural Adaptation of the Liturgy* (NY: Paulist Press, 1982); id., *Liturgies of the Future: The Process and Methods of Inculturation* (New York: Paulist Press, 1989); id., *Liturgical Inculturation: Sacramentals, Religiosity and Catechesis* (Collegeville, MN: The Liturgical Press, 1992); id., "Liturgical Inculturation and the Search for Unity," in *So We Believe, So We Pray: Towards Koinonia in Worship,* ed. Thomas F. Best and Darmar Heller, Faith and Order Paper No. 171 (Geneva: WCC Publications, 1996: 55–64).

8. See, for example, Giuseppe Alberigo, Jean-Pierre Jossua, and Joseph A. Komonchak, eds., *The Reception of Vatican II,* trans. Matthew J. O'Connell (Washington, DC: The Catholic University of America Press, 1987). Chapter 5 by Komonchak, "The Local Realization of the Church," is an excellent analysis of the implications of seeing the Church not as an abstract, universal concept but as a vibrant reality actualized within and by the local celebrations of the particular churches which make up a community. Komonchak and others see the ecclesiology introduced in *Lumen Gentium, Sacrosanctum Concilium,* and *Christus Dominus* as "something of a Copernican revolution in ecclesiology (loc. cit., 78)." See also Komonchak, "The Theology of the Local Church: State of the Question," in *The Multicultural Church: A New Landscape in U. S. Theologies,* ed. William Cenkner, OP. (New York: Paulist Press, 1996), 35–49, where Komonchak assesses more recent Roman concern about a priority of the local church over the universal Church, especially in basic Christian communities. In addition, see Downey and Fragomeni, 316–17 for Power's writings pertaining to "Worship: Theology, History, Interpretation"; and, Patrick Granfield, OSB, *The Limits of the Papacy: Authority and Autonomy in the Church* (New York: Crossroad, 1990). Granfield's chapter 5, "The Church of Rome and the local Church," is also an informative analysis of the tension between the universal and local church and how this tension has been perceived in recent, i.e., late nineteenth-century Church history as well as after the Second Vatican Council.

9. David N. Power, OMI, "Liturgy and Culture," *East Asian Pastoral Review* 4 (1984): 348–60. This essay forms the basis for chapter 5 in *Worship: Culture and Theology.* The citations that follow are taken from the 1990 publication and not the original essay. See David N. Power, OMI, *Worship: Culture and Theology* (Washington, DC: The Pastoral Press, 1990). The bibliographical references in Downey and Fragomeni (above) reveal that Power contributed significantly to the study of the relationships between church and world, liturgy and culture.

cultures, such diversity did not prevail in the liturgical celebrations.[10] In fact, observed Power, a rather homogenous liturgical experience might greet the visitor no matter what the country![11] Power's summary observation about this interrelationship between culture and liturgy merits closer attention:

> This experience of cultural diversity contrasts sharply with the apparent homogeneity of most liturgical celebrations throughout the world. Even given such differences as that in one place the assembly are seated on benches and in another on the floor, one gets the impression of a common liturgical pattern universally repeated in slightly different colors.[12]

The preceding observation by Power demonstrates the necessity for understanding the terminology of evangelical and liturgical inculturation,[13] i.e., how the Gospel was initially preached and received within a respective culture and how the local church continues to celebrate its belief in the Gospel in liturgical worship.

In January of 1994, the Vatican Congregation for Divine Worship and the Discipline of the Sacraments issued a document entitled *On The Roman Liturgy and Inculturation: Fourth Instruction for the Right Application of the Conciliar Constitution on the Liturgy (Nos. 37–40)*. This recent *Fourth Instruction* highlights some areas within liturgical celebrations that it proposes to regulate: language, music, gesture, and posture.[14] These elements of ritual worship will necessarily be incorporated into the liturgical life of their respective local churches in a variety of ways reflecting the same variety of cultures. And yet, the *Fourth Instruction* also envisions that the substantial unity of the Roman rite should be maintained [*inculturationis processus perficiendus est Ritus romani **unitate substantiali** (original emphasis) servata*], that inculturation does not imply the creation of new families of rites [*inculturationis inquisitio non contendit ad novas familias rituales creandas*], and finally, that any cultural adaptations remain

---

10. Power, *Worship: Culture and Theology*, 67.

11. Ibid.

12. Ibid.

13. The introduction of the term *inculturation* at this juncture in no way implies that the term appears in the documents of Vatican II. In fact, it is notably absent from *Sacrosanctum Concilium* and related documents. The importance of this term will be considered later.

14. Cf., CDWDS, *De Liturgia Romana et inculturatione*, nos. 39, 40, and 41.

part of the Roman rite [*consulens autem culturae datae exigentiis, aptationes inducit, quae semper pars manent Ritus romani*].[15]

It would appear, then, that an examination of *Sacrosanctum Concilium* might serve both as the starting point and background for any consideration of the question of inculturation within the liturgy. As this work progresses, significant opinions from theologians and from Pope John Paul II regarding the term *inculturation* will also be examined to determine their relationship to the process of inculturation within the liturgy.

Before examining *Sacrosanctum Concilium* as a basis for liturgical inculturation, however, it must be acknowledged that *Sacrosanctum Concilium* and other documents from the Second Vatican Council are written for the Roman Catholic Church. Thus, when the words *liturgy, Church, rite(s)*, and so on are used herein, their reference is to the Roman Catholic context and not to a broader one, unless specified by the writer. In addition, the word *liturgy* throughout this work is not to be equated merely with the celebration of the Eucharist but is to be understood as encompassing all that belongs to liturgical celebration.

SACROSANCTUM CONCILIUM: THE BASIS FOR LITURGICAL ADAPTATION

The importance that *Sacrosanctum Concilium* ascribes to the liturgical celebration as essential to the life of the universal and local church can never be underestimated. For example, from the opening numbers of the liturgical constitution, one finds statements such as "The liturgy is each day building up those who are within into a holy temple in the Lord, into a dwelling place for

---

15. Ibid., no. 36. It is interesting to note that the references cited above refer in the *Fourth Instruction* itself to SC 37–40 and to John Paul II's address on January 26, 1991 to the plenary assembly of the Congregation for Divine Worship and the Discipline of the Sacraments: "This is not to suggest to the particular churches that they have a new task to undertake following the application of liturgical reform, that is to say, adaptation or inculturation. Nor is it intended to mean inculturation as a creation of alternative rites. . . . It is a question of collaborating so that the Roman Rite, maintaining its own identity, may incorporate suitable adaptations" (Ibid., footnote 77). Cf. Ioannis Pauli, "Allocutio ad eos qui plenario coetui Congregationis de Cultu Divino et Disciplina Sacramentorum interfuerunt," AAS 83 (1991): 940: "Il senso di tale indicazione non è di proporre alle Chiese particolari l'inizio di un nuovo lavoro, successivo all'applicazione della riforma liturgica, che sarebbe l'adattamento o l'inculturazione. E neppure è da intendersi l'inculturazione come creazione di riti alternativi. . . Si tratta, pertanto di collaborare affinché il rito romano, pur mantenendo la propria identità, possa accogliere gli opportuni adattamenti."

God in the Spirit, until they reach the stature of the age of Christ's fullness. . . ."[16] In addition, it is Christ present in the worshipping assembly, in the Word of God proclaimed within its midst, in the presiding minister, in the eucharistic species and the sacraments which show that "every liturgical celebration, inasmuch as it is the act of Christ the priest and his body which is the church, is above all an activity of worship. No other activity of the church equals it in terms of its official recognition or its degree of effectiveness."[17]

These same ideas are echoed later in *Sacrosanctum Concilium* in what is perhaps the most frequently quoted section of the constitution: "The liturgy is, all the same, the high point towards which the activity of the Church is directed, and, simultaneously, the source from which all its power flows out."[18] Since the manner in which people worship not only expresses their faith but also contributes to the building up of that same faith, participation in the liturgical celebrations of the Church is an important consideration in any discussion of inculturation. In setting out the principle that participation is not only desirable but also quite essential, *Sacrosanctum Concilium* states: "The church very much wants all believers to be led to take a full, conscious, and active participation in liturgical celebration. This is demanded by the very nature 'of the liturgy itself.'"[19] This principle is so important that only a few lines later, it is restated with even more vigor: This full active sharing on the part of the whole people is of paramount concern in the process of renewing the liturgy and helping it to grow, because such sharing is the first and necessary source from which believers can imbibe the true Christian spirit.[20]

When number 41 of *Sacrosanctum Concilium* states that the liturgical life of the diocese centered around the bishop (i.e.,

---

16. SC, no. 2: ". . . cum liturgia eos qui intus sunt cotidie aedificet in templum sanctum in Domino, in habitaculum Dei in Spiritu, usque ad mensuram aetatis plenitudinis Christi."

17. Ibid., no. 7: ". . . omnis liturgica celebratio, utpote opus Christi sacerdotis eiusque corporis quod est ecclesia, est actio sacra praecellenter, cuius efficacitatem eodemque titulo eodemque gradu nulla alia actio ecclesiae adaequat."

18. Ibid., no. 10: ". . . Attamen liturgia est culmen ad quod actio ecclesiae tendit et simul fons unde omnis eius virtus emanat."

19. Ibid., no. 14: "Valde cupit mater ecclesia ut fideles universi ad plenam illam, consciam, atque actuosam liturgicarum celebrationum participationem ducantur, quae ab ipsius liturgiae natura postulatur."

20. Ibid. ". . . Quae totius populi plena et actuosa participatio, in instauranda et fovenda sacra liturgia, summopere est attendenda: est enim primus, isque necessarius fons, e quo spiritum vere christianum fideles hauriant; et ideo in tota actione pastorali, per debitam institutionem, ab animarum pastoribus est sedulo adpetenda."

the diocesan bishop) in the cathedral church should be held in the highest regard, it nevertheless repeats the importance of the participation of all present in such celebrations:

> Therefore, everyone should regard the liturgical life of the diocese centering on the bishop, above all in the cathedral church, as of the highest importance. They should be convinced that the church is displayed with special clarity when the holy people of God, all of them, are actively and fully sharing in the same liturgical celebrations—especially when it is the same eucharist—sharing one prayer at one altar, at which the bishop is presiding, surrounded by his presbyterate and his ministers.[21]

Number 50 also repeats this important principle: "There is to be a revision of the way the Mass is structured so that the specific ideas behind the individual parts and their connection with one another can be more clearly apparent, and so that it becomes easier for the people to take a proper and active part."[22] This prescription raises one of the main issues to be dealt with in liturgical inculturation: how the rites are to be revised.

The importance of the revision of the rites for the liturgy occupies a primary place in *Sacrosanctum Concilium*. In number four of the liturgical constitution we read: "Moreover, where necessary, it (the Council) wants them (the rites) to be revised carefully in the light of sound tradition, and to be given new vigor in order to meet today's circumstances and needs."[23] Lest so important a principle as the revision of the rites be misguided or unfocused, *Sacrosanctum Concilium* further refines how such revision may take place in number 34, stating: "the rites should radiate a rich simplicity; they should be brief and lucid, avoiding pointless repetitions; they should be intelligible to the people and should not in general require much explanation."[24] The shift

---

21. Ibid., no. 41: "Quare omnes vitam liturgicam dioeceseos circa episcopum, praesertim in ecclesia cathedrali, maximi faciant oportet: sibi persuasum habentes praecipuam manifestationem ecclesiae haberi in plenaria et actuosa participatione totius plebis sanctae Dei in iisdem celebrationibus liturgicis, praesertim in eadem eucharistia, in una oratione, ad unum altare cui praeest episcopus a suo presbyterio et ministris circumdatus."

22. Ibid., no. 50: "Ordo missae ita recognoscatur, ut singularum partium propria ratio necnon mutua connexio clarius pateant, atque pia et actuosa fidelium participatio facilior reddatur."

23. Ibid., no. 4: ". . . atque potat ut, ubi opus sit, caute ex integro ad mentem sanae traditionis recognoscantur et novo vigore, pro hodiernis adiunctis et necessitatibus donentur."

24. Ibid., no. 34: "Ritus nobili simplicitate fulgeant, sint brevitate perspicui et repetitiones inutiles evitent, sint fidelium captui accommodati, necque generatim multis indigeant explanationibus."

from Latin to the vernacular in liturgical celebrations was probably the first concrete implementation of this principle.[25] Some simplification of the liturgical celebrations, however, preceded the use of the vernacular.

ADAPTATION OF THE LITURGY: TERMINOLOGY AND PRINCIPLES

Numbers 37–40 of *Sacrosanctum Concilium* present the norms for adapting the liturgy to the native character and traditions of people in the section entitled *"Normae ad aptationem ingenio et traditionibus populorum perficiendam."* These four numbers in the liturgical constitution form the basis for any discussion of liturgical adaptation and/or inculturation. As with many other documents, sometimes the best hermeneutic for interpretation is found in the document itself. Thus, numbers 37–40 of *Sacrosanctum Concilium* need to be interpreted in light of the principles stated in *Sacrosanctum Concilium* numbers 21–23; namely, 1) the liturgy is made up of changeable and unchangeable elements;[26] 2) regulation of the liturgy depends on the authority of the Apostolic See and, as law permits, on the local bishop;[27] 3) in order that healthy tradition may be preserved while yet allowing room for legitimate development, a thorough investigation—theological, historical, and pastoral—of the individual parts of the liturgy to be revised is always done first;[28] and finally, 4) changes should not be made unless a real and proven need of the Church requires them, and new forms grow organically in some way out of those already in existence.[29]

In addition, numbers 37–40 introduce a terminology which will occur again in the first three postconciliar instructions on the proper implementation of *Sacrosanctum Concilium;* namely, *Inter*

---

25. See SC, nos. 26, 54, 118.

26. Ibid., no. 21: ". . . Nam liturgia constat parte immutabili, utpote divinitus instituta et partibus mutationi obnoxiis."

27. Ibid., no. 22:1: "Sacrae liturgiae moderatio ab ecclesiae auctoritate unice pendet: quae quidem est apud apostolicam sedem, et ad normam iuris, apud episcopum."

28. Ibid., no. 23: "Ut sana traditio retineatur et tamen via legitime progressioni aperiatur, de singulis liturgiae partibus recognoscendis accurata investigatio theologica, historica, pastoralis semper praecedat."

29. Ibid. ". . . Innovationes, demum, ne fiant nisi vera et certa utilitas ecclesiae id exigat et adhibita cautela ut novae formae ex formis iam exstantibus organice quodammodo crescant."

oecumenici (1964);[30] *Tres abhinc annos* (1967);[31] and, *Liturgicae instaurationes* (1970).[32] The Latin title that precedes numbers 37–40 in *Sacrosanctum Concilium* presents the first important term, *aptatio*, in the accusative singular: *aptationem*. Numbers 38[33] and 39[34] each contain one use in the ablative and accusative plural respectively, while number 40 presents the term in four distinct places. Although what follows may appear to be a rather lengthy inclusion from *Sacrosanctum Concilium*, the repeated use of the Latin term *aptatio* in number 40 below, rendered as "adaptation(s)" in the English translation, merits close attention. The entire citation is included here for the reader's convenience:

> However, in some places or in some situations, there may arise a pressing need for a more profound [translation corrected] adaptation of the liturgy. This will turn out to be more difficult. Wherefore:
>
> 1. The competent, territorial ecclesiastical authority mentioned in art. 22 § 2 should carefully and consciously consider which elements from the traditions and natural character of individual peoples can be brought appropriately into divine worship. Adaptations which are judged useful or necessary should be proposed to the apostolic see, and introduced with its consent.
>
> 2. In order that the adaptation be made with the necessary and careful consideration, the apostolic see will, if necessary, give to the territorial ecclesiastical authority mentioned above the power to allow and direct the necessary prior experimentation for a fixed period of time among certain gatherings suitable for this purpose.
>
> 3. Because liturgical laws often involve special difficulties with respect to *adaptation* (emphasis added), particularly in mission

30. Sacra Rituum Congregatio (hereafter, SRC), "Instructio (prima)," *Inter oecumenici* AAS 56 (1964): 877–900. [The ICEL translation may be found in DOL 23, nos. 293–391.]

31. SRC, "Instructio altera," *Tres abhinc annos* AAS 59 (1967): 442–48. [The ICEL translation may be found in DOL 39, nos. 445–74.]

32. Sacra Congregatio pro Cultu Divino, (hereafter SCCD), "Instructio tertia," *Liturgicae instaurationes* AAS 62 (1970): 692–704. [The ICEL translation may be found in DOL 52, nos. 509–31.]

33. SC, no. 38: "Provided that the fundamental unity of the Roman rite is preserved, room is to be left, even when the books used in the liturgy are revised, for legitimate variations and *adaptations* (emphasis added) to meet the needs of different gatherings, areas, and peoples, especially in mission territories." ["Servata substantiali unitate ritus romani, legitimis varietatibus et *aptationibus* (emphasis added) ad diversos coetus, regiones, populos, praesertim in missionibus, locus relinquatur."]

34. SC, no. 39: "Within limits to be laid down in the standard editions of the books used in the liturgy, it will be the job of the competent local church authority (see article 22, section 2) to specify *adaptations* (emphasis added). . . ." ["Intra limites in editionibus typicis librorum liturgicorum statutos, erit competentis auctoritatis ecclesiasticae territorialis, de qua in art, 22, 2, *aptationes* (emphasis added) definire."]

lands, experts [*viri*] in these matters must be employed to formulate them.[35]

The repeated use of *adaptation(s)* in the citation above is of utmost importance in this section of the liturgical constitution. In the first place, there is an explicit acknowledgment in this number that the current liturgical rites may need "an even more profound adaptation." Commenting on this fact as well as on the truly exceptional nature of this inclusion in *Sacrosanctum Concilium,* the Italian scholar R. Falsini observes that number 40 also contains within itself both the implicit (albeit distant) possibility of new rites slowly emerging as well as the potential for future difficulties in the area of liturgical adaptation.[36] Falsini also considers the inclusion of this article in *Sacrosanctum Concilium* as both courageous and revolutionary, corresponding to the true nature of Christianity's being enfleshed in every people and land.[37] Finally, he concludes that the inclusion of number 40 is reminiscent of the ancient Church's long-standing liturgical tradition, especially during the first millennium, of accommodating the tradition to the various people with whom the Church came into contact.[38]

---

35. SC, no. 40: "Cum tamen variis in locis et adiunctis, *profundior liturgiae aptatio urgeat* (emphasis added), et ideo difficilior evadat: (1) A competenti auctoritate ecclesiastica territoriali, de qua in art 22, 2, sedulo et prudenter consideretur, quid, hoc in negotio, ex traditionibus ingenioque singulorum populorum opportune in cultum divinum admitti possit. *Aptationes* (emphasis added) quae utiles vel necessariae existimantur, apostolicae sedi proponantur, de ipsius consensu introducendae. (2) Ut autem *aptatio* (emphasis added) cum necessaria circumspectione fiat, eidem auctoritati ecclesiasticae territoriali ab apostolica sede facultas tribuetur, si casus ferat, ut in quibusdam coetibus ad id aptis et per determinatum tempus necessaria praevia experimenta permittat et dirigat. (3) Quia leges liturgicae difficultates speciales, quoad *aptationem* (emphasis added) praesertim in missionibus, secum ferre solent, in illis condendis praesto sint viri, in re de qua agitur, periti." The use of the masculine plural (*viri*) of the Latin word for male human person (*vir, -i*) in no. 40:3 indicates that the provision for "experts" in these matters of adapting the liturgy would be limited to men and would not include women.

36. Cf. R. Falsini, "Commento," in *Costituzione conciliare sulla sacra liturgia: Introduzione, testo Latino-Italiano, commento,* Sussidi Liturgico-Pastorali 7, ed. F. Antonelli and R. Falsini (Roma: Società Editrice "Vita e Pensiero," 1964), 200: "Il caso previsto da questo articolo è del tutto eccezionale. Il Concilio ha tenuto presente la possibilità che 'in alcuni luoghi e in particolari circostanze' si renda urgente un adattamento più profondo, più radicale del rito romano, cioè oltre il quadro o limite posto dai libri liturgici. Non si esclude addirittura l'eventualità de intaccare la stessa unità sostanziale del rito romano e quindi l'ipotesi, si pur lontana, della lenta creazione di nuovi riti. Tale adattamento offre non poche difficoltà."

37. Ibid., no. 201: ". . . un gesto di grande coraggio, che può apparire persino rivoluzionario ma che in realtà corrisponde alla vera natura del Cristianesimo di "incarnarsi" in ogni popoli ed in ogni terra. . . ."

38. Ibid. ". . . e alla antica e sana tradizione liturgica, che ha accolto, specialmente durante il primo millennio, usi tradizioni dei vari popoli con i quali venne a contatto."

It is clearly visible from number 40 above that the term *aptatio* is translated by the English "adaptation" in the singular or by "adaptations" when the Latin indicates the use of the plural. However, in the two instructions that follow, the Latin *accommodatio* is also used in its place and is rendered in English as "adaptation(s)" as well. While this may at first appear to be semantic hair-splitting, a more detailed study of this use of words in *Sacrosanctum Concilium* may shed light on subsequent usage and intended meaning in the English translation.

THE DIFFERENCES IN MEANING AND USES OF *APTATIO* AND *ACCOMMODATIO* IN *SACROSANCTUM CONCILIUM* AND POST-CONCILIAR DOCUMENTS

In his book *Liturgies of the Future: The Process and Methods of Inculturation*, Anscar J. Chupungco, OSB, documents that the word *aptatio* is consistently used throughout Chapter I (*Sacrosanctum Concilium*, numbers 38–40), Chapter IV (*Sacrosanctum Concilium*, number 90), Chapter VI (*Sacrosanctum Concilium*, number 120), and Chapter VII (*Sacrosanctum Concilium*, number 126). *Aptatio*, however, does not appear in Chapter III of the same document.[39] Rather, *accommodatio* is used in the third chapter on the sacraments and the sacramentals. Chupungco concludes:

> The hermeneutical analysis of the text of *Sacrosanctum Concilium* leads us to the conclusion that the two words were used interchangeably. The use of *accommodatio* in the section on the sacraments and sacramentals was decidedly a form of compromise, a via media meant to calm anxieties over a suspected design to overhaul the church's sacramental system. It is evident that the change in terminology did not affect the meaning intended by the framers of *Sacrosanctum Concilium*. *Aptatio* and *accommodatio* meant the same thing. In fact, once it had been made clear that these words had the same meaning, there was no further need to subject the other sections of *Sacrosanctum Concilium* to this kind of change.[40]

While Chupungco's conclusion quoted above may apply throughout *Sacrosanctum Concilium*, later documents, e.g., the

---

39. Chupungco, *Liturgies of the Future: The Process and Methods of Inculturation*, 23–24.
40. Ibid., 24–25.

second and third of the four instructions on the proper implementation of the liturgical constitution, will use similar terminology but with a slightly different nuance. In this regard, Chupungco also notes that "the neat distinction between *aptatio*, as the competence of the conferences of bishops, and *accommodatio*, as the competence of the minister, began to evolve only with the publication of the new *editio typica* of the liturgical books."[41]

Given the provisions included in *Sacrosanctum Concilium* for experiments and adaptation within the liturgy which had remained basically unchanged for some three hundred years prior to the promulgation of *Sacrosanctum Concilium*, it is not surprising that excesses, abuses, and irregularities would occur in the celebration of the liturgy in the years that followed. In an attempt to define and clarify the parameters for the implementation of liturgical adaptations within the liturgy, three instructions were issued between 1964 and 1970. These documents, as well as the *Fourth Instruction*, issued in January of 1994, must be analyzed in light of the terminology and principles contained in *Sacrosanctum Concilium*.

---

41. Ibid., 25. Chupungco concludes: "Both words are used by SC to express Vatican II's general program 'to adapt more suitably to the needs of our times those institutions that are subject to change,' as read in SC 1." Although the translation into English of either the singular or plural of *aptatio* and *accommodatio* (and of their verbal equivalents, *aptare* and *accommodare* in all of their possible forms) remains difficult, Chupungco's opinion above may be valid insofar as *Sacrosanctum Concilium* is concerned. However, the fact that *aptatio* may mean more than what the English translation "adaptation" conveys may account for substituting *accommodatio* (perhaps translated better as "arrangement" or "adjustment") for *aptatio*.

CHAPTER II

THE FIRST THREE INSTRUCTIONS ON THE CORRECT IMPLEMENTATION OF *SACROSANCTUM CONCILIUM*

The intention of this chapter is to present an overview of the first three instructions on the correct implementation of *Sacrosanctum Concilium*. These documents represent the initial steps taken in the reform and revision of the rites of the Roman Catholic Church and also serve as the genetic origins of the *Fourth Instruction*. The preceding chapter presented the background necessary to begin an examination of these documents with a view toward the adaptation(s) permissible within liturgical celebrations. In this chapter, we will look more closely at these initial instructions from 1964–1970 to determine how these instructions laid the groundwork for subsequent liturgical inculturation. This chapter will examine, insofar as possible, the genesis of each instruction and the instruction itself, with its appropriate divisions and sub-divisions, paying particular attention to permissible adaptation(s) of the liturgy. Finally, this chapter will also include the critical opinions of scholars in the field of liturgy in the discussion of these first three instructions.

THE FIRST INSTRUCTION: *INTER OECUMENICI*, SEPTEMBER 26, 1964

The *First Instruction on the orderly carrying out of the Constitution on the Liturgy* issued by the Consilium, under the auspices of the Sacred Congregation of Rites, appeared on September 26, 1964.[1]

---

1. Officially established by Paul VI in the *Motu Proprio, Sacram Liturgiam* and promulgated on January 13, 1964 in a letter from the Vatican Secretariat of State, the Consilium, made up of cardinals, bishops, and a variety of liturgical consultants, was instrumental in writing some of the documents of the initial stages of the postconciliar liturgical reform. It was later disbanded and ultimately replaced, in stages: a) by the Sacred Congregation of Rites, which itself was replaced by b) the Congregation for Divine Worship and the Discipline of the Sacraments. Cf. Bernard Botte, OSB, *From Silence to Participation: An Insider's View of Liturgical Renewal*, trans. John Sullivan, OCD. (Washington, DC: The Pastoral Press, 1988), 126–27; Bugnini, *The Reform of the Liturgy 1948–1975*, 37–39; and Paul VI, *Motu Proprio, Sacram Liturgiam*, AAS 56 (1964): 139–44. [The ICEL translation of the *motu*

Various commentaries and assessments of the instruction surfaced almost immediately. Bugnini, who served as secretary for the Consilium, for example, noted that "it [i.e., the instruction] took six months and a series of schemas to produce and was discussed at length in two general meetings of the Consilium."[2] After several months of discussions, the members of the Consilium opted to follow the order of the chapters in *Sacrosanctum Concilium* as a guideline for the present document, listing under each heading in the *First Instruction* the liturgical innovations and changes it contained.[3]

Like Bugnini, his Vincentian confrere and theologian Charles Braga noted that the *First Instruction* should be weighed as an "interim document, . . . a second step—and a broad one—toward the full renewal of the liturgy."[4] In addition, he related the *First Instruction* directly to *Sacrosanctum Concilium*, stating that the former follows the latter "faithfully and fully, in spirit and in letter."[5]

Pastoral theologian J. D. Crichton, in his *Changes in the Liturgy: Considerations on the Instruction for the Right Ordering and Execution of the "Constitution on the Sacred Liturgy"* began his assessment of the document with the following observation:

> The Instruction inaugurates a new era in which much more freedom will be left to individual churches, whether dioceses or parishes, to order their services according to the fundamental laws of the liturgy and in light of their own circumstances.[6]

The eminent French liturgist Pierre Jounel commented that the *First Instruction* was produced partly out of necessity.[7] The

---

proprio may be found in DOL 20, nos. 276–289. See nos. 49–54 for the initial formation and membership of the Consilium; nos. 54–60 for its initial promulgation; and nos. 60–69 for a detailed outline of its initial work and effect on the renewal of the liturgy.]

2. Bugnini, *The Reform of the Liturgy 1948–1975*, 825.

3. Ibid., 827.

4. Charles Braga, C.M., "Commentary on the Instruction," in T*he Commentary on the Constitution and on the Instruction on the Sacred Liturgy,* ed. C. Braga and A. Bugnini, trans. Rev. Vincent P. Mallon (New York: Benziger Brothers, 1965), 327.

5. Ibid., 328.

6. J. D. Crichton, *Changes in the Liturgy: Considerations on the Instruction for the Right Ordering and Execution of the "Constitution on the Sacred Liturgy"* (Staten Island, NY: Alba House, 1965), vii.

7. Pierre Jounel, *Les premières étapes de la réforme liturgique: I: L'Instruction du 26 septembre 1964,* Traduction officielle et commentaire (Paris: Desclée, 1965), 13: "L'Instruction pour l'exécution de la Constitution sur la liturgie est née, en partie, de la nécessite où se trouvait le Conseil de définir clairement les fonctions des assemblées épiscopales en matière liturgique, de manière à faciliter l'oeuvre législative de ces assemblées."

Consilium needed to define the role which episcopal conferences were to have in legislating liturgical matters. He also reasoned that the instruction would resolve doubts regarding the interpretation of *Sacrosanctum Concilium* and its mandate for liturgical revision.[8] Finally, Jounel stated that the instruction would allow certain liturgical principles from *Sacrosanctum Concilium* to ground the subsequent liturgical and pastoral practice of ritual revisions which were sure to attract the attention of both clergy and laity.[9]

The instruction itself contains an introduction that is divided into three sections and five chapters. The introduction "recalls the essential doctrinal principles and explains the nature of the document."[10] Braga highlights certain principles in the introductory section which, he believes, are necessary as the "foundation for the whole liturgical reform and for pastoral activity."[11] Among these principles, Braga notes the importance of adapting the rites to the circumstances of place and time, of instructing the faithful as to the centrality of the liturgy in the living out of the Paschal Mystery, and finally, of engaging in liturgical, pastoral activity to promote the more perfect, active participation of the faithful in the liturgy.[12]

THE *FIRST INSTRUCTION* AND LITURGICAL ADAPTATION

Paralleling the schema of *Sacrosanctum Concilium*, the chapters within this first instruction follow the divisions of *Sacrosanctum Concilium* and are then subdivided to highlight liturgical innovations and ceremonial changes presented in the instruction. Bugnini notes that the first chapter is a rather lengthy presentation of "a sizable set of general norms that apply the Constitution to the practical order."[13] For our purposes, two areas merit closer

---

8. Ibid. "Elle a aussi pour but de résoudre les doutes éventuels qui pourraient surgir sur l'interprétation de la Constitution *De sacra Liturgia* et du motu proprio du 25 janvier 1964. C'est ce deuxième objectif qui a valu son plan à l'Instruction."

9. Ibid., 13–14: "L'Instruction se propose enfin de préciser certains principes contenus dans la Constitution et de 'fixer certains points qui peuvent entrer en vigueur dès maintenant.' Ce sont évidemment ces modifications rituelles qui attireront d'abord l'attention du clergé et des fidèles, mais elles n'auront une efficacité pastorale que si elles sont reçues par tous comme des applications des principes établis par la Constitution conciliaire."

10. Bugnini, *The Reform of the Liturgy 1948–1975*, 832.

11. Braga, "Commentary on the Instruction," in *The Commentary on the Constitution and on the Instruction on the Sacred Liturgy*, ed. A. Bugnini and C. Braga, 332.

12. Ibid.

13. Bugnini, *The Reform of the Liturgy 1948–1975*, 832.

examination; namely, a) numbers 20–23, regarding competent authority in liturgical matters [*De competenti auctoritate in re liturgica*], and b) numbers 40–45, regulating the vernacular translations of liturgical texts [*De popularibus textuum liturgicorum interpretationibus (ad Const. art 36, 3)*]. Concerning the competent authority for the regulation of liturgical matters, the instruction states clearly that the Holy See reserves the right to approve the general liturgical books.[14] In addition, the instruction also prescribes that the diocesan bishop has the authority to regulate the liturgy within his own diocese, respecting, of course, those principles enunciated in *Sacrosanctum Concilium* regarding the Holy See and the competent territorial authority.[15] In this regard, there was an interesting query made concerning the variety to be allowed within what were then referred to as "territorial authorities" and are currently called "episcopal conferences." The principle involved in the query pertains directly to what will later come to be called liturgical inculturation:

> Query: When the rubrics provide several options, may the competent territorial authority for the sake of the whole region or the bishop for his diocese direct all to observe a single way of doing things, for the sake of uniformity? Reply: Strictly speaking, this is lawful. But always to be kept in mind is the preservation of that freedom, envisioned by the new rubrics, *to adapt the celebration* (emphasis added) *in an intelligent way* (original emphasis) to the particular church and assembly of the faithful in such a way that the whole rite is a living reality for living people.[16]

What is of interest and importance in this query is the reference to adaptation [*aptandi*] and the reason for it; namely, that

---

14. SRC, *Inter oecumenici*, no. 21: "Apostolicae Sedis est tum libros liturgicos generales instaurare atque approbare. . . ."

15. Ibid., no. 22: "Episcopi est Liturgiam intra fines suae dioeceseos, iuxta normas et spiritum Constitutionis de sacra Liturgia, necnon decretorum Apostolicae Sedis et competentis auctoritatis territorialis, moderari."

16. Quoted in DOL 23:314, footnote R, 5. SRC, *Inter oecumenici*, no. 22: f: "Ad dubium propositum, 'utrum, ad informitatem obtinendam, quando a rubricis plures dantur possibilitates, auctoritas territorialis competens pro universa regione, vel Episcopus pro sua dioecesi statuere possit ut unica ratio ab omnibus teneatur,' responsio huiusmodi invenitur in *Notitiae* 1 (1965) 254: "Per se licet. Attamen, semper prae oculis habendo quo non tollatur illa libertas, quae a novis rubricis praevidetur, *aptandi* (emphasis added), *modo intelligenti* (original emphasis), celebrationem sive ecclesiae sive coetui fidelium, ita ut sacer ritus universus sit revera quid vivum pro hominibus vivis." " Quoted in Reiner Kaczynski, ed., *Enchiridion Documentorum Instaurationis Liturgicae*, 2 vols. (Roma: Casa Editriche Marietti, 1976–1988), 56, footnote f. [Hereafter, the shortened form for the author, i.e., Kaczynski, will be used without the abbreviation *ed.* The volume number will precede the page(s) when they cited and the abbreviation *no./nos.* will be used when specific numbers of a document are mentioned.]

the liturgical celebration, whether an action of the Church or of the assembly of the faithful, be done in such a way that the ritual is seen as a living reality for living people [*celebrationem sive ecclesiae sive coetui fidelium, ita ut sacer ritus sit revera quid vivum pro hominibus vivis*].

In addition, in this first chapter, there is also an interesting example of an adaptation (although the word is not mentioned directly) of the liturgy for foreign language groups living within the confines of a territorial region:

> Liturgical services held anywhere for people of a foreign language, especially for immigrants, members of a personal parish, or other like groups, may, with the consent of the local Ordinary, lawfully be celebrated in the native tongue of these faithful. Such celebrations are to conform to the limits for use of the vernacular and to the translation approved by the competent territorial ecclesiastical authority for the language in question.[17]

The prescription quoted above, especially with its provision for immigrants, is worthy of note for two reasons. In the first place, this adaptation relegated to the local ordinary the freedom to use his own discretion regarding the implementation of the use of the vernacular under special circumstances. Secondly, it reaffirmed what had been stated several times in *Sacrosanctum Concilium*; namely, that the liturgy is first and foremost a full, conscious, and active celebration of the local community's vibrant faith.[18]

Chapter two deals more specifically with "The Mystery of the Eucharist" [*De Sacrosancto Eucharistiae Mysterio*] and is replete with rubrical changes within the liturgy. What is noteworthy, however, is that once again the use or adaptation of the vernacular appears to occupy a central position in this instruction. In particular, number 57 allows that certain parts of the Mass, whether recited or sung, may now be in the vernacular; namely:

---

17. DOL 23:333. SRC, *Inter oecumenici*, no. 41: "In actionibus liturgicis quae concurrente populo, alius linguae alicubi, praesertim adstante coetu emigrantium, paroeciae personalis hisque similium, celebrantur, adhibere licet de consensu Ordinarii loci, linguam vernaculam iis fidelibus notam, iuxta modum et versionem a competenti auctoritate ecclesiastica territoriali illius linguae legitime approbata."

18. Cf. DOL 1:14 and Braga, in *The Commentary on the Constitution and on the Instruction on the Sacred Liturgy*, ed. A. Bugnini and C. Braga, 353. Commenting on numbers 40–43 of this *First Instruction*, but more particularly on number 41, Braga observes: "This is part of that *adaptation* (emphasis added) which should make the liturgy a thing completely in accord with the genius of each people, no matter where they may live."

the proclaiming of the lessons, epistle, and gospel; the universal prayer or prayer of the faithful; as befits the chants of the place, the chants of the Ordinary of the Mass; namely, the *Kyrie, Gloria, Credo, Sanctus-Benedictus,* and *Agnus Dei* as well as the introit, offertory, and communion antiphons and chants between the readings; acclamations, greetings, and dialogue formularies, the *Ecce Agnus Dei, Domine non sum dignus, Corpus Christi* at the communion of the faithful, and the Lord's prayer with its introduction and embolism.[19]

Chapter three, "The Other Sacraments and the Sacramentals," presents an extension of permission to use the vernacular in sacraments in addition to the Eucharist. While there are many points of interest in this chapter regarding sacramental theology, what is of note for our purposes is a statement regarding the sacrament of the Anointing of the Sick and how it is to be administered. Number 68 of this instruction states:

> When the anointing of the sick and viaticum are administered at the same time, *unless a continuous rite already exists in a local ritual* (emphasis added), the sequence of the rite is to be as follows. . . .[20]

The provision for the continuance of local rituals within the administration of the sacrament is but another indication of an adaptation of the liturgy within a local culture.

Commenting on local rituals that were already in existence prior to the reform, in particular, local rituals that already reflected a restoration of the more traditional order of Penance, Anointing, and Viaticum in the administration of this sacrament, Pierre Jounel noted that for the past 15 years (1949–1964), under the influence of the liturgical renewal and in light of a more traditional sacramental theology, several local rituals had already been restored. As a result, the universal practice in the Western

---

19. DOL 23:349. SRC, *Inter oecumenici,* no. 57: "In Missis sive cantu sive lectis, quae cum populo celebrantur, competens auctoritas ecclesiastica territorialis linguam vernaculam admittere potest, actis ab Apostolica Sede probatis seu confirmatis: (a) praesertim in proferendis Lectionibus, Epistola et Evangelio, necnon in oratione communi seu fidelium; (b) pro condicione autem locorum etiam in cantibus Ordinarii Missae, nempe: *Kyrie, Gloria, Credo, Sanctus-Benedictus et Agnus Dei,* et in antiphonis ad introitum, ad offertorium et ad communionem, necnon in cantibus inter lectiones occurrentibus; (c) insuper in acclamationibus, salutationibus et formulis dialogi, in formulis: *Ecce Agnus Dei; Domine non sum dignus, et Corpus Christi* in communione fidelium, et in oratione dominica cum sua admonitione et embolismo." In addition, see footnote R 20 in DOL 23:349, page 101 for a very detailed explanation of how the principles enunciated in *Sacrosanctum Concilium* as well as the prescriptions set forth in the first instruction are interrelated.

20. DOL 23:360. SRC, *Inter oecumenici,* no. 68: "Cum Unctio infirmorum et Viaticum simul administrantur, *nisi in Rituali particulari ritus continuus iam habeatur* (emphasis added), res ita ordinentur."

Church was finally conforming to what has always been in effect in the Eastern Church.[21]

Finally, chapters four and five of the *First Instruction* deal with changes in the Divine Office and the design of churches and altars to facilitate the participation of the faithful. These later chapters are, therefore, not directly related to the subject matter at hand. Suffice it to say that this *First·Instruction*, issued within nine months of the promulgation of *Sacrosanctum Concilium*, provides concrete evidence of the initial stages of liturgical adaptation in at least two areas: first and foremost in the more widespread use of the vernacular throughout liturgical celebrations, notably in the celebration of the Eucharist; and secondly, in the importance attached to existing local rites in the administration of the sacraments and sacramentals.

THE SECOND INSTRUCTION: *TRES ABHINC ANNOS*, MAY 4, 1967

The work of producing the *Second Instruction* had taken place in meetings of the Consilium between April 1965 and its promulgation in May of 1967.[22] However, a significant change is observable at the beginning of the document in a subtle shift in vocabulary used to refer to liturgical adaptation. Prior to this second instruction, the Latin *aptatio* and *accommodatio* were used almost interchangeably in *Sacrosanctum Concilium*[23] and rendered in English translation as "adaptation(s)." In the previous instruction, *Inter oecumenici*, there does not appear to be any significant use of either word.

---

21. Pierre Jounel, "Commentaire: L'Instruction du 26 septembre 1964," *La Maison-Dieu* 80 (1964): 94: "Depuis une quinzaine d'années, sous l'influence du renouveau liturgique et dans la lumière d'une théologie sacramentaire plus traditionnelle, plusieurs rituels particuliers avaient déjà restauré l'ordre ancien: pénitence, onction, viatique. [C'est le cas du rituel allemand *Collectio rituum* (1959), I, 3, 4, et de la deuxième édition du Rituel latin-français (1956), p. 98]. Ce sera désormais la discipline universelle de l'Occident, comme elle a toujours été de l'Orient."

22. Bugnini, *The Reform of the Liturgy 1948–1975*, 837: Bugnini notes that the principles at work in the decree (read: *Second Instruction*) should be to allow simplifications and norms that do not introduce any changes into the structural development of the rites.

23. Chupungco, *Liturgies of the Future: The Process and Methods of Inculturation*, 24. Regarding the terminology of inculturation vis-à-vis adaptation, see G. Arbuckle, "Inculturation Not Adaptation: Time to Change Terminology," *Worship* 60 (1986): 519. Arbuckle states that the term "inculturation" is to be preferred to the term "adaptation" because: "Adaptation is another pejorative word. It is too closely associated with a dated theology and the missionary experiences of a Eurocentric church. It connotes a one-way manipulation of cultures, not an openness to receive on the part of both parties in the dialogue."

THE *SECOND INSTRUCTION* AND
LITURGICAL ADAPTATION

In this *Second Instruction*, however, the plural of the word *accommodatio* appears three times in the short introduction. The first appearance of *accommodatio* relates the two instructions to each other and to the issue of adaptation of the liturgy: "Three years ago the Instruction *Inter oecumenici*, issued by the Congregation of Rites, 26 September 1964, established a number of *adaptations* (emphasis added) for introduction into the sacred rites."[24] The second time that *accommodatio* occurs, the reference is to the purpose for making adjustments to the liturgy: ". . . to increase this participation even more and to make the liturgical rites, especially the Mass, clearer and better understood, the same bishops have proposed certain other *adaptations* (emphasis added)."[25] Finally, the last occurrence of *accommodatio* refers to the ongoing adaptation and reform of the liturgy: ". . . the following *adaptations* (emphasis added) and changes are instituted to achieve the more specific actualization and measured progress of the liturgical reform."[26] It is important to be cognizant of the context and use of the terminology for liturgical adaptation in these initial instructions, since there is a significant interplay in the vocabulary of inculturation and adaptation in the *Fourth Instruction*.[27]

In a way similar to its predecessor, the *Second Instruction* begins with a short introduction explaining the reasons and principles involved in the liturgical reform. Pierre Jounel notes that its official title, *Instructio Altera ad exsecutionem Constitutionis de sacra Liturgia recte ordinanda*, indicates that the *Second*

---

24. DOL 39:445. SRC, *Tres abhinc annos*, Intro. "Tres abhinc annos, per Instructionem *Inter Oecumenici*, ab hac sacra Rituum Congregatione die 26 septembris 1964 datam, variae *accommodationes* (emphasis added), in sacros ritus inducendae. . . ."

25. Ibid. "Ad hanc vero participationem augendam atque ad ipsorum rituum, Missae praesertim, pleniorem perspicuitatem et intellegentiam comparandas, iidem Episcopi nonnullas alias proposuerunt *accommodationes*. . . (emphasis added)."

26. Ibid., 39:446: "Ut autem liturgica instauratio pressius ad rem deducatur et progressive procedat, sequentes *accommodationes* (emphasis added) et variationes statuuntur."

27. Cf. David N. Power, OMI, "Liturgy and Culture Revisited," *Worship* 69 (1995): 225–43; especially 226 for the distinction above. Power notes the curious interplay between the use of both *inculturatio* and *aptatio* in the *Fourth Instruction*. He suggests that *inculturatio* may express something deep rooted and permanent, rather than accommodations that are purely formal and temporary, while *aptatio* may be more suited to the desire to have the whole process of inculturation in non-Eurocentered cultures take place "within the unity of the Roman Rite," or "within the context of the Roman Rite."

Instruction has a relationship with its predecessor.[28] In addition, he states that the present document represents an important step in the general reform of the liturgy promulgated by the Second Vatican Council.[29] Finally, Jounel observes that the appearance of a second instruction corresponded to a perceived need on the part of both the laity and the clergy to adapt the liturgical celebration of the Eucharist to the changes in posture, gesture, and language. In particular, Jounel believes that the celebration of Mass facing the people made it quite unacceptable to continue the multiple kisses of the altar, genuflections, and signs of the cross.[30] Moreover, concelebration had afforded the clergy other than the principal celebrant the opportunity to recite the Canon with a minimum of gesture and even with a sung Eucharistic prayer.[31] Finally, observes Jounel, the Mass celebrated with the people had given both clergy and laity an appreciation of the daily Lectionary.[32]

Bugnini, on the other hand, noted that although the *First Instruction* was well received, it also "caused people to feel more keenly the lack of logic still found in some details and the need of taking steps to eliminate it."[33] In addition, he also observed that in the short space of time between the first instruction and the second one, two important changes in the ritual celebration of the Eucharist (i.e., the use of the vernacular and the Mass celebrated facing the people) could be made harmoniously along the lines of the reform, without changing the contemporary liturgical books.[34]

The instruction then lists eight areas which are directly affected by the current prescriptions: Options in the texts for

---

28. Pierre Jounel, "Les principes directeurs de l'instruction," *La Maison-Dieu* 90 (1967), 17: "Le Titre même de l'Instruction du 4 mai 1967: *Deuxième Instruction pour une juste application de la Constitution sur la liturgie* la rattache à celle du 26 septembre 1964."

29. Ibid. "L'Instruction *Tres abhinc annos* (4 mai 1967) va constituer, elle aussi, une étape importante dans la restauration générale de la liturgie promulguée par le Concile."

30. Ibid., 19: ". . . . le fait de célébrer face au peuple leur (c.-à.-d., aux prêtres) rendait difficilement supportable la multiplicité des baisers de l'autel, des génuflexions et des signations. . . ."

31. Ibid. ". . . la concélébration comme célébrant non principal leur a fait expérimenter un type d'eucharistie où l'on dit le Canon avec un minimum de gestes et où l'on chante la prière eucharistique."

32. Ibid. ". . . la messe avec le peuple leur a donné le goût du lectionnaire quotidien."

33. Bugnini, *The Reform of the Liturgy 1948–1975*, 836.

34. Annibale Bugnini, "Commentaire," *Documentation Catholique* 64 (1967): 894: "L'expérience de la langue du peuple et la célébration vers le peuple ont montré que certains détails des rites ne sont plus admissibles et peuvent être amendés sans toucher aux livres liturgiques actuels, et en harmonie avec les lignes directrices de la réforme."

Mass;[35] Prayers in the Mass;[36] Changes in the Order of Mass;[37] Some Special Cases (nuptial Masses and those celebrated by a priest with failing sight or otherwise infirm);[38] Variations in the Divine Office;[39] Some Variations in Rites for the Dead;[40] Vestments;[41] and finally, Use of the Vernacular.[42] In this final section, the permission to use the vernacular is extended to include: a) the Canon of the Mass; b) all the rites of Holy Orders; and c) the readings of the Divine Office, even in choral recitation.[43]

Jounel observes that there are two distinct motifs in the introductory section of this *Second Instruction*. In the first place, Jounel asserts that the introduction reveals three rules [*règles*] for the choice of the liturgical adaptations allowed up to this point: a) all adaptations proposed in the *Second Instruction* are consistent with what had been called for thus far in the liturgical reform; b) this *Second Instruction* is utilitarian and practical and thus secondary innovations are not dealt with herein; and c) no adaptations proposed in this second instruction require the publication of new liturgical books.[44]

---

35. DOL 39:447; SRC, *Tres abhinc annos*, I: De Missae formulis eligendis.

36. Ibid., 450: II: De orationibus in Missa.

37. Ibid., 453: III: De quibusdam in variationibus in ordine Missae.

38. Ibid., 463: IV: De quibusdam circumstantiis particularibus (In missis "Pro sponsis" et in missa celebrata a sacerdote caecutiente vel infirmo).

39. Ibid., 465: V: De quibusdam variationibus in Officio divino.

40. Ibid., 469: VI: De quibusdam variationibus in Officiis defunctorum.

41. Ibid., 471: VII: De sacris vestibus.

42. Ibid., 474: VII: De lingua vernacula adhibenda.

43. Ibid. SRC, *Tres abhinc annos*, no. 28: ". . .ut lingua vernacula adhiberi valeat, in actionibus liturgicis cum populo celebrantis, etiam: (a) in Canone Missae; (b) in universo ritu sacrarum Ordinationum; (c) in lectionibus divini Oficii, etiam in recitatione chorali."

44. Jounel, "Les principes directeurs de l'instruction," 19–20: "La première règle consiste dans la conformité des adaptation proposées avec les projets déjà retenus pour la réforme générale. . . . la deuxième règle est celle de l'utilité: plusieurs mesures suggérées n'ont pas été retenues, parce que l'autorité a voulu s'en tenir à l'essentiel et ne pas multiplier les innovations secondaires dans un document qui a un but pratique. . . . Enfin, la troisième règle tient dans le fait qu'on n'a pas voulu toucher aux livres liturgiques actuels: les adaptations 'peuvent être appliquées par des dispositions rubricales.'"

Similarly, in accord with Bugnini,[45] Jounel notes that the introductory section also contains an important reminder[46] of what is stated clearly in *Sacrosanctum Concilium*, number 22:3: "Therefore, no other person, not even if he is a priest, may on his own add, remove, or change anything in the liturgy."[47] This norm concerning the regulation of the liturgy refers not only to the authority of the Apostolic See but also to other authorities mentioned in this number, i.e., the diocesan bishop [*apud episcopum*] and the legally established competent territorial groupings of various kinds of bishops [*ad competentes varii generis territoriales episcoporum coetus legitime constitutos*].[48] Although these prescriptions (*Sacrosanctum Concilium*, number 22 §2, §3) urge that all respect the authority of the Church in matters liturgical, the reaffirmation in the *Second Instruction* of not allowing the addition, removal, or changing of anything in the liturgy is a significant point of interest in the development and chronological overview of the four instructions. The question of both apostolic and episcopal authority relating to the regulation of adaptation of the liturgy will play a significant role in the *Fourth Instruction*.

THE THIRD INSTRUCTION: *LITURGICAE INSTAURATIONES*, SEPTEMBER 5, 1970

The *Third Instruction* on the orderly carrying out of the Constitution on the Liturgy is different both in format and in style from its two predecessors. There are no significant chapter divisions or headings in the document. Rather, the *Third Instruction* comprises an introduction and a presentation of 12 principles. The latter, in turn, offer suggestions and mandates for the correction of some abuses which had arisen in the intervening years.

Bugnini provides information relevant to the genesis of this third instruction and its place in the liturgical renewal. In the

---

45. Bugnini, "Commentaire," 898: "Il convient de souligner le rappel. . . dans l'introduction du document, du caractère sacral de la loi liturgique. La liturgie n'est pas l'affaire de tout un chacun, mais action ecclésiale, hiérarchique, communautaire. Il n'est pas permis à personne de léser ou de diminuer cette valeur sacré, pleine de mystère, par des initiatives personnelles et arbitraires."

46. Jounel, "Les principes directeurs de l'instruction," 20: "La seconde partie du préambule de l'Instruction consiste dans un rappel solennel du 'principe capital de la discipline,' si explicitement formulé dans l'article 22 de la constitution liturgique."

47. DOL 1: 22, 3: "Quapropter nemo omnino alius, etiamsi sit sacerdos, quidquam proprio marte in liturgia addat, demat, aut mutet."

48. Ibid., 22, 2: "Ex potestate a iure concessa, rei liturgicae moderatio inter limites statutos pertinet quoque ad competentes varii generis territoriales episcoporum coetus legitime constitutos."

three years that intervened between the second and the third instructions, Bugnini notes that the *Consilium* had been collecting a number of reports from various sources regarding certain arbitrary changes introduced into liturgical celebrations.[49] In addition, Bugnini also observes that as early as February of 1968, the *Consilium* had written to the Secretariat of State regarding a forthcoming instruction which would be based largely upon the *General Instruction of the Roman Missal;* this instruction would address the areas where the greatest abuses in the Mass had occurred.[50] A first draft of the proposed instruction, in Italian, was sent to the Congregation for the Doctrine of the Faith on July 12, 1969.[51] What is noteworthy, however, is the response of this same Congregation, particularly in the areas which they listed as deserving special consideration: 1) the inviolability of the texts of the Mass and especially of the Eucharistic prayer; 2) the importance of bishops' correcting liturgical abuses even if they must resort to penal remedies; 3) the need to emphasize the link between liturgy and faith in the introduction to the instruction; 4) the preference for terms such as "the Mass," "the Eucharistic sacrifice" rather than the Lord's Supper or the Memorial of the Lord, these latter terms considered as more Protestant than Catholic in their meaning; 5) the strong recommendation of the use of the traditional host rather than bread; and finally 6) the need to regulate vesture at liturgies, even if this means granting permission for the chasuble-alb.[52]

A new draft with the corrections above was submitted to Pope Paul VI on September 6, 1969. In his response, dated November 8, he noted three points which are of interest to the present study because they represent a limitation on liturgical adaptation of the liturgy: no type of dialogue homily was to be introduced into the Mass; the bread used for the Mass should preferably be the small hosts; and finally, all experiments in the liturgy were to cease with the publication of this *Third Instruction.*[53]

---

49. See Bugnini, 840; Gy, "La troisième instruction pour une juste application de la Constitution conciliaire sur la liturgie," *La Maison-Dieu* 104 (1970): 167: "On rencontre souvent aujourd'hui, et dans tous les pays, des négligences ou des désordres par rapport aux lois liturgiques, et beaucoup de catholiques s'en plaignent."

50. Ibid.

51. Ibid., 840–43.

52. Ibid., 840–41.

53. Ibid., 842.

In addition, Bugnini also states that a new version of the instruction was submitted to the Holy Father on May 16, 1970. After some additional emendations and revisions, Paul VI gave his final approval for the printing of the *Third Instruction* on October 2, 1970.[54] Bugnini's comments about the reception of the document serve as a fitting segue into an examination of the details contained therein:

> The instruction was not well received. It was to be expected, of course, that a document urging a return to discipline would not be warmly greeted. In this case, however, the reactions were stronger than anticipated. The meaning of the document was distorted, and the values it urged were not understood. The general interpretation was that it represented a "brake" on reform and a return to the preconciliar situation, and that in it, Rome was showing its determination "to do away with and repress all initiative." This was a difficult time.[55]

According to Bugnini, the most positive part of the *Third Instruction* is its introduction consisting of some ten paragraphs recalling the purposes of the liturgical reform, exhorting bishops to exercise their proper duties in the regulation of the liturgy within their domains, and finally extolling the virtues of diocesan liturgical commissions as an aid to the bishops in the execution of their duties.[56]

Like Bugnini, the distinguished liturgist A. Tegels finds the introductory section of this *Third Instruction* to be quite positive.[57] More specifically, Tegels notes that the instruction itself contains an urgent recommendation for bishops to fulfill their roles as leaders in the liturgical renewal.[58] The introduction to the *Third Instruction* refers to this recommendation as an episcopal duty:

> The first appeal must be made to the authority of the individual bishops. . . . They have the duty of governing, guiding, encouraging, or sometimes reproving, of lighting the way for the carrying out of true reform, and also of taking counsel, so that the whole Body of the Church may be able to move ahead single-mindedly and with the unity of charity in the diocese, the nation, and the entire world.

---

54. Ibid., 843.

55. Ibid.

56. Ibid., 844.

57. A. Tegels, "Chronicle: A Third Instruction," *Worship* 44 (1970): 623.

58. Ibid.

Such efforts of the bishops are the more necessary and urgent because the link between liturgy and faith is so close that service to the one redounds to the other.[59]

Tegels also highlights the importance of the role of the local bishop in guiding the liturgical life of the diocese to facilitate the priests' working together in a hierarchical fellowship.[60]

After assessing the positive contributions of the introductory section of the document, in a manner reminiscent of Bugnini, Tegels analyzes the 12 "principles and suggestions" that the *Third Instruction* contains and concludes that some of the norms therein are too unnecessarily restrictive.[61] In this regard, Tegels lists, among several prescriptions of the document, the prohibition regarding nonbiblical readings in the Liturgy of the Word.[62] He does observe, however, that while the instruction forbids the substitution of such readings, it does not forbid the addition of nonbiblical readings.[63] In addition, Tegels notes the prohibition of dialogue homilies,[64] the insistence upon the celebration of the Liturgy of the Word and the eucharistic action in the same place,[65] and the lack of provision for spontaneous offering of intentions in

---

59. DOL 52:511. SCCD, *Liturgicae instaurationes*, Intro. "Ac primum ad singulorum auctoritatem Episcoporum est appellandum. . . . Ipsorum enim est moderari, dirigere, instimulare, quandoque etiam arguere, semper vero illustrare rectae renovationis exsecutionem, pariterque consulere, ut universum Ecclesiae corpus eadem mente, in unitate caritatis, procedere valeat in dioecesi, in natione, in mundo. Quae Episcoporum opera hac in re necessaria et urgentior est ob intimas, quae Liturgiam inter et Fidem intercedunt, necessitudines, adeo ut, quod obsequium alteri exhibetur, in alteram redundet."

60. Tegels, 623. Cf. DOL 52:511: "The bishops' mastery of the knowledge needed greatly assists priests in the ministry they exercise in due hierarchic communion and facilitates that obedience required as a fuller sign of worship and for the sanctification of souls." SRC, *Liturgicae instaurationes*, Intro. "Congrua enim rerum cognitio, quam Episcopi habent, non parve auxilio est sacerdotibus in ministerio, quod sane in communione hierachica est exsequendum, eaque debitam reddit obedientiam faciliorem, quae ad perfectiorem cultus significationem atque animarum santificationem postulatur."

61. Tegels, 624.

62. Ibid. Cf. DOL 52:513. SCCD, *Liturgicae instaurationes*, nos. 2–2a: "Inter sacros textus, qui in coetu liturgico recitantur, divinae Scripturae libri peculiari pollent dignitate. . . . Liturgia verbi summa cura excolenda est. Numquam licet pro ea alias lectiones substituere, sive a sacris sive a profanis auctoribus, veteribus vel recentioribus, depromptas."

63. Ibid., 624.

64. Ibid. Cf. DOL 52:513. SCCD, *Liturgicae instaurationes*, no. 2a: "Homiliae finis est nuntiatum Dei verbum fidelibus explanare et ad huius aetatis sensum accommodare. Ipsa proinde ad sacerdotem spectat; christifideles vero notationibus dialogis, hisque similibus sese abstineant."

65. Ibid. Cf. DOL 52:520. SCCD, *Liturgicae instaurationes*, no. 2b: "Liturgia verbi eucharisticam liturgiam preparat et ad eam ducit, quacum unum actum cultus efficit. Quapropter alteram ab altera separare non licet, easque diverso tempore et loco celebrare."

the general intercessions by members of the assembly.[66] Finally, Tegels observes that although there is a mandate that the bread used for Eucharist should look and taste like bread, "the instruction prescribes that it must always be made in the traditional form,"[67] that is, from wheaten flour and unleavened bread.[68]

In his commentary on this *Third Instruction*, French liturgist P.-M. Gy presents a differing analysis. He insists that the present document is not so much a negative list of prescriptions as a reaffirmation of what had already been stated in the two previous instructions.[69] In addition, Gy believes that the *Third Instruction* is consistent with the letter and spirit of previous liturgical documents and the two prior instructions.[70] Finally, Gy asserts that the *Third Instruction* represents a call to order, an affirmation of the importance of the role of the local bishops in the reform of the liturgy, and an insistence upon certain principles which had been enunciated in the years intervening between the *First Instruction* and the present one.[71] For Gy, then, the *Third Instruction* represents not so much a restricting of the liturgical reform but rather

---

66. Ibid. Cf. DOL 52:521. SCCD, *Liturgicae instaurationes*, no. 3g: "In oratione universali seu oratione fidelium. . . . Illae autem intentiones sint antea et paratae et scriptae, atque huic generi dicendi consentaneae."

67. Ibid. Cf. DOL 52:523. SCCD, *Liturgicae instaurationes*, no. 5: "Panis ad Eucharistiam celebrandam triticeus et, iuxta perantiquum Ecclesiae latinae morem, azymus est. Quamvis veritas signi postulet ut tamquam verus cibus appareat, qui frangitur et dividitur inter fratres, tamen *semper* (original emphasis) forma tradita conficiendus est, iuxta normam Institutionis generalis Missalis romani (n. 283) sive agatur de parvis hostiis pro fidelium Communione sive de hostiis maioris formae, in partes deinde frangendis." The supposition here is the prevailing use of small and large hosts for the people and clergy respectively. The traditional form which the instruction postulates for the confection of the bread is *triticeus* and *azymus*.

68. Tegels, 625.

69. P.-M. Gy, "La troisième instruction pour une juste application de la Constitution conciliaire sur la liturgie," 167: "Il serait tout à fait injuste et inexacte de voir dans cette Instruction un contenu principalement négatif. Cela fausserait la lecture de tout le document."

70. Ibid. "Non seulement c'est une règle élémentaire de toujours situer un document législatif dans l'ensemble des documents connexes auxquels il se rattache en les rappelant et les complétant, mais, de fait, l'Instruction est homogène à la lettre et à l'esprit des différents documents de la réforme liturgique et des Instructions précédentes."

71. Ibid. "Trois points que nous considérons successivement: (1) un 'rappel à l'ordre' d'une certaine ampleur n'était pas opportun avant que l'essentiel de la réforme liturgique soit achevé; (2) le bon ordre de la liturgie incombe encore plus aux évêques qu'au Siège apostolique et dépend de la qualité de leur pastorale liturgique; (3) Presque toutes les normes contenues dans l'Instruction ne sont que le rappel des règles déjà établies au cours de la réforme liturgique des dernières années."

a restatement and reaffirmation of what had already been clearly legislated in previous instructions.[72]

THE *THIRD INSTRUCTION* AND LITURGICAL ADAPTATION

Before concluding the study of this *Third Instruction*, some of the 12 principles merit closer examination because they will reappear in a slightly different, albeit more nuanced manner in the *Fourth Instruction*. For example, the first principle situates the relationship between experimentation and ritual celebration of the liturgy vis-à-vis the individual celebrant:

> The effectiveness of the liturgy does not lie in experimenting with rites and altering them over and over, nor in a continuous reductionism, but solely in entering more deeply into the word of God and the mystery being celebrated. It is the presence of these two that authenticates the Church's rites, not what some priest decides, indulging his own preference.[73]

While one could suspect that such a prescription might lead to a reduction of the options of the priest celebrant and/or to a limitation on any adaptations, the same instruction also states in a subsequent principle:

> The priest may say a very few words to the congregation at the beginning of the Mass and before the readings, the preface, and the dismissal, but should give no instruction during the eucharistic prayer.[74]

---

72. Ibid. "Les différents avertissements contenus aux nos. 2 à 12 de l'Instruction, qui concernent le plus souvent la messe, ne font dans la plupart des cas que rappeler une discipline déjà édictée ailleurs, et c'est à peine si ici ou là s'y ajoute dans le détail une précision restrictive ou au contraire l'amorce d'une évolution."

73. DOL 52:512. SCCD, *Liturgicae instaurationes*, no. 1: "Actionum liturgicarum vis non continentur in ritibus frequenter experiendis renovandisque vel etiam ad simpliciorem usque formam redigendis, verum tantum in verbo Dei et in mysterio, quod celebratur, altius perscrutandis, quorum praesentia rituum Ecclesiae observantia confirmatur, non vero iis, quae aliquis sacerdos, suo indulgens ingenio, statuat."

74. Ibid., 52:520. SCCD, *Liturgicae instaurationes*, no. 3f: "Inter Missae celebrationem sacerdos quam brevissime populum alloqui potest, scilicet in ipso initio, ante lectiones, ante praefationem et antequam populum dimittat. Attamen in liturgia eucharistica a monitionibus includendis abstineat." This option was included in the *Ordo Missae* of 6 April 1969. Cf. Kaczynski, no. 96:1406: ". . . Ipsi insuper licet, brevissimis verbis, introducere fideles in Missam diei, antequam celebratio inchoetur; in liturgiam verbi, ante lectiones; in Precem eucharisticam, ante praefationem; necnon universam actionem sacram, ante dimissionem, concludere." Cf. Sacred Congregation for Divine Worship, *General Instruction of the Roman Missal*, 4th ed. (Vatican City: Vatican Polyglot Press, 1975), no. 11.

Additional latitude appears in the area of the choice of musical instruments used in the liturgy of the local churches. Referring
back to a principle stated in *Musicam sacram*;[75] namely, that the
Church does not bar any style of sacred music from the liturgy,[76]
the instruction reaffirms that principle and situates the regulation of such musical adaptations within the purview of the local
bishop, when there are no prior norms established:

> More specific determinations belong to the conferences of bishops
> or, where there are no general norms as yet, to the bishop within his
> diocese. Every attention is to be given to the choice of musical
> instruments; limited in number and suited to the region and to com-
> munity culture, they should prompt devotion and not be too loud.[77]

Finally, the instruction contains important references in
principles 11 and 12 regarding further experimentation and adaptation of the liturgy. Principle 11 states clearly:

> Should any conference of bishops judge it necessary and timely to
> add further formularies or to make *particular adaptations* (emphasis
> added), these are to be incorporated after the approval of the Holy
> See, and by means of a distinctive typeface are to be clearly set off
> as separate from the original Latin text.[78]

Principle 12 contains an interesting play on words in the
Latin text between *aptationes* and *accommodationes*, calling to
mind the distinction made earlier in this work by Chupungco.[79]
After abrogating all prior permission for experimentation within
the Mass, the instruction goes on to state in principle 12:

> The conferences of bishops are to draw up in detail *any adaptations*
> (emphasis added) envisioned in the liturgical books and submit them

---

75. SRC, "Instructio," *De musica in sacra Liturgia (Musicam sacram)*, AAS 59 (1967):
300–20; Kaczynski, 1:275–91.

76. Ibid. *Musicam sacram*. no. 9; Kaczynski, 1:277: ". . . Nullum genus musicae sacrae
Ecclesia ab actionibus liturgicis arcet. . . ."

77. DOL, 52:517. SCCD, *Liturgicae instaurationes*, no. 3c: "Nam, quamvis Ecclesia
nullum genus musicae sacrae ab actionibus liturgicis arceat. . . . Res pressius determinare
ad Conferentias Episcopales vel, normis generalibus deficientibus, ad episcopos in propriae
dioecesis finibus spectat. Omni cura insuper seligantur instrumenta musica, numero
circumscripta, loco et indoli communitatis congruentia, quae pietatem foveant neque
nimium strepitum edant."

78. DOL, 52:529. SCCD, *Liturgicae instaurationes*, no. 11: "Si Conferentia Episcopalis
alias formulas addi necessarium opportunumque duxerit, aut quasdam *accommodationes*
(emphasis added) afferre, hae post Sanctae Sedis approbationem inducantur, et a primigeno
textu latino peculiaribus notis distinguantur."

79. Chupungco, *Liturgies of the Future: The Process and Methods of Inculturation*, 23–25.

for confirmation to the Holy See. . . . Should further *adaptations* (emphasis added) become necessary, in keeping with the norm of the Constitution *Sacrosanctum Concilium* art. 40, the conference of bishops is to examine the issue thoroughly, attentive to the character and traditions of each people and to specific pastoral needs.[80]

This same principle continues to state that any experimentation must be done prudently, on a small scale within a controlled environment, and last no longer than one year in duration. Finally, it concludes with a rather perplexing restriction for any proposed adaptation:

> A report then is to be sent to the Holy See. While a reply is pending, use of the petitioned *adaptation* (emphasis added) is forbidden.[81]

It is not surprising, then, that this final principle allows for a variety of opinions regarding its interpretation. Tegels takes an optimistic view and asserts that the instruction does not prohibit further experimentation with the liturgy but rather makes provision for it according to the conditions expressed in principle 12.[82] In addition, he observes the dichotomy that principle 12 also contains:

> The problem is that it is impossible to know if you want any basic changes without first experimenting with them. The procedure is a bit cumbersome. But at least the principle of experimentation is accepted.[83]

Gy, on the other hand, maintains that limiting experimentation not only falls within the purview of the Apostolic See but that it is also its sacred charge and duty.[84] Moreover, according to Gy, the duty of the bishops goes beyond merely assuring good order in liturgical celebrations; he maintains, rather, that good order within the liturgical celebration is essential for ecclesial

---

80. DOL, 52:530. SCCD, *Liturgicae instaurationes,* no. 12: *"Aptationes* (emphasis added), de quibus in libris liturgicis agitur, ipsae Conferentiae Episcopales pressius definiant et Apostolicae Sedis confirmationi subiciant. Si adhuc amplioribus *aptationibus* (emphasis added), ad normam n. 40 Constitutionis *Sacrosanctum Concilium,* opus fuerit, Episcoporum Conferentia rem penitus perspiciat, ingenium et traditiones cuisque gentis ac peculiares necessitates pastorales expendens."

81. Ibid. "Postea res ad Apostolicam Sedem deferatur. Non licet, dum Apostolicae Sedis responsum expectatur, petitas *accommodationes* (emphasis added) in usum inducere."

82. Tegels, 626.

83. Ibid.

84. Gy, "La troisième instruction pour une juste application de la Constitution conciliaire sur la liturgie," 171: "Mais revenons à l'essentiel. Déjà l'Apôtre Paul exhortait l'Église de Corinthe à célébrer l'Eucharistie de manière bien ordonnée et signalait les inconvénients qu'il y avait à mêler celle-ci à un repas ordinaire."

communion.[85] Finally, while it is true that in Gy's opinion, the Congregation for Worship regards the *Third Instruction* as a means of imposing order once again on the liturgical reform of the post-conciliar period, he nevertheless agrees with Tegels that the future will present its own problems in this area.[86]

In conclusion, while the overall import of the *Third Instruction* was one of curbing experimentation and correcting abuses and excesses, this *Third Instruction* represented yet another stage in the process of liturgical adaptation. Bugnini, like Tegels, believed that the document could have taken a more positive tone.[87] Perhaps his summary comments on the final article of the *Third Instruction* may provide the focus and lenses needed to approach the revisions and adaptations of the liturgy which occurred in the subsequent years:

> The press laid great emphasis on this number (12) of the instruction, interpreting it as putting "an end to all experimentation." In fact, the instruction was simply bringing clarifications. It said once more that the Holy See alone gives permission, in writing, for experiments. . . . In addition, the instruction says that since the Roman Missal has now been published, no further experimentation with the Mass is permitted—a logical prohibition. On the other hand, the instruction speaks of *adaptations possibly being needed and explains the procedure to be followed* (emphasis added).[88]

Finally, as we now turn to an examination of some of the revisions in the rites and more particularly to the question of inculturation, the closing words of the *Third Instruction* provide an excellent *point de départ:*

---

85. Ibid. "Parmi les tâches de l'office apostolique de Pierre et des évêques envers la liturgie, rappeler l'ordre de la célébration n'est ni la principale ni la seule, mais c'est l'une d'elles, et elle est nécessaire à la communion ecclésiale."

86. Ibid. "La Congrégation pour le culte divin, sans préjuger de ce qui devra être fait demain, demande qu'aujourd'hui le bon ordre soit observé. Mais elle n'ignore pas que demain presse."

87. Bugnini, *The Reform of the Liturgy 1948–1975*, 843–44: "It must be admitted, however, that the document would have had a better reception if the style had been different (except in introduction): less harsh, more persuasive, more expansive in giving reasons for admonitions, and also a little more open on certain points. In addition, it would have been more effective. But, as we saw above, this more relaxed approach was not possible. On the other hand, even though it met with a somewhat humiliating reception, the document had to be published; it was necessary to say something about the points raised, and the pressures being brought to bear from within the Curia and from outside were many, strong, and justified."

88. Ibid., 847.

The contemporary reform aims at making available liturgical prayer that has its origin in a living and honored tradition. Once available, this prayer must appear clearly as the work of the entire people of God in all their orders and ministries. The effectiveness and authenticity of this reform has as its sole guarantee the unity of the whole ecclesial organism.[89]

---

89. DOL, 52:531. SCCD, *Liturgicae instaurationes*, no. 13: "Praesens instauratio liturgicam precem proferre contendit, e viva et vetustissima spirituali traditione exortam. Et cum profertur, ipsa manifestanda est ut opus totius populi Dei, in suis diversis ordinibus et ministeriis constituti. Tantummodo enim in hac totius compaginis ecclesialis unitate certa servatur vis et authenticitas." It is unfortunate that ICEL did not render a more accurate translation of the closing lines. Perhaps a better rendering of the last two sentences might read: "Once available, this prayer must appear clearly as the work of the entire people of God, constituted in its diverse orders and ministries. Solely in the unity of the whole ecclesial organism is the effectiveness and authenticity of the tradition maintained."

CHAPTER III

THE REVISIONS OF CERTAIN SACRAMENTS AND RITUALS

When the formal sessions of the Second Vatican Council ended in 1965, the work of revising the Roman rite was already in process. As early as spring of 1964,[1] the Consilium had been meeting on a regular basis to establish procedures and guidelines that were to regulate the revision and adaptation of the rites according to the prescriptions of *Sacrosanctum Concilium*.[2] Bugnini notes that at the sixth general meeting of the Consilium in the fall of 1965, B. Fischer and P.-M. Gy submitted a report regarding the revision and adaptations for sacraments, sacramentals, and for religious profession.[3] In this report, the relators called attention to four areas requiring special consideration: 1) the relation between future rituals and particular rituals;[4] 2) the extent of adaptations;[5] 3) the

---

1. See Bugnini, *The Reform of the Liturgy 1948–1975*, 579–82.

2. In Bugnini's *The Reform of the Liturgy 1948–1975*, chapters 2, 5, 6, 7, and 8 provide detailed information regarding the step-by-step procedures undertaken in the implementation of the council's mandate for the revision of the rites.

3. Cf. B. Fischer and P.-M. Gy, "De recognitione Ritualis Romani," *Notitiae* 2 (1966): 220–30. This document is divided into three major areas; namely, "I: Character Proprius Novi Ritualis Romani; II: Normae Generales Instaurationis Liturgicae in Ritualis Recognitione Servandae; and finally, III: De Aliquibus Sacramentorum et Sacramentalium Ritibus In Specie." There are further subdivisions of each larger section. See below and also Bugnini, *The Reform of the Liturgy 1948–1975*, 580–81, especially footnote 2 on 581 regarding Fischer and Gy.

4. Bugnini, The Reform of the Liturgy 1948–1975, 581. Bugnini notes: "The Roman ritual, though complete in itself, will therefore have to serve as norm and model for the particular rituals (SC, no. 68). Consequently, possibilities of adaptation and variation must be left open for the particular rituals 'provided the substantial unity of the Roman Rite is preserved' (SC, no. 38)." Cf. Fischer and Gy, "De recognitione Ritualis Romani," "I:1: Relatio inter futurum Rituale Romanum et Ritualia particularia," 220.

5. Ibid. Bugnini continues: "The liturgical constitution looks upon rituals as the privileged place for adaptations." Footnotes 2 and 3, which accompany this citation, refer the reader to SC, no. 22, 2; no. 39. Reference is also made to adaptations in the rites of baptism (SC, nos. 65, 68), marriage (SC, no. 77), new sacramentals (SC, no. 79), and funerals (SC, no. 81). Cf. Fischer and Gy, "De recognitione Ritualis Romani," "II:2: Speciale Momentum aptationis in campo Ritualis," 221; also "III: De Aliquibus Sacramentorum et Sacramentalium Ritibus in Specie," 223, especially (1) "De Baptismo," 223–25; (6) "De Exsequiis," 228; (7) "De

instructions to be prefixed to each rite;[6] and finally, 4) the General Norms.[7] With these considerations in mind, the work of revision was divided among the members of the Consilium.

Following the directives of number 63b[8] of the liturgical constitution (which mandated that a new edition of the Roman book of rites be prepared), the study groups of the Consilium prepared new *editiones typicae* of the various sacramental rites. In the *praenotanda* of most of the revised *editiones typicae*, principles and guidelines for cultural adaptations were usually given.

The newly revised books of the individual sacramental rites did not appear as a single book but rather as separate volumes, giving the *editiones typicae* for different sacramental usages. The *editiones typicae* of the sacramental rites are not of their nature cultural adaptations but include norms for such endeavors alongside more general theological and pastoral norms. These norms provide the focus for the present chapter.

Matrimonio," 228–29; (8) "De Sacramentalibus et specialiter de Benedictionibus," 229–30. It should also be noted that the English translation of the Latin titles (above) used in Bugnini could, perhaps, be rendered better as: "II:2: Special Consideration in the area of Ritual adaptations; III: Concerning some rites of the sacraments and sacramentals." Also, the material presented in the English translation of Bugnini does not follow the sequential order of presentation in the Latin.

6. Ibid., 582: Bugnini observes: "The liturgical constitution attaches special importance to the instructions that are to open each section of the Ritual and even each rite (SC, no. 63b). . . . The instructions should be included in particular rituals, but a suitable adaptation of them is not prohibited. What is done must, of course, receive proper approval from the Holy See." Cf. Fischer and Gy, "De recognitione Ritualis Romani," "I:3, Instructiones singulis ritibus praeponendae," 222.

7. Ibid. Bugnini concludes: "Like the other reforms, that of the Ritual was to follow the broad guidelines set down in no. 23 of the liturgical constitution, and, generally, all the principles set forth in Chapter I of the constitution on the priority of communal celebrations over individual ones, participation by the congregation, simplicity in the rites, reading of the word of God, brief comments, instruction of the faithful, and the elimination of all special honors for private persons." Cf. Fischer and Gy, "De recognitione Ritualis Romani," "II: Normae Generales Instaurationis Liturgicae in Ritualis Recognitione Servandae," 222.

8. SC, 63b in Tanner, 833: "There is to be a new edition of the Roman book of rites, and, following this as a model, each competent local church authority (see article 22 §2) should prepare its own, adapted to the needs of individual areas, including those to do with language, as soon as possible. Once these have been reviewed by the Apostolic See, they should be introduced in the appropriate areas. However, when these books or local collections of rites are being drawn up, the instructions put in the Roman ritual before each individual rite are not to be left out, whether these be instructions of a pastoral and practical kind or instructions which have some special social concern." ["Iuxta novam ritualis romani edtionem ritualia particularia, singularum regionum necessitatibus, etiam quoad linguam, accommodata, a competenti ecclesiastica auctoritate territoriali de qua in art. 22 §2 huius constitutionis quam primum parentur, et, actis ab apostolica sede recognitis, in regionibus ad quas pertinet adhibeantur. In iis autem ritualibus vel particularibus collectionibus rituum conficiendis, ne omittantur instructiones, in rituali romano singulis ritibus praepositae, sive pastorales et rubricales, sive quae peculiare momentum sociale habent."]

Since a consideration of the norms for the revision of all the sacraments lies beyond our scope in this work, this chapter will limit its consideration to the *editiones typicae* of three sacraments and one ritual: The Rites of Ordination of Deacons, Priests, and Bishops[9] and the Rites of Ordination of a Bishop, of Priests, and of Deacons;[10] the Rite of Marriage;[11] The Rite of Funerals;[12]

---

9. *Pontificale Romanum* ex decreto Sacrosancti Oecumenici Concilii Vaticani II instauratum auctoritate Paul Pp. VI promulgatum, *De Ordinatione Diaconi, Presbyteri et Episcopi*, editio typica (Vatican City: Typis Polyglottis Vaticanis, 1968). [*Roman Ritual* and *Pontifical* revised by Decree of the Second Vatican Ecumenical Council and published by authority of Pope Paul VI and Pope John Paul II, *Ordination of Deacons, Priests, and Bishops*, in *The Rites of the Catholic Church*, vol. 2, prepared by the International Commission on English in the Liturgy: A Joint Commission of Catholic Bishops' Conferences, approved for use in the Dioceses of the United States of America by the National Conference of Catholic Bishops and confirmed by the Apostolic See, Study Edition, trans. by ICEL, 1975 (Collegeville, MN: The Liturgical Press, 1991). The second volume of *The Rites of the Catholic Church* (above) presents *De Ordinatione Diaconi, Presbyteri et Episcopi* in a format conducive for reference and study.]

10. *Pontificale Romanum* ex decreto Sacrosancti Oecumenici Concilii Vaticani II renovatum auctoritate Paul Pp. VI editum Ioannis Pauli Pp. cura recognitum, *De Ordinatione Episcopi, presbyterorum, et diaconorum*, editio typica altera, *Notitiae* 26 (1990): 74–95. (A single volume edition of this editio typica altera is available from Vatican City: Typis Polyglottis Vaticanis, 1990). The *Decretum* of promulgation from CDWDS is dated June 29, 1989. The decree allows the editio typica altera to be used at a date determined by the conferences of bishops. [*The Roman Pontifical* As Renewed By Decree of the Second Vatican Ecumenical Council Published By Authority of Pope Paul VI And Further Revised At the Direction of Pope John Paul II, *Rites of Ordination of a Bishop, of Priests, and of Deacons*, Second Typical Edition, (Washington, DC: USCCB, 2003). The English translation of the *Rites of Ordination of a Bishop, of Priests, and of Deacons* 1999, International Committee on English in the Liturgy, Inc. All rights reserved.]

11. *Rituale Romanum* ex decreto Sacrosancti Oecumenici Concilii Vaticani II instauratum auctoritate Pauli Pp. VI promulgatum, *Ordo celebrandi Matrimonium*, editio typica (Vatican City: Typis Polyglottis Vaticanis, 1969) [hereafter OCM, 1969]. [*Roman Ritual* revised by Decree of the Second Vatican Ecumenical Council and published by authority of Pope Paul VI, *Rite of Marriage*, English translation approved by the National Conference of Catholic Bishops and confirmed by the Apostolic See, trans. by ICEL, 1969 (New York: Catholic Book Publishing Co., 1969), (hereafter, *Rite of Marriage*, trans. by ICEL, 1969).] *Rituale Romanum* ex decreto Sacrosancti Oecumenici Concilii Vaticani II renovatum auctoritate Pauli Pp. VI editum Ioannis Pauli Pp. II cura recognitum, *Ordo celebrandi Matrimonium*, editio typica altera (Vatican City: Typis Polyglottis Vaticanis, 1991) [hereafter OCM, 1991]. [*Roman Ritual* revised by Decree of the Second Vatican Ecumenical Council and published by authority of Pope Paul VI revised at the direction of Pope John Paul II, *Order of Celebrating Marriage*, second typical edition for Study and Comment by the Bishops of the Member and Associate-Member Conferences of the International Commission of English in the Liturgy), approval pending (Washington, DC: ICEL, 1996), (hereafter: *Rite of Marriage*, Provisional text, ICEL, 1996). At the time of submission of this manuscript (July, 2003), an officially approved translation was unavailable.].

12. *Rituale Romanum* ex decreto Sacrosancti Oecumenici Concilii Vaticani II instauratum auctoritate Pauli Pp. VI promulgatum, *Ordo exsequiarum* editio typica (Vatican City: Typis Polyglottis Vaticanis, 1969), (hereafter OE), in Kaczynski, 1:606–13. [*Rite of Funerals* in *The Rites of the Catholic Church* as revised by Decree of the Second Vatican Ecumenical Council and published by authority of Pope Paul VI Study Edition,

and the Rite of the Anointing of the Sick.[13] The first two of these do not belong to the revision of the Roman Ritual but to the Revised Pontifical. Since both the Rite of Ordination and the Rite of Marriage have undergone two revisions, this will be taken into account.

DE ORDINATIONE DIACONI, PRESBYTERI ET EPISCOPI, 1968

The 1968 *editio typica* of the ordination rites does not contain provisions for the cultural adaptation of liturgical celebration. The purpose for mentioning it in this study is to acknowledge its existence as the first of the rites to be revised and promulgated.[14]

The apostolic constitution *Pontificalis Romani*,[15] which precedes the ordination rites themselves, discusses the "matter and form" of each sacramental order. The "matter" in all cases consists in the imposition of hands.[16] The apostolic constitution also

---

trans. by ICEL, 1970 (New York: Pueblo Publishing Co., 1983); *Roman Ritual* revised by Decree of the Second Vatican Ecumenical Council and published by authority of Pope Paul VI, *Order of Christian Funerals,* approved for use in the Dioceses of the United States of America by the National Conference of Catholic Bishops and confirmed by the Apostolic See, prepared by the International Commission on English in the Liturgy: A Joint Commission of Catholic Bishop's Conferences, Presider's Edition, (Collegeville, MN: The Liturgical Press, 1989)].

13. *Rituale Romanum* ex decreto Sacrosancti Oecumenici Concilii Vaticani II instauratum auctoritate Pauli Pp. VI promulgatum, *Ordo Unctionis infirmorum eorumque pastoralis curae,* editio typica (Vatican City: Typis Polyglottis Vaticanis, 1972) [hereafter OI]. [*Roman Ritual* revised by Decree of the Second Vatican Ecumenical Council and published by authority of Pope Paul VI, *Pastoral Care of the Sick: Rites of Anointing and Viaticum,* approved for use in the dioceses of the United States of America by the National Conference of Catholic Bishops and confirmed by the Apostolic See, trans. by ICEL, [hereafter OI, trans. by ICEL, 1983] (New York: Catholic Book Publishing Co., 1983)]. It must be noted from the start that the 1983 ICEL text is an example of an official adaptation, Approved by the Apostolic See, and a translation.

14. Bugnini, *The Reform of the Liturgy 1948–1975,* 696. Cf. Annibale Bugnini, *La riforma liturgica 1948–1975* (Roma: Edizioni Liturgiche, 1983), 676: "Il rito sacramentale del matrimonio fu uno dei primi ad essere messo a studio e il primo che fu pubblicato." The precise dates of publication of the *editiones typicae* of both rites are March 19, 1969 for the *Ordo celebrandi Matrimonium* and August 15, 1968 for *De Ordinatione Diaconi, Presbyteri, et Episcopi.* The former was effective as of July 1, 1969; the latter as of April 6, 1969. The 1968 *editio typica* for *De Ordinatione Diaconi, Presbyteri, et Episcopi* appeared without any *praenotanda.*

15. The Decree of promulgation by the Congregation for Rites may be found in Kaczynski, 1:392–95.

16. Ibid. For bishops, see 392–93: "Ex traditione enim, quae praesertim liturgicis ritibus et Ecclesiae tum Orientis tum Occidentis usu declaratur, perspicuum est manuum impositione. . . ."

specifies that the essential part of each of the three prayers of ordination is the "form" of the sacrament.[17] The general structure of the Rite of Ordination follows the same pattern in all three cases. After the presiding bishop has delivered the homily, the rites are then celebrated.[18] In short, the revision of the Rite of Ordination in 1968 was an initial step in the process of revising all the sacramental rites and as such, it suffered from some deficiencies.[19] This revision serves herein not so much as an example of a new *editio typica* dealing with cultural adaptations of the liturgy but rather as a point of departure for a consideration of the *editio typica altera* of 1989.

DE ORDINATIONE EPISCOPI, PRESBYTERORUM, ET DIACONORUM, 1989[20]

INTRODUCTION

The 1989 title of the ritual itself, i.e., *De Ordinatione Episcopi, presbyterorum et diaconorum*, reveals a shift in both theological

---

17. Ibid. "et verbis consecrationis gratiam Spiritus Sancti ita conferri et sacrum characterem ita imprimi." For Deacons see ibid., 394: "In Ordinatione Diaconorum materia est Episcopi mannum impositio, quae silentio fit super singulos ordinandos ante precationem consecratoriam; forma autem constat verbis eiusdem precationis consecratoriae, quorum haec ad naturam rei pertinent, atque adeo ut actus valeat exiguntur: 'Emitte in eos, Domine, quaesumus Spiritum Sanctum, quo in opus ministerii fideliter exsequendi munere septiformis tuae gratiae roborentur' "; for priests see ibid.: "In Ordinatione Presbyterorum, item materia est Episcopi mannum impositio, quae silentio super singulos ordinandos fit ante precationem consecratoriam; forma vero constat verbis eiusdem precationis consecratoriae, quorum haec ad naturam rei pertinent, atque adeo ut actus valeat exiguntur: 'Da, quaesumus, omnipotens Pater, his familiis tuis Presbyterii dignitatem; innova in visceribus eorum Spiritum sanctitatis; acceptum a te, Deus, secundi meriti munus obtineant, censuramque morum exemplo suae conversationis insinuent.'"

18. Ibid. See Bugnini, *The Reform of the Liturgy 1948–1975*, 719–20 for a brief summary of the rite itself.

19. Ibid., 721. Concerning the deficiencies of the reformed rites of ordination, Bugnini notes: "The reformed rites of ordination were generally accepted as satisfactory. Use of them, however, also brought to light some deficiencies. These were felt at two points in particular: the lack of an Introduction *(praenotanda)* comparable to those in the liturgical books published later on (i.e., after 1968), and the ordination prayer for priest, which, it was objected, was not very meaningful, inasmuch as it focuses more on Old Testament priesthood than on the priesthood of Christ."

20. *The Roman Pontifical* As Renewed By Decree of the Second Vatican Ecumenical Council Published By Authority of Pope Paul VI And Further Revised At the Direction of Pope John Paul II, *Rites of Ordination of a Bishop, of Priests, and of Deacons*, Second Typical Edition, trans. by ICEL, 1999 (Washington, DC: USCCB, 2003).

and ecclesiological perspective.[21] The decree of promulgation[22] from the Congregation for Divine Worship and the Discipline of the Sacraments which introduces the second typical edition addresses the reason for the change in terminology:

> The structure of this book is changed in such a way that it begins with the Bishop, who has the fullness of the sacrament of Holy Orders, in order to convey more clearly the idea that priests are the Bishop's co-workers and that deacons are ordained for his ministry.[23]

The same decree addresses other areas of change from the previous *editio typica*. Concerning cultural adaptations of the liturgy, there are two indications in the closing paragraphs of the decree which indicate that the *praenotanda* in the second typical edition make provision for the conferences of bishops to prepare adaptations according to the law:

> It will be the concern of the Conferences of Bishops to introduce into practice and into the editions prepared for the vernacular languages the texts, rites, and norms which are found in this edition.
> The Latin edition of these texts and rites may be used as soon as it is published. Vernacular versions, when these have been approved by the Conferences of Bishops and confirmed by the Apostolic See, become effective on the date to be decreed by those Conferences.[24]

It is not surprising, therefore, that the threefold division of the "General Introduction" (i.e., *praenotanda generalia*) contains a section entitled "Adaptations for Different Regions and Circumstances."[25]

---

21. Cf. *De Ordinatione Diaconi, Presbyteri et Episcopi* in 1968 with *De Ordinatione Episcopi, presbyterorum et diaconorum* in 1989.

22. *De Ordinatione Episcopi, presbyterorum et diaconorum*, editio typica altera, *Decretum* Notitiae 26 (1990):74–75.

23. Eduardo Cardinal Martínez, Prefectus (CDWDS) *Decretum*, editio typica altera *Notitiae* 26 (1990): 75: "Dispositio libri immutata est, ita ut initium sumendo ab Episcopo, qui plenitudinem sacri Ordinis habet, melius intellegatur quomodo presbyteri eius sint cooperatores et diaconi ad eius ministerium ordinentur."

24. *The Roman Pontifical* As Renewed By Decree of the Second Vatican Ecumenical Council Published By Authority of Pope Paul VI And Further Revised At the Direction of Pope John Paul II, *Rites of Ordination of a Bishop, of Priests, and of Deacons*, Second Typical Edition, 9. Cf. Latin text: "Conferentiis Episcoporum curae erit textus, ritus et normas, quae in hac editione inveniuntur, in praxim et in editiones linguis vernaculis apparandas inducere. Iidem ritus ac textus, lingua latina exarati, statim ac prodierint erunt adhibendi; linguis autem vernaculis, cum interpretationes a Conferentiis Episcoporum approbatae ab Apostolica Sede sint recognitae, a die quem ipsae Conferentiae statuerint."

25. *De Ordinatione Episcopi, presbyterorum, et diaconorum*, editio typica altera, in *Notitiae* 26 (1990): 74–78: "Prenotandae Generalia: (I) De Sacra Ordinatione; (II) De Structura Celebrationis; (III) De Aptationibus ad Varias Regiones et Adiuncta."

ADAPTATIONS ALLOWED BY THE *PRAENOTANDA*

In the third section of the *praenotanda*, "Adaptations for Different Regions and Circumstances" [*De aptationibus ad varias regiones et adiuncta*], the first sentence of number 11 enunciates a principle concerning the right of the conferences of bishops to adapt [*accommodare*] the rites of ordination of a bishop, of priests, and of deacons to the needs of the particular regions, so that after the Apostolic See has reviewed the decisions of a conference, the rites may be used in the region of that conference.[26] The Latin text includes both *aptatio* and *accommodatio* (in its verbal form, *accommodare*). The former describes the overall project, i.e., the work of adapting and/or accommodating the liturgy. The latter refers more particularly to the adjustments made in the ritual celebration in relation to the constraints and peculiarities of each particular region [*singularum regionum necessitatibus*].[27]

The second sentence of number 11 recalls similar prescriptions from the *praenotanda* of earlier *editiones typicae* of other sacraments.[28] Three reasons for accommodating the liturgy are then mentioned in succession:

1. Due regard for local circumstances and conditions [*adiunctis locorum et rerum*]

2. The character or native talents of the peoples [*ingenio populorum*]

3. The traditions of the peoples [*necnon et traditionibus populorum*]

---

26. Ibid., no. 11: "Conferentiis Episcoporum competit, ritus Ordinationum Episcopi, presbyterorum et diaconorum *accommodare* (emphasis added) singularum regionum necessitatibus, ut, actis ab Apostolica Sede recognitis, in regionibus ad quas pertinet, adhibeatur. Qua in re Conferentiae Episcoporum, attentis locorum et rerum adiunctis necnon ingenio et traditionibus populorum, possunt: . . ." It is, however, interesting to note that despite the similarity between this statement in the 1989 editio typica altera of *De Ordinatione Episcopi, presbyterorum et diaconorum* and a similar one in the 1972 *Ordo unctionis infirmorum*, the 1989 text omits the words "vi Constitutionis de sacra Liturgia (art. 63b)." This phraseology is included, however, in the *1991 Ordo celebrandi Matrimonium*. The latter postdates *De Ordinatione Episcopi, presbyterorum et diaconorum*. However, one cannot help but wonder why the reference to *Sacrosanctum Concilium* was not included here.

27. The use of *aptatio* in the heading, "De Aptationibus ad Varias Regiones et Adiuncta," recalls the vocabulary used in *Sacrosanctum Concilium*, number 40, where *aptatio* is used throughout the three subsections. Its use here also is consistent with the revisions of other sacramental rites, especially in the section of the *praenotanda* dealing with the competency to make adaptations to the liturgy as well as the manner in which such proposals are to be made. However, curiously enough, in the first sentence of no. 11, *De Ordinatione Episcopi, presbyterorum et diaconorum*, *accommodare* is used to describe the very same phenomenon.

28. See footnote 25 above.

The terminology above reveals the importance of the relationship between the celebration of the liturgical rite and local culture. First of all, since the prevailing values of any given culture affect liturgical celebrations, the conferences of bishops should be attentive to the *adiuncta locorum et rerum*, i.e., to the particular constraints or needs that may be found in any given place. For example, the prevailing values in place in a given culture may mitigate against a question/answer format relating to the candidate's promise of obedience. Perhaps the *formulae Ritus Romani* of the *editio typica altera* for a particular episcopal region might consider omitting the question/answer pattern altogether and substituting a declarative statement on the part of the candidate as he promises obedience to his lawful bishop, or, in the case of religious who are to be ordained, to his lawful superior.[29] The declarative statements may perhaps be more suited to both the *adiuncta locorum et rerum* and to the *ingenium et traditiones populorum*.[30]

Secondly, the *ingenium populorum* reflects the overall cultural outlook or world-view of particular peoples, e.g., the way in which priesthood fits into a particular culture's view of religion. Thus, episcopal conferences should be attentive to both the theological and cultural currents in a given society regarding the understanding of the role of priesthood in the culture.[31]

---

29. *De Ordinatione Episcopi, presbyterorum, et diaconorum*, no. 153: "Promittis mihi et successoribus meis reverentiam et obedientiam?" "Promitto," are the formulas to be used when the diocesan bishop ordains candidates for the diocesan priesthood in his own diocese. (The formula is slightly altered to "ordinario tuo" when the ordaining bishop is not the Ordinary of the diocese.) However, there is an interesting addition to the 1989 *Ordo* when religious are to be ordained. The words *Episcopo diocesano*, which were absent from the formula in the 1968 *Ordo*, have now been added so that the new formula now asks: "Promittis *Episcopo dioecesano* (emphasis added) necnon legitimo Superiori tuo reverentiam et obedientiam?" "Promitto."

30. See OCM, 1991 in footnotes 60 and 62 below for a provision regarding the adaptation or omission of questions in the rite of marriage.

31. For the changing perspective on the priesthood, see Daniel Donovan, *What Are They Saying About the Ministerial Priesthood?* (New York: Paulist Press, 1992), especially 134–40. Donovan summarizes several different contemporary theological perspectives on the priesthood. Although he is presenting various theological perspectives, they are, nevertheless, a reflection of how priesthood is perceived and even lived within various cultures: "The broadening of the notion of priesthood beyond the cultic demanded a rethinking that does not seem to have taken place. The confusion [i.e., about priesthood and priestly identity] was related to some degree to the multiplicity of functions that were now [i.e., post Vatican II] said to be part of the priestly office. (. . .) Theologians developed a variety of theologies of ministry. Some like Rahner and Ratzinger stress preaching and the word; others like John Paul II emphasized specifically cultic functions; and others still like Kasper and O'Meara gave the priority to pastoral leadership. (. . .) At the present time there is obviously no single Roman Catholic theology of the ministerial priesthood. This should be neither surprising

The *traditiones populorum* are the customs and practices such as those used to express assent or to offer obedience to the competent authority. This terminology is subsequently reflected in the prescriptions that follow concerning the authority of the Conference of Bishops to establish in what way the community, in keeping with regional customs, is to indicate its assent to the elections of the candidates in the ordination of a bishop (nos. 38 and 74), of priests (nos. 122, 150, 266, 307), of deacons (nos. 198, 226, 264, 305).[32]

Furthermore, as circumstances may suggest, the conferences of bishops are to see that before the ordination other questions be added to those already provided in the various rites of ordination (for a bishop, nos. 40 and 76; for priests, nos. 124, 152, 270, 311; for deacons, nos. 200, 228, 268, 309).[33] The conferences should also specify the form by which the elect for the diaconate and the presbyterate are to promise respect and obedience (nos. 125, 153, 201, 228, 269, 271, 310, 312).[34] In a similar vein, the episcopal conferences should ensure that in addition to the response to the respective question on celibacy, the candidate manifest in some external way the resolve to accept commitment to the obligation of celibacy (in the ordination of a deacon, nos. 200, 228, 268, 309).[35]

Concerning the music to be used in the ritual celebration, it also falls to the Conference of Bishops to approve songs to be used instead of those in this book, i.e., the Roman Pontifical containing

---

nor disheartening. The ordained ministry is a rich and many-sided reality, and there are a variety of legitimate approaches to it." Ibid., 136, 138.

32. *De Ordinatione Episcopi, presbyterorum, et diaconorum:* "(a) formare definire qua communitas, iuxta morem regionis, electioni candidatorum assentit (in Ordinatione Episcopi, nn. 38 et 74; in Ordinatione presbyterorum, nn. 122, 150, 226, 307; in Ordinatione diaconorum, nn. 198, 226, 264, 305)."

33. Ibid. "(b) statuere ut interrogationibus ante Ordinationem in ritibus praevisis (in Ordinatione Episcopi, nn. 40 et 76; in Ordinatione presbyterorum, nn. 124, 152, 270, 311; in Ordinatione diaconorum, nn. 200, 228, 268, 309) aliae, pro opportunitate, addantur."

34. Ibid. "(c) definire formam, qua electi ad diaconatum et presbyteratum reverentiam et oboedientiam promittunt (nn. 125, 153, 201, 228, 269, 271, 310, 312)." In lieu of questions, for example, perhaps declarative statements on the part of the candidates for ordination may be substituted in cultures that are more democratic than monarchical.

35. Ibid. "(d) statuere ut propositum assumendi obligationem caelibatus (in Ordinatione diaconorum, nn. 200, 228, 268, 309), praeter resonsionem ad quaestionem respectivam, froma aliqua externa manifestetur." The directive to have the candidates manifest, in some external way, their resolve to accept their commitment to celibacy may prove to be more difficult than it may first appear. For example, in the commitment to celibacy, the external manifestation may require more than a simple question/answer formula, or even a declarative sentence.

the ordination rite.[36] Finally, it is up to the conferences of bishops to propose to the Apostolic See other adaptations that will be introduced with its consent.[37] However, the laying on of hands cannot be omitted, nor the prayer of ordination shortened or replaced by other, alternative texts. The general structure of the rites and the proper character of each element are to be retained.

It would appear that the prescriptions in 11b regarding the addition of other questions before the ordination of the candidate [*aliae (i.e., interrogationes), pro opportunitate, addantur*], and 11d concerning the manifestation in some external way of the candidate's resolve to accept commitment to the obligation of celibacy [*forma aliqua externa*] correspond more closely to the *necessitates* and *adiuncta* mentioned in the opening statement in number 11. The prescriptions of 11a in relation to the way in which the community, in keeping with the regional customs, indicates its assent to the election of candidates [*formam definire qua communitas, iuxta morem regionis*] and 11c, concerning the form in which candidates for the diaconate and priesthood promise respect and obedience [*definire formam*], appear to be more in accord with the *traditiones populorum*.

Finally, in the rites of ordination, certain invariables, e.g., the laying on of hands and the prayer of ordination, have enjoyed a long-standing presence in the ritual celebration of ordination. With the exception of the restrictions stated within it, the last prescription in 11f remains intentionally broad. Consequently, while other adaptations may be presented to the Apostolic See for consideration, these two moments of ritual prayer (with an accompanying gesture) must remain unchanged. Thus, number 11 presents a summary of the significant adaptations by way of additions and/or changes from the previous *editio typica* of the rites of ordination.

---

36. Ibid. "(e) approbare quosdam cantus peragendos loco ipsorum qui in hoc libro indicantur." The permission to approve songs different from those that appear in the *editio typica* not only reiterates the central role that music and song occupy in the celebration of the Roman liturgy, but also foreshadows some of the prescriptions that will appear in the Fourth Instruction concerning music and song. Cf. *Fourth Instruction*, nos. 40–42.

37. Ibid. "(f) proponere Apostolicae Sedi alias aptationes rituum, de ipsius consensu introducendas. Attamen manuum impositio omitti nequit; Prex Ordinationis nec reduci nec substituti potest cum aliis textibus alternativis. Structura generalis ritus et indoles propria uniuscuiusque elementi serventur."

ORDO CELEBRANDI MATRIMONIUM, 1969

INTRODUCTION

The mandate to revise the *Rite of Marriage* contained in *Sacrosanctum Concilium*, numbers 77 and 78, and the accompanying general guidelines regarding the revision of the *Rite of Marriage* reveal the purpose for revising the marriage ritual. The significant points are listed below:

1. The rite of celebrating marriage in the Roman book of rites is to be revised, and made richer, in such a way that it will express the grace of the sacrament more clearly, and emphasize the duties of wife and husband.[38]

2. "If any parts of the world . . . use other praiseworthy customs and ceremonies" while celebrating the sacrament of matrimony, "the synod is very concerned that they be preserved in their entirety."[39]

3. Moreover, in accordance with article 63, the competent local church authority (see article 22:2 of this constitution) has been delegated the power to compose its own rite, one that is matched to the customs of the places and of the people that come under it. However, the law which requires the priest witnessing the marriage to ask for and obtain the consent of the parties contracting it should remain.[40]

The principles enunciated above in number 77 are peculiar to the revisions in the sacrament of matrimony because they appear to go further than the general principles on adaptation stated early in the liturgical constitution. Moreover, although

---

38. SC, no. 77: "Ritus celebrandi matrimonium, qui exstat in rituali romano, recognoscatur et ditior fiat, quo clarius gratia sacramenti significetur et munera coniugum inculcentur."

39. Ibid. "Si quae provinciae . . . aliis laudabilibus consuetudinibus et caeremoniis" in celebrando matrimonii sacramento, "utuntur eas omnino retineri sancta synodus vehementer optat." [The direction of the quotation marks in SC, no. 77 follows what occurs in Tanner, 834.] It is interesting to note that the provision for retaining local customs dates back to the Council of Trent, Session 24, *Canons on the Reform of Marriage*, Chapter I, November 11, 1563: "Finally, the holy synod earnestly desires that, if any provinces have praiseworthy customs and ceremonies in this [read matrimony] matter, over and above those here mentioned, these should by all means be retained." "Si quae provinciae aliis, ultra praedictas laudabilibus consuetudinibus et caeremoniis hac in re utuntur, eas omnino retineri sancta synodus vehementer optat." [Both of the preceding citations in English and Latin are from Tanner, vol. 2, 756.]

40. Ibid. "Insuper competenti auctoritati ecclesiasticae territoriali, de qua in art. 22, 2 huius constitutionis, relinquitur facultas, ad normam art. 63, exarandi ritum proprium usibus locorum et populorum congruentem, firma tamen lege ut sacerdos assistens requirat excipiatque contrahentium consensum."

some of the mandates in *Sacrosanctum Concilium* to revise the other sacraments express a similar concern for local culture and customs, the language used in numbers 77 and 78 is unique to the mandate for the revision of the rite of celebrating marriage.

The second paragraph of number 77 quotes an important principle from the Council of Trent, recognizing the existence of local rites that date back over centuries [*Si quae provinciae . . . aliis laudabilibus consuetudinibus et caeremoniis . . . utuntur*].[41] Secondly, the third paragraph of number 77 uses a stronger term to describe the task of the competent territorial authority, i.e., "*relinquitur facultas . . . exarandi ritum proprium usibus locorum et populorum congruentem.*"[42] The phraseology here is clearly different from that which appeared previously in the liturgical constitution when it addressed the area of adaptation of the liturgy. In addition, number 77 not only urges the retention [*eas omnino retineri*] of marriage rituals that are already in use; it also requires the "writing," i.e., the composing of a new rite for celebrating marriage [*vehementer optat exarandi ritum*].

At the same time that it fosters attention to local culture and customs regarding the liturgical celebration of the sacrament of matrimony, the innovative principle enunciated in number 77 preserves an important canonical provision [*firma tamen lege*] of the Roman rite: it requires that the priest (witnessing the marriage) ask for and receive the consent of those contracting marriage [*ut sacerdos assistens requirat excipiatque contrahentium consensum*].

THE *PRAENOTANDA* AND THE ADAPTATIONS OF THE RITE OF MARRIAGE ALLOWED BY THE *PRAENOTANDA*: NUMBERS 12–16; 17–18

The 18 numbers comprising the *praenotanda* contain two categories of directives: numbers 1–10 are intended more for use by all pastors, while numbers 12–18 are directed to episcopal conferences and their work of creating particular and local rituals. It is the second category that is of special interest for our purposes.

---

41. See footnote 39 above.

42. See Charlton T. Lewis and Charles Short, *A Latin Dictionary Founded on Andrew's Edition of Freund's Latin Dictionary*, ed. and rev. Charlton T. Lewis and Charles Short (Oxford: The Clarendon Press, 1879; reprint, New York: Oxford University Press, Inc., 1993), 673 and 164 respectively (page citations are to the reprint edition). The verb *exaro, -are* comes from the Latin root, *aro-are*, meaning to plow, to dig up, to till.

After stating in number 12 that particular rituals suitable for the customs and needs of individual areas should be prepared according to the principle of *Sacrosanctum Concilium* 63b and 77, numbers 13–16 list specific areas for adaptations:[43]

13. The formulas of the Roman Ritual may be *adapted* (emphasis added) or, as the case may be, filled out (including the questions before the consent and the actual words of consent). When the Roman Ritual has several optional formulas, local rituals may add other formulas of the same type.[44]

14. Within the rite which strictly expressed the sacrament of matrimony, the arrangement of its parts may be varied. If it seems more suitable even the questions before the consent may be omitted as long as the priest asks and receives the consent of the contracting parties.[45]

There are several interesting considerations in the provisions made above. Number 13 provides for the adaptation of the Roman rite [*Formulae Ritualis Romani aptari possunt*]. It also stipulates that the rite may be filled out (i.e., completed/finished) by adapting the questions before the consent and the expression of the consent itself [*etiam quaestiones ante consensum et ipsa verba consensus*]. Going further than the permission given in the Rite of Ordination, the second paragraph of number 13 envisions local rituals adding other formulas of the same nature to the liturgical celebration [*Formulae Ritualis Romani, si casus fert, compleri*]. Number 14 of the *praenotanda* respects the canonical provision concerning the essential components of the Rite of Marriage referred to above and repeats them verbatim: [*sed firma lege ut sacerdos assistens requirat excipiatque contrahentium consensum*]. Thus, numbers 13 and 14 serve as examples of adaptation

---

43. OCM, 1969, no. 12: "Firma manente facultate de qua infra, sub n. 17, in regionibus in quibus Rituale Romanum Matrimonii viget, Ritualia particularia singularum regionum consuetudinibus et necessitatibus *aptata* (emphasis added) parentur, ad normam art 63b et 77 Constitutionis de sacra Liturgia actis ab Apostolica Sede recognitis."

44. *Rite of Marriage*, trans. by ICEL, 1969 no. 13: "Formulae Ritualis Romani *aptari* (emphasis added) possunt vel, si casus fert, compleri (etiam quaestiones ante consensum et ipsa verba consensus). Quando Rituale Romanum plures exhibet formulas ad libitum, Ritualia particularia possunt etiam alias formulas eiusdem generis adicere." For an example of local rituals of the same type being added as an optional formula, see *Rite of Marriage*, trans. by ICEL, 1969, no. 25:12–13, both alternatives "B" for use in the dioceses of the United States of America.

45. Ibid., no. 14: "In ritu Sacramenti Matrimonii proprie dicto, *ordo partium accommodari* (emphasis added) potest, omissis etiam, si opportunius videbitur, quaestionibus ante consensum, sed firma lege ut sacerdos assistens requirat excipiatque contrahentium consensum."

of the Rite of Marriage which take into account both the long-standing tradition of the Church and local, ritualized customs.

The prescriptions of numbers 15 and 16 are also very significant examples of adaptations sensitive to the local culture of the people. The former permits that when the exchange of rings has been completed [*Traditione anulorum expleta*], "either the crowning or the veiling of the bride" [*vel coronatio sponsae, vel eius velatio*] may be included according to the local customs [*attentis locorum consuetudinibus, haberi potest*].[46] The next part of the paragraph refers to the possibility of 1) omitting the joining of hands or 2) the blessing and exchange of rings; it also specifies that the Conference of Bishops may substitute other rites in their place [*possunt Conferentiae Episcopales. . . vel aliis ritibus suppleantur*].[47]

Echoing the prescriptions of *Sacrosanctum Concilium* (no. 37), number 16 of OCM, 1969 allows that "whatever is good and is not indissolubly bound up with superstition and error be sympathetically considered and, if possible, preserved intact" [*quidquid honestum est, nec indissolubili vinculo superstitionibus erroribusque adstipulatur*] in the celebrations of marriage in countries receiving the Gospel for the first time [*apud populos, qui nunc primum Evangelium recipiunt*]. Secondly, number 16 prescribes that such things may be admitted into the liturgy itself [*immo in ipsam etiam Liturgiam admittatur*], provided they are in harmony with the true and authentic spirit of the liturgy [*dummodo cum rationibus veri et authentici spiritus liturgici congruat*].[48] The fact that the *praenotanda* of OCM, 1969 indicated an openness to "preserve intact" and "sympathetically consider whatever is good and not bound up with superstition" in a local culture which was receiving the Gospel for the first time represents a remarkable shift in what was once a staunchly conservative view on the part of the institutional church regarding "pagan" cultures. Moreover, that "such elements may be admitted into the liturgy" (provided they are in harmony, etc.)

---

46. Ibid., no. 15: "Traditione anulorum expleta, attentis locorum consuetudinibus, haberi potest vel coronatio sponsae vel eius velatio."

47. Ibid. "Sicubi iunctio manuum vel benedictio vel traditio anulorum cum ingenio populorum componi nequeunt, possunt Conferentiae Episcopales statuere ut hi ritus omittantur, vel aliis ritibus suppleantur."

48. Ibid., no. 16: "In usibus et modis celebrandi Matrimonium vigentibus apud populos, qui nunc primum Evangelium recipiunt quidquid honestum est, nec indissolubili vinculo superstitionibus erroribusque adstipulatur, benevole perpendatur ac, si fieri potest, sartum tectumque servetur, immo in ipsam etiam Liturgiam admittatur, dummodo cum rationibus veri et authentici spiritus liturgici congruat."

seems to indicate an equal willingness on the part of the institutional church to engage culture without prejudice.

Numbers 17 and 18 comprise the final section of the *praenotanda,* entitled "The Power to Compose a Particular Rite" [*De facultate exarandi ritum proprium*]. Indeed, the prescriptions of these two numbers envision more than mere adaptations of the liturgical celebration. Number 17 begins with the provision that allows the Conference of Bishops to draw up its own rite of marriage [*Unaquaeque Conferentia Episcopalis facultatem habet exarandi ritum proprium Matrimonii*] suited to the use of the people and place they serve [*locorum et populorum usibus congruentem*] and approved, of course, by the Apostolic See [*actis ab Apostolica Sede probatis*].[49] However, as we noted above in regard to number 14, the invariables in the liturgical celebration of the rite, whether composed anew or celebrated according to the Roman ritual, are the priest's asking for and receiving consent of the contracting parties and the nuptial blessing.[50]

The final prescription for adaptation occurs in the *praenotanda,* number 18.[51] However, here the *aptatio* is reversed. No longer is it a question of adapting a Roman rite to a culture; it is, rather, the situating or adapting the customary rites of a people to the Christian spirit and liturgy [*In populis apud quos caeremoniae Matrimonii . . . oportet illas ad spiritum christianum ac liturgiam aptare*]. There is also an interesting ecclesiological emphasis contained in number 18 in its recognition of the *domus ecclesiae* as a place for the liturgical celebration of the marriage rite [*In populis . . . ex consuetudine in domibus habentur, etiam per plures dies*]. The mention of both the place for and the duration of the celebration is one of the broadest and richest adaptations of the liturgical celebration of a sacramental rite.[52]

---

49. Ibid., no. 17: "Unaquaeque Conferentia Episcopalis facultatem habet *exarandi ritum proprium Matrimonii,* (emphasis added) locorum et populorum usibus congruentem, actis ab Apostolica Sede probatis."

50. Ibid. ". . . firma tamen lege ut sacerdos assistens requirat excipiatque contrahentium consensum et benedictionem nuptialem impertiatur."

51. OCM, 1969, no. 18: "Among peoples where the marriage ceremonies customarily take place in the home, sometimes over a period of several days, these customs should be adapted to the Christian spirit and to the liturgy. In such cases the Conference of Bishops, according to the pastoral needs of the people, may allow the sacramental rite to be celebrated in the home."

52. Ibid., no. 18: "In populis apud quos caeremoniae Matrimonii ex consuetudine in domibus habentur, etiam per plures dies, opportet illas ad spiritum christianum ac liturgiam *aptare* (emphasis added). Quo in casu potest Conferentia Episcopalis, iuxta necessitates pastorales populorum, statuere ut ipse ritus Sacramenti in domibus celebrari possit."

Thus, numbers 12–18 of *Ordo celebrandi Matrimonium* allow adaptations of the marriage rite, permit the composition of particular rituals and other formulas that are suited for the customs and needs of individual areas, endorse the rearrangement of the parts of the 1969 marriage ritual, and allow broad latitude to the conferences of bishops to draw up their own rites and to supplement them as suited to the pastoral needs of the people. Nevertheless, it must still be noted that whatever adaptations are made by the particular conference of bishops, the adapted rite must always be approved by the Apostolic See and conform to the law.[53]

ORDO CELEBRANDI MATRIMONIUM, 1991

There is a considerable difference in the number of entries in the *praenotanda* in the *editio typica altera* of 1991 over that of 1969. The 1969 edition contained 18 entries, subdivided into groupings of two or more; the 1991 edition contains a total of 44 *praenotanda*, subdivided in a similar but enriched pattern: (I) Concerning the Importance and Dignity of the Sacrament of Marriage; (II) Concerning Offices and Ministries; (III) Concerning the Celebration of Marriage: (A) Concerning Preparation, (B) Concerning the Rite to be Used; (IV) Concerning the Adaptations to be Arranged under the Care of the Conferences of Bishops.[54] Although it is this final section concerning adaptations that is pertinent to our considerations in the present study, there are very significant additions to OCM, 1991 which have theological, pastoral, and cultural implications.

PASTORAL ADAPTATIONS ADDED TO OCM, 1991

Numbers 25 and 26, for example, illustrate two ways in which lay participation in the sacramental rite has been enhanced. The former

---

53. Cf. no. 17 of OCM, 1969 (concerning the right of the Conference of Bishops to draw up its own rite of marriage suited to the usage of the place and of the people). Note that no such provision is allowed in any part of *De Ordinatione Diaconi, Presbyteri et Episcopi.*

54. OCM, 1991: "I: De Momento et Dignitate Sacramenti Matrimonii; II: De Officiis et Ministeriis; III: De Celebratione Matrimonii: De Praeparatione, De ritu adhibendo; IV: De Aptationibus Conferentiarum Episcoporum Cura Parandis." Again, I am indebted to ICEL for providing me a draft of the *Order of Celebrating Marriage*, (For Study and Comment by the Bishops of the Member and Associate-Member Conferences of the International Commission of English in the Liturgy), Second Typical Edition (Washington, DC: ICEL, 1996), approval pending (hereafter: *Rite of Marriage,* Provisional text, ICEL, 1996). Throughout the remainder of this study, I have chosen, at times, to deviate from their translation and provide my own English translation. When the translation is from ICEL, it shall be so indicated.

states: "In places where priests and deacons are lacking, the diocesan bishop, after a prior favorable decision of the Conference of Bishops and having obtained the permission of the Apostolic See, may delegate laypersons to assist at marriages. The delegated layperson "asks for and receives the consent of the couple in the name of the church."[55] The layperson's role is also extended in the rite to include "aiding in the spiritual preparation of the couple and in the preparation of the liturgical celebration."[56] The same number ends with an echo of *Sacrosanctum Concilium* number 26, wherein the entire Christian community is called upon to give testimony to faith and to demonstrate to the world the love of Christ in the celebration of Marriage.[57] It will be very interesting to see how the provision for laypersons assisting at marriages will be incorporated (inculturated) into the various national editions of the Latin *Ordo*, especially in those countries where priests and/or deacons are not readily available.[58]

---

55. *Rite of Marriage*, Provisional text, ICEL, 1996. no. 25. OCM, 1991, no. 25: "Ubi desunt sacerdotes et diacni, potest Episcopus dioecesanus, praevio voto favorabili Episcoporum Conferentiae et obtenta licentia Apostolicae Sedis, laicos delegare, qui Matrimoniis assistant. . . Exquirit sponsorum consensum eumque nomine Ecclesiae recipit." It would appear from the wording of the text regarding the prior favorable vote of the Conference of Bishops and the necessity for prior license from the Apostolic See, that delegation of a layperson to assist at marriages is not the ideal situation. (Cf. *Codex Iuris Canonici auctoritate Ioannis Pauli Pp. II promulgatus* (Vatican City: Librería Editrice Vaticana, 1983), can. 1108, 2 (hereafter CIC). Concerning laypersons assisting at marriages, see Julián López, "La segunda edición del ritual del Matrimonio," *Phase* 203 (1994): 415. López points out that the provisions for laypersons in the 1991 *Ordo* are very different from previous permissions allowing laypersons as Eucharistic ministers or as officiants at blessings or funerals. The difference here is rooted not in the capacity of laypersons to fulfill some function or liturgical ministry arising from their baptismal priesthood, but rather on the conditions that the Church establishes about the form for the celebration of Matrimony, i.e., the conditions which can affect the validity of the sacrament as they are reflected in the Revised 1983 *Code of Canon Law*. "No se trata, por tanto, de una concesión equiparable a la del ministro extraordinario de la Eucaristía, o a las que permiten a los laicos dirigir algunas celebraciones de sacramentales (exsequias o bendiciones). La diferencia radica no en la capacidad de los laicos parar desempeñar algunas funciones u oficios litúrgicos, sobre la base de su sacerdocio bautismal, sino en las condiciones que la Iglesia establece acerca de la forma de celebrar el Matrimonio, condiciones que pueden afectar a la validez del sacramento, como son los requisitos contemplados en el canon 1112, §1."

56. Ibid., no. 26: "Alii vero laici variis modis partem exercere possunt tum in praeparatione spirituali nupturientium, tum in ipsa celebratione ritus."

57. Ibid. "Tota autem communitas christiana cooperetur oportet ad fidem testificandam et amorem Christi mundo significandum."

58. López, 416: "Será interesante comprobar el puesto que se da a este rito en los rituales nacionales. Sin duda figurará en todos, dado que estos rituales deben recoger lo que se encuentra en la edición típica latina, pero no ocupará el mismo lugar ni el mismo relieve en un ritual editado en Europa que en uno preparado para unas Iglesias en las que no es fácil contar con la presencia del sacerdote o del diácono y será preciso recurrir a lo establecido en

---

ADAPTATIONS ALLOWED TO
THE CONFERENCES OF BISHOPS

It must be stated from the start that there are differences between OCM, 1969 and OCM, 1991 concerning the adaptations of the marriage rite that are proper to the conferences of bishops. In the former, the effort was made to include under one heading for numbers 12–16 the entire process and possibility of adaptations [*De ritualibus particularibus parandis*], inclusive of what belongs to the adaptations of the Roman rite, and under another heading for numbers 17 and 18 the composition of new liturgies [*De facultate exarandi ritum proprium*]. In the analysis below of OCM, 1991, it will become clear that in a comparison of the fourth section of the *praenotanda* of OCM, 1991, "Concerning the Adaptations to be provided under the care of the Conference of Bishops" [*De aptationibus Conferentiam episcoporum cura parandis*], numbers 39–41 will correspond to OCM, 1969 numbers 12–16; numbers 42–44 in OCM, 1991 will correspond to numbers 17–18 of OCM, 1969.

This final section of the *praenotanda* of OCM, 1991 is replete with references to adaptation. Number 39 of the 1991 *Ordo* begins with an allusion to numbers 37–40 and 63b of *Sacrosanctum Concilium* wherein the background for adaptation is established. The right of the Conference of Bishops to adapt this (i.e., the Rite of Marriage) Roman Ritual to the customs and needs of the regions is established after the acta have been reviewed by the Apostolic See.[59]

---

el CDC, c. 1112." It is also interesting that López alone notes this pastoral adaptation in his consideration of the *praenotanda*. José M. Rodríguez in "Nueva edición del ritual del Matrimonio" mentions the adaptation in a section concerning who can be considered the official, delegated witness of the Church at the ritual celebration. He and López both note that Chapter III in the editio typica altera, "Ordo celebrandi Matrimonium coram assistente laico" is devoted to how a delegated layperson presides over the entire celebration. See José M. Rodríguez, "Nueva edición del ritual del Matrimonio: Teología y Pastoral," *Phase* 32 (1992): 24–25 and German Martinez, "The Newly Revised Roman Rite for Celebrating Marriage," *Worship* 69 (1995): 129–30. Martinez does not even mention this adaptation. In fact he omits it from his list of new elements. Moreover, the insight on the part of López must be seen in relation to the theological and canonical principle that the Church in the West has always understood that the couple to be married are the ministers of the sacrament with the priest as the official witness.

59. OCM, 1991, no. 39: "Conferentis Episcoporum competit, vi Constitutionis de sacra Liturgia (nn. 37–40 et 63b) hoc Rituale Romanum, singularum regionum consuetudinibus et necessitatibus *accommodare* (emphasis added), ut, actis ab Apostolica Sede recognitis, in regionibus ad quas pertinet adhibeatur." It is important to notice that the vocabulary used herein is not that of *aptare* (used in OCM, 1969) but rather that of *accommodare*.

Number 40 of the *praenotanda* lists the specific responsibilities of the Conference of Bishops in the area of adaptation:

1. To decide on the *adaptations* (emphasis added) indicated here (cf. below, nos. 41–44)

2. As circumstance suggests, to *adapt* (emphasis added) and supplement the *praenotanda* (translation corrected) of the Roman Ritual from no. 36 on (rite to be used), so as to achieve the conscious and active participation of the faithful

3. To prepare translations of the texts, so that they are truly *adapted* (emphasis added) to the genius of the different languages and cultures, and to add, whenever appropriate, suitable melodies for singing

4. In preparing editions, to arrange the material in a form that will be suitable for pastoral use[60]

Number 41 specifies the areas (i.e., guidelines) that must be kept in view in the preparation of adaptations. First, it allows for the formularies of the Roman Ritual (even the questions before the consent and the very words of consent) to be adapted [*Formulae Ritualis Romani aptari possunt*] and, as circumstances suggest, even supplemented [*vel, si casus fert, compleri*].[61] Secondly, number 41 specifies that whenever the Roman Ritual provides several texts from which to choose [*plures exhibet formulas ad libitum*], other formulas (texts) of the same kind may be added [*alias formulas eiusdem generis adicere licet*].[62] Provided that the structure of the sacramental rite be maintained [*servata structura ritus sacramentalis*], the arrangement of the order of the parts of the rite may also be adjusted [*ordo partium accommodari potest*]; for example, if it seems more suitable, the omission of the questions before the

---

60. *Rite of Marriage*, Provisional text, ICEL, 1996, no. 40. Cf. OCM, 1991, no. 40: "Qua de re, Conferentiarum Episcoporum erit: (1) *Aptationes* (emphasis added) definire, de quibus infra (nn. 41–44); (2) Praenotanda quae in Rituali Romano habentur inde a n. 36 et sequentibus (De ritu adhibendo), si casus fert, *aptare* (emphasis added) et complere ad participationem fidelium consciam et actuosam reddendam; (3) Versiones textuum parare, ita ut indoli variorum sermonum atque ingenio diversarum culturarum vere *accommodentur* (emphasis added), additis, quoties opportunum fuerit, melodiis aptis; (4) In editionibus parandis, materiam ordinare modo qui ad usum pastoralem aptior videatur."

61. Ibid., no. 41:1. Cf. OCM, 1991, no. 41:4: "In *aptationibus* (emphasis added) apparandis, prae oculis habeantur ea quae sequuntur: Formulae Ritualis Romani *aptari* (emphasis added) possunt vel, si casus fert, compleri (etiam interrogationes ante consensum et ipsa verba consensus)."

62. Ibid., 41:2. Cf. OCM, 1991, no. 41:2: "Quando Rituale Romanum plures exhibet formulas ad libitum, alias formulas eiusdem generis adicere licet."

reception of consent is permitted [*interrogationes ante consensum omitti possunt*], provided that the consent be clearly asked for and received [*tamen lege ut assistens requirat excipiatque contrahentium consensum*].[63] Although this adaptation echoes what was contained in the previous rite,[64] there is a significant change in vocabulary from the 1969 *Ordo* wherein the assisting minister is specified as the "priest assisting" [*sacerdos assistens*] at Marriage. In the 1991 *Ordo* the assisting minister may be either a delegated lay man/woman, or a priest or a deacon, since the word *sacerdos* is dropped from the provision in number 42 [*firma tamen lege ut assistens requirat excipiatque contrahentium consensum*].[65]

Number 41:4 allows that in the case of pastoral need, the consent of the contracting parties may always be asked for by questioning [*potest . . . contrahentium consensus semper interrogatione*].[66] Thus, what formerly was a rubric in the 1969 *Ordo* is now placed in the *praenotanda* of the second edition.[67]

LITURGICAL ADAPTATIONS DEPENDING ON LOCAL CUSTOMS, THE TRADITIONS, AND CULTURES OF PEOPLES ALLOWED TO THE CONFERENCES OF BISHOPS

The three remaining guidelines in number 41 suggest ways in which the Rite of Marriage may be adapted according to the local customs, traditions, and cultures of the peoples.[68] Number 41:5 concerning the local customs, exchanging of rings and the crowning or veiling of the bride, or the veiling of the bride and groom[69]

---

63. Ibid., 41:3. Cf. OCM, 1991, no. 41:3: "Servata structura ritus sacramentalis, ordo partium *accommodari* (emphasis added) potest. Si opportunius videbitur, interrogationes ante consensum ommiti possunt, firma tamen lege ut assistens requirat excipiatque contrahentium consensum."

64. Cf. OCM, 1969, nos. 13 and 14.

65. OCM, 1969, Cf. nos. 6, 14, and 17 for the words *sacerdos assistens*.

66. OCM, 1991, no. 41:4: "Necessitate pastorali id exigente, statui potest ut contrahentium consensus semper interrogatione requirat."

67. OCM, 1969, nos. 25, 45, and 60.

68. Cf. Martinez, "The Newly Revised Roman Rite for Celebrating Marriage," 136–37: "Another important fact in regard to the liturgical structure of the ritual is the enrichment of creativity and inculturation. All Christian traditions have always included the local culture in their rites of marriage."

69. OCM, 1991, no. 41:5: "Traditione anulorum expleta, attentis locorum consuetudinibus haberi potest vel coronatio sponsae vei sponsorum velatio."

is almost a verbatim inclusion of number 15 of the *praenotanda* from the 1969 *Ordo*. There is, nevertheless, a subtle change from the phrase "either the crowning or the veiling of the bride" to "either the crowning of the bride or the veiling of the bride and the groom."[70] This change may reflect a contemporary attention to inclusiveness (different from OCM, 1969's exclusive mention of the "bride" only) as well as a more contemporary understanding of the roles of husband and wife in the living out of their marriage promises as equals.[71]

The provision in number 41:6 for the omission or replacement of the joining of hands and exchanging and blessing of rings by other rites, when they are incompatible with the culture,[72] is yet another example of how the liturgical celebration respects the local customs and traditions. OCM, 1991 does not repeat the specific reference to the Conference of Bishops as those who allow the omission or substitution; rather, it is presumed that all adaptations are subject to their competence as stated in the heading to Part IV of the *praenotanda*.[73]

The final guideline in number 41:7 is an excellent example of a principle of liturgical inculturation that will be enunciated in the *Fourth Instruction*; namely, that it is to be carefully and prudently considered [*Sedulo et prudenter consideretur*] what may be opportunely admitted [*opportune admitti possit*] from the customs and native character of individual peoples [*quid ex traditionibus ingenioque singulorum populorum*].[74]

---

70. Cf. OCM, 1969, no. 15: ". . . vel coronatio sponsae, vel *eius* (emphasis added) velatio" OCM, 1991, no. 41: 5: ". . . . vel coronatio sponsae vel *sponsorum* (emphasis added) velatio."

71. This change, i.e., the inclusion of a mention of the groom where formerly only the bride was mentioned, will also be evident in the revisions of the nuptial blessings from OCM, 1969 to OCM, 1991.

72. OCM, 1991, no. 41:6: "Sicubi iunctio manuum vel benedictio anulorum eorumque traditio cum ingenio populorum componi nequeunt, statui potest ut his ritus omittantur, vel aliis ritibus suppleantur." This adaptation is a verbatim inclusion of number 15 from the 1969 Ordo.

73. OCM, 1969, no. 15: "Sicubi iunctio manuum vel benedictio vel traditio anulorum cum ingenio populorum componi nequeunt, possunt Conferentiae Episcopales statuere ut hit ritus . . . ." with OCM, 1991, no. 41:6: "Sicubi iunctio manuum vel benedictio anulorum eorumque traditio cum ingenio populorum componi nequeunt, statui potest ut hi ritus. . . ."

74. OCM, 1991, no. 41:7: "Sedulo et prudenter consideratur qui ex traditionibus ingenioque singulorum populorum opportune admitti possunt." Cf. *Fourth Instruction*, nos. 56–57, especially footnote 122 regarding the *Order of Christian Initiation of Adults and the Baptism of Children*.

THE CONFERENCES OF BISHOPS
AND THE COMPOSITION OF A NEW RITE
OF MARRIAGE

The remaining three numbers of the fourth section of the *praeno-tanda* in OCM, 1991 have to do with composing new rites. They represent a significant repetition of some prescriptions of OCM, 1969, with slight clarifications added. For example, in contrast to OCM, 1969, number 17 which specifically designates the assisting minister as *sacerdos assistens,* in number 42 of OCM, 1991, the one who acts as the assisting minister in asking for and receiving the consent of the contracting parties is left unspecified.[75] There is also a repetition of the importance of the imparting of the nuptial blessing [*benedictio nuptialis impertiatur*] by the assisting minister during the liturgical celebration.[76]

However, in number 43, the repetition of the phrase "for the marriage customs of nations that are now receiving the Gospel for the first time" [*qui nunc primum Evangelium recipiunt*] from the 1969 *editio typica* is quite significant.[77] The *Fourth Instruction* will make a similar distinction between adaptations among such peoples and those in more traditional Christian cultures.[78] In number 44 of the 1991 *Ordo,* the permission for celebrating the marriage ceremonies that take place customarily in the homes, sometimes over a period of days, is repeated.[79] It is also significant, however, that the OCM, 1991 retains the emphasis of OCM,

---

75. Ibid., no. 42. Cf. OCM, 1969, no. 17: ". . . firma tamen lege ut *sacerdos assistens* (emphasis added) requirat excipiatque contrahentium consensum" with OCM, 1991, no. 42: "firma tamen lege ut *assistens* requirat et excipiatque contrahentium consensum. . . ." This number is also essentially a repetition of OCM, 1969, no. 17, with the exception of the addition in the 1991 version of the phrase, *ad normam Constitutionis de sacra liturgia* (n. 63b), to specify the basis for the right of the Conference of Bishops to draw up its own marriage rite.

76. Ibid. ". . . ut assistens . . . benedictio nuptialis impertiatur." Note that in Chapter III, "Ordo Celebrationis Matrimonium Coram Assistente Laico," nos. 139 "Tunc assistens prosequitur, manibus iunctis:

Nunc super hos sponsos,
Dei benedictionem súpplices invocémos
Ut ipse suo fóveat benignus auxilio
Quos ditávit connúbi sacraménto

and 140, "Deinde super sponsos genuflexos assistens, dicit, manibus iunctis, orationem benedictionis nuptialis, omnibus participantibus." leave no doubt that the presiding layperson (assistens) imparts the nuptial blessing but with hands joined.

77. Ibid., no. 43: "In usibus et modis celebrandi Matrimonium vigentibus apud populos, qui nunc primum Evangleium recipiunt. . . ."

78. See De Liturgia Romana et inculturatione, nos. 6–8.

1969 (number 18); namely, that the local marriage rituals are to be adapted to the Christian spirit and to the liturgy and not vice-versa [oportet illas (i.e., caeremoniae Matrimonii)] ad spiritum christianum ac Liturgiam aptare].

It would appear from the considerations above that the praenotanda are very important in the creation and revision of new rites. Reading and reflecting upon the praenotanda can and should lead to a better quality of celebrations of the sacraments in their ritual context.

ORDO EXSEQUIARUM, 1969

THE PRAENOTANDA

From the opening numbers of the praenotanda in the revised rite of funerals, it is evident that the focus of the liturgical celebration is envisioned as a present action which affects the future. Thus, the praenotanda consistently use the present indicative to stress the importance of the actual celebration of the funeral rites: "In the funeral rites, the Church celebrates [celebrat Ecclesia] the paschal mystery of Christ. . . . The Church offers the eucharistic sacrifice of Christ's passover for the dead and pours out prayers and intercessions on behalf of the dead [Ideo sacrificium eucha-risticum Paschatis Christi pro defunctis offert Ecclesia, pre-cesque atque suffragia pro illis effundit]."[80] When the text uses the present subjunctive, it always occurs in the purpose clause introduced by ut, expressing a hope that the present day celebrations may bring spiritual help to some and the consolation of hope to others [ut . . . aliis impetrent spiritualem opem, aliis offerant spei solacium].[81]

Number 2 of the praenotanda states that when Christians celebrate funeral rites, the celebration should be an affirmation not only of their hope in eternal life but should also meet contemporary needs and respect the local customs and native character of various peoples:

---

79. OCM, 1991, no. 44: "In populos apud quos caeremoniae Matrimonii ex consuetudine in domibus habentur, etiam per plures dies, oportet illas ad spiritum christianum ac Liturgiam aptare (emphasis added). Quo in casu, potest Conferentia Episcoporum, iuxta necessitates pastorales populorum, statuere ut ipse ritus Sacramenti in domibus celebrari possit." This is a verbatim repetition (with the exception of the modification of OCM, 1969 Conferentia Episcopalis to Conferentia Episcoporum in OCM, 1991) of OCM, 1969, no. 18.

80. Rite of Funerals in The Rites of the Catholic Church, no. 1. OE, no. 1.

81. Ibid.

In celebrating the funeral rites of their brothers and sisters, Christians should certainly affirm their hope in eternal life in such a way that they do not seem to neglect or ignore the feeling and practice of their own time and place [*ita tamen ut mentem modumque agendi hominum suae aetatis suaeque regionis circa defunctos nec ignorare nec neglegere videantur*]. Whether, therefore, it may be a question of family traditions or of local customs or of societies established to take care of funerals, anything that is good may be used freely [*quidquid bonum invenerint*]; but anything alien to the Gospel should be transformed [*quidquid vero Evangelio contradicere videatur, ita transformare nitantur*] so that funeral rites for Christians may proclaim the paschal faith and the spirit of the Gospel.[82]

In addition, depending on local customs, the revised rite also recognizes the importance of the following areas: a) the vigil in the home of the deceased; b) the time between death and burial and also the time when the body is laid out; c) the assembly of relatives and, if possible, of the whole community to receive hope and consolation in the Liturgy of the Word, to offer the Eucharistic sacrifice, and to bid farewell to the deceased in the final commendation, followed by the carrying of the body to the grave or tomb.[83]

The *praenotanda* also show the importance in some places of the "home" of the deceased as a "station" for the celebration of a funeral rite:

The funeral rite, according to the third plan, is to be celebrated in the home of the deceased. In some places this plan is not at all useful; but in some regions it is actually necessary. In view of the variety of circumstances, specific points have not been considered; but it seemed desirable to mention this rite so that it may include

---

82. Ibid., no. 2. OE, no. 2: "In fratrum suorum exsequiis celebrandis spem vitae aeternae christiani utique affirmare satagant, ita tamen ut mentem modumque agendi hominum suae aetatis suaeque regionis circa defunctos nec ignorare nec neglegere videantur. Sive ergo de familiarum traditionibus agitur, sive de locorum consuetudinibus, sive de societatibus ad funera curanda constitutis, quidquid bonum invenerint, libenter probent, quiquid vero Evangelio contradicere videatur, ita transformare nitantur, ut, quae exsequiae pro christianis celebrentur, et fidem paschalem ostendant et evangelicum spiritum vere demonstrent." This prescription recalls the principles of SC, no. 37.

83. OE, no. 3: "Potiora autem momenta, iuxta locorum consuetudines, haec numerari possunt: vigilia in domo defuncti, corporis depositio in feretro et ipsius translatio ad sepulcrum, praemissa tum propinquorum tum, si fieri potest, totius etiam communitatis adunatione ad audiendam in liturgia verbi consolationem spei, ad sacrificium eucharisticum offerendum et ad defunctum ultima valedictione consalutandum." The importance of the celebration and duration of the Rite of Funerals in the "home" recalls a similar adaptation from the celebration of the *Rite of Marriage* in OCM, 1969 and 1991, nos. 18 and 44, respectively.

elements common to the others, for example, in the Liturgy of the Word and in the rite of final commendation and farewell. For the rest, the conference of bishops may make their own arrangements.[84]

Number 9, which follows immediately, stipulates that when particular rituals are prepared in harmony with the new Roman Ritual, the Conference of Bishops may either a) retain the three plans for funeral rites or b) change the order or c) omit one or other of them.[85] The remainder of this article grants wide latitude to conferences of bishops (after considering pastoral needs) to allow for the existence of a variety of types of funeral celebrations within the same country.[86] The provision for the simultaneous existence in the same country of a variety of types of liturgical celebrations is particularly significant in the *praenotanda* since the *editiones typicae* of the sacramental rites we have considered to this point do not contain a similar prescription. It would appear that a more pastoral approach to adaptations permeates the *praenotanda* of the *Ordo exsequiarum* and both *editiones typicae* of *Ordo celebrandi Matrimonium*.

ADAPTATIONS ALLOWED TO
THE CONFERENCES OF BISHOPS

Numbers 21–22 list the "Adaptations by the Conferences of Bishops" and the responsibilities for the episcopal conferences in preparing particular rituals for funerals. It is interesting to note that the prescriptions herein appear to form the basis for what will be included (more or less verbatim) in the section "Adaptations by the Conferences of Bishops" in subsequent revisions of

---

84. *Rite of Funerals*, no. 8. OE, no. 8: "Ritus exsequialis iuxta typum tertium, in domo defuncti celebrandus, qui fortasse alicubi omnino inutilis censebitur, necessarius [9] tamen videtur in nonnullis regionibus. De rebus singulis, diversis adiunctis prae oculis habitis, consulto non agitur. Attamen convenire visum est ut quaedam saltem indicationes proponerentur, ita ut et in hoc casu haberi possent elementa communia cum ceteris typis, v. gr. in liturgia verbi et in ritu ultimae commendationis seu valedictionis. Ceterum, Conferentiae Episcopales poterunt providere."

85. OE, no. 9: "Quando Ritualia particularia iuxta novum Rituale Romanum praeparabuntur, Conferentiae Episcopalis erit sive tres typos exsequiarum retinere, sive ordinem mutare, sive unum typum alterumve omittere."

86. Ibid. "Nam fieri potest ut in aliqua natione unus typus, e. gr. typus primus cum tribus stationibus, sit exclusive in usu et qua talis, ceteris exclusis, retinendus; in alia vero omnes tres sint necessarii. Ideo Conferentia Episcopalis, attentis necessitatibus particularibus, opportune providebit."

the sacramental rites.[87] As was the case in the *Ordo celebrandi Matrimonium,* 1969 and 1991, there are three areas addressed in this section: the concern for adaptations of the rites that follow in the *editio typica,* the retention of rites already existing, and the composition of new rites and formulas suitable for and adapted to the needs of individual regions.

Number 21, for example, begins in a general way, stating that according to number 63b of *Sacrosanctum Concilium,* the conferences of bishops have the right to prepare a section of their particular rituals that will correspond to this section of the Roman Ritual but which is to be adapted to the needs of each region. After review by the Apostolic See, the ritual may be used in the regions for which it has been prepared.[88] A list of responsibilities of the conferences of bishops regarding the preparation and adaptation of particular rituals follows immediately.[89] The responsibilities reveal a concern for adapting the liturgical celebration of the funeral rites to the needs of each region; they also propose an initial methodology for adapting the liturgy.

Number 21:1, for example, prescribes that in making adaptations, it is for the Conference of Bishops to define the adaptations, within the limits stated in this section of the Roman Ritual.[90] Once the adaptations are defined, (21:1), the conferences of bishops are to consider carefully and prudently which elements from the traditions and cultures of individual peoples may be appropriately admitted (into the liturgy); they may also propose other adaptations which they believe are useful or necessary to the Apostolic See, by whose consent they may be introduced.[91]

Number 21:3 requires retaining or adapting special elements of existing particular rituals, if any exist, provided that they can be brought into harmony with *Sacrosanctum Concilium* and

---

87. Cf. OI , nos. 21 and 22; OCM, 1991, nos. 39, 40, and 41.

88. OE, no. 21: "Conferentiis Episcopalibus competit, vi Constitutionis de sacra Liturgia (art. 63b), in Ritualibus particularibus parare titulum qui huic titulo Ritualis Romani respondeat, singularum tamen regionum neccesitatibus *accommodatum* (emphasis added), ut, actis Apostolica Sede recognitis, in regionibus ad quas pertinet adhibeatur."

89. Ibid. "Qua in *aptatione,* (emphasis added), Conferentiarum Episcopalium erit: . . ."

90. Ibid., no. 21:1: "*Aptationes definire,* (emphasis added) intra limites in hoc titulo statutos."

91. Ibid., no. 21:2: "Sedulo et prudenter considerare quid ex traditionibus ingenioque singulorum populorum opportune admitti possit; ideoque alias *aptationes* (emphasis added), quae utiles vel necessariae existimentur, Apostolicae Sedi proponere, de ipsius consensu inducendas."

contemporary needs.[92] This concern for attentiveness to contemporary needs projects a forward movement of the methodology advocated herein. Number 21:4 directs the conferences of bishops to "prepare translations of the texts which are truly suited to the genius of the various languages and cultures adding, wherever appropriate, suitable melodies for singing."[93]

Number 21:5 instructs the bishops to "adapt and supplement the *praenotanda* of the Roman Ritual so that the ministers will fully understand the significance of the rites and celebrate them effectively."[94] Number 21:6 prescribes that "the arrangement of the material in the liturgical books be prepared under the direction of the conferences of bishops so that the order is best suited to pastoral purposes, and in such a way that none of the material contained in this typical edition is to be omitted."[95] The final sentence in number 21 deals with the addition of rubrics to the liturgical texts; additional rubrics and texts should be distinguished typographically from the rubrics and the texts of the Roman Ritual.[96]

Number 22 is directed more to the pastoral adaptations of the funeral rites. It further clarifies the tasks before the conferences of bishops for adaptations of the *Rite of Funerals*. In the first place, the rite may be arranged according to one of the plans (number 9 of the *praenotanda*).[97] Secondly, the conferences of bishops may substitute [*alias, si opportunum visum fuerit, substituere*], if preferred, texts from Chapter VI for those that appear

---

92. Ibid., no. 21:3: "Propria autem Ritualium particularium iam exstantium elementa, si quae habentur, retinere, dummodo cum Constitutione de sacra Liturgia et necessitatibus hodiernis componi possint, vel ea *aptare* (emphasis added)."

93. *Rite of Funerals* in *The Rites of the Catholic Church,* no. 21:4. OE, no. 21:4: "Versiones textuum parare, ita ut ingenio variarum linguarum culturarumque vere sint *accommodatae* (emphasis added), additis, quotiescumque opportunumn fuerit, melodiis cantui aptis."

94. Ibid., no. 21:5: "Praenotanda, quae in Rituali Romano habentur, *aptare* (emphasis added) atque ita ut ministri significationem rituum plene intellegant et effectu compleant."

95. Ibid., no. 21:6: "In editionibus librorum liturgicorum cura Conferentiarum Episcopalium parandis, materiam ordinare modo qui ad usum pastoralem aptissimus videatur, tamen, ut de materia, quae in hac editione typica continentur, nihil omittatur."

96. OE, no. 21:6: "Si quae vero rubricas vel textus adicere opportunum videatur, congruo signo vel charactere typographico distingantur a rubricis et textibus Ritualis Romani."

97. Ibid., no. 22:1: "In parandis Ritualibus particularibus de exsequiis, Conferentiarum Episcopalium erit: (1) Ritum ordinare iuxta unum vel plures typos, prout indicatum est supra, n. 9."

in the basic rite.[98] They may also add (according to 21:6) other formulas of the same kind [alias etiam formulas eiusdem generis adicere] whenever the Roman Ritual provides a choice of texts.[99] In addition, the conferences of bishops may judge whether laypersons are to be deputed to celebrate the funeral rites (cf. number 19 of the praenotanda).[100]

Numbers 22–25 deal with the priest minister and the suitable layout of rituals to accommodate good pastoral practice. Thus, number 22:5 states that if pastoral reasons exist, the sprinkling with holy water and the incensation may be omitted or another rite substituted.[101] The final provision allows the conferences of bishops to determine the liturgical color for funerals in accordance with the character of the people [ingenio populorum]; the color should not be offensive to human sorrow but should express Christian hope enlightened by the Paschal Mystery.[102]

The closing numbers of the praenotanda, 23–25, present pastoral suggestions for the preparation of each ritual and a variety of textual suggestions for liturgical use in the celebration of the funeral rites. It is noteworthy, however, that the Ordo exsequiarum contains numerous references to the importance of the role of cultural adaptations in the liturgical celebrations of the rite. The prescriptions contained in the praenotanda and in the introductory sections appear to expand on the methodology for adapting the liturgy that we find in the initial editiones typicae of the sacramental revisions. They also demonstrate a consistent concern for the interchange between local culture (traditions, language, and so on) and the liturgy. However, unlike the praenotanda of the Ordines celebrandi Matrimonium, 1969 and 1991, the praenotanda of Ordo exsequiarum do not envisage the composition of new rites based on culture and custom.

---

98. Ibid., no. 22:2: "Pro formulis in ipso ritu principali propositis, alias, si opportunum visum fuerit, substituere ex iis quae in capite VI habentur."

99. Ibid., no. 22:3: "Quoties Rituale Romanum plures exhibet formulas ad libitum eligendas, alias etiam formulas eiusdem generis adicere (ad normam n. 21:6)."

100. Ibid., no. 22:4: "Iudicare an laici deputandi sint ad celebrandas exsequias (Cf. supra, n. 19)." Cf. OCM, 1991, no. 25.

101. Ibid., no. 22:5: "Sicubi ratio pastoralis id suadeat, statuere ut aspersio censatio omitti possint, vel alio ritu suppleri."

102. Ibid., no. 22:6: "Colorem illum liturgicum pro exsequiis statuere, qui sit ingenio populorum, quique et dolorem humanum non offendum et spem christianam ostendat mysterio paschali illuminatam."

ORDO UNCTIONIS INFIRMORUM EORUMQUE PASTORALIS CURAE, 1972

THE *PRAENOTANDA* AND ADAPTATIONS ALLOWED TO THE CONFERENCES OF BISHOPS

An extensive examination of the theological and pastoral principles found in the *praenotanda* of this rite is far beyond the scope of the present work. Suffice it to say that beginning with a modern awareness of the Christian meaning of sickness,[103] and continuing with a more biblical, ecclesial, and Christocentric understanding of the suffering of the sick,[104] the *praenotanda* present theological and pastoral principles for the celebration of the rite.

Section IV of the *praenotanda*, concerning the adaptations that the conferences of bishops may make [*De aptationibus quae conferentiis episcopalibus competunt*] is of particular interest for our purposes. Numbers 38 and 39 parallel the prescriptions expressed in the *Ordo exsequiarum*, numbers 21 and 22, with slight changes of vocabulary in the *Ordo unctionis infirmorum*. Number 38, for example, repeats *Ordo exsequiarum*, number 21 concerning the right of the conferences of bishops to prepare a section in particular rituals [*in Ritualibus particularibus parare titulum . . . accommodatum singularum regionum necessitatibus*] corresponding to the present section of the Roman Ritual and adapted to the needs of the different parts of the world.[105] As we noted previously concerning the rites of Ordination and Marriage, although the section uses the vocabulary of *aptatio*, the general principle is stated in the language of *accommodatio*.

The six duties of the conferences of bishops that follow repeat those enunciated in the *Ordo exsequiarum*, numbers 21:1–6 with slight modifications. The six areas are worth noting for their content regarding possible adaptations in the celebration of the rite. Number 38a, for example, mentions the responsibility of the conferences of bishops to "decide on the adaptations [*apta-*

---

103. OI, 1972, nos. 1 and 4. See P.-M. Gy, "Le nouvel rituel des malades," *La Maison-Dieu* 113 (1973): 32–33.

104. OI, nos. 2–3.

105. Ibid., no. 38: "Conferentiis Episcopalibus competit Constitutionis de sacra Liturgia (art. 63b), in Ritualibus particularibus parare titulum qui huic Ritualis Romani titulo congruat, *accommodatum* (emphasis added) singularum regionum neccesitatibus, ut, actis Apostolica Sede recognitis, in regionibus ad quas pertinet adhibeatur." This prescription is also found in OE, no. 21.

tiones definire] according to the principles of *Sacrosanctum Concilium*, number 39."[106] Number 38b expands on this task: Once the decisions (38a) are made, the conferences of bishops are to weigh carefully and prudently [*sedulo et prudenter considerare quid ex traditionibus ingenioque singulorum populorum opportune admitti possit*] what elements from the traditions and cultures of individual peoples may be admitted into the liturgy; then, they may propose to the Apostolic See other adaptations considered useful or necessary that will be introduced (into the liturgy) with the same consent [*alias aptationes, quae utiles vel necessariae existimantur, Apostolicae Sedi proponere, de ipsius consensu inducendas*].[107] These prescriptions correspond to those contained in the *Ordo exsequiarum*, numbers 21:1 and 21:2.

Number 38c mandates "retaining or adapting the elements in the rites that now exist in particular rituals [*Ritualium particularium circa infirmos iam exstantium elementa, si quae habentur, retinere*] as long as they are compatible with *Sacrosanctum Concilium* and with contemporary needs."[108] As we also noted above, the principle here recognizes the existence of local rites that may date back over centuries and therefore are to be retained. However, unlike a similar prescription in the *Ordines celebrandi Matrimonium*, 1969 and 1991, the language used herein does not indicate that the *praenotanda* provide for the creation of new rites for anointing.[109]

Number 38d directs the conferences of bishops to "prepare translations of the texts so that they are truly adapted to the

---

106. Ibid., no. 38a: "Aptationes definire, *de quibus in art. 39 Constitutionis de sacra Liturgia* (emphasis added)." Number 39 of SC refers not only to the competence of the local church authority and its competence regarding adaptations; it also directs that the local authority specify the adaptations regarding the administration of the sacraments, the sacramentals, processions, liturgical language, and the art and music of worship. It would appear that in OI, there is a subtle movement in methodology in 38a; i.e., the prescription herein reminds the conferences of bishops that there are specific areas for adapting the liturgy to which they should be more attentive.

107. Ibid., no. 39b: "Sedulo et prudenter considerare quid ex traditionibus ingenioque singulorum populorum opportune admitti possit; ideoque alias aptationes quae utiles vel necessariae *existimantur* (emphasis added), Apostolicae Sedi proponere, de ipsius consensu inducendas." OE, no. 21:2 uses the present subjunctive form, *existimentur*.

108. Ibid., no. 38c: "Quaedam propria Ritualium particularium circa infirmos iam exstantium elementa, si quae habentur, retinere, dummodo cum Constitutione de sacra Liturgia et necessitatibus hodiernis componi queant, vel ea aptare (emphasis added)." The content of this subsection is essentially a repetition of OE, no. 21:3 with one notable exception, a change from OE, no. 21:3: "si quae habeantur retinere," to OI, 38c: "si quae habentur."

109. Cf. OCM, 1969, no. 17; OCM, 1991, no. 42.

native character [*versiones textuum parare, ita ut indoli vario-*
rum sermonum atque ingenii culturarum vere accommodentur]
of different languages and cultures and to add, whenever appropriate, suitable melodies for singing [*additis, quoties opportunum*
fuerit, melodiis cantui aptis]."[110] This prescription reflects both
a sensitivity to local culture as well as a continuity with the principles of *Sacrosanctum Concilium*, number 14 concerning fostering the full, active, and conscious participation of the people in
the liturgical celebration of the rite.

Number 38e directs the bishops to "adapt and enlarge, if
necessary, the *praenotanda* in the Roman Ritual [*Praenotanda,*
quae in Rituali Romano habentur, si casus fert, aptare et com-
plere] in order to encourage the conscious and active participation
of the faithful [*ad participationem fidelium consciam et actu-*
osam]."[111] This is an example of a major change from *Ordo exse-*
quiarum, number 21:5. The latter specifies that the *praenotanda*
are to be adapted and completed so that the ministers fully understand and fulfill the meaning of the rites as they are being celebrated [*Praenotanda . . . aptare atque complere, ita ut ministri*
significationem rituum plene intellegant et effectu compleant]. In
Ordo Unctionis infirmorum, number 38e, the emphasis recalls
the principles stated in *Sacrosanctum Concilium*, number 14 and
the insistence on the full, active, and conscious participation of
all the faithful in the celebration of the liturgical rite.[112]

Number 38f prescribes that the editions of liturgical books
prepared under the direction of the conferences of bishops be read-
ied in as suitable a format as possible for pastoral use [*materiam*
ordinare modo qui ad usum pastoralem aptissimus videatur].[113]

Number 39 repeats the same permission granted in OCM,
1969, number 13, that "whenever the Roman Ritual gives several

---

110. OI, no. 38d: "Versiones textuum parare, ita ut indoli variorum sermonum atque
ingenii culturarum vere *accommodentur* (emphasis added), additis, quoties opportunumn
fuerit, melodiis cantui *aptis* (emphasis added)." What is stated in this subsection is essentially
a verbatim repetition of OI, no. 21:4 with minor and negligible vocabulary changes.

111. Ibid., no. 38e: "Praenotanda, quae in Rituali Romano habentur, si casus fert, *aptare*
(emphasis added) et complere ad participationem fidelium consciam et actuosam reddendam."

112. Cf. SC, no. 14: "Quae totius populi plena et actuosa participatio, in instauranda et
fovenda sacra liturgia, summopere est attendenda: est enim primus. . ." and OI, no. 38e.

113. Ibid., no. 38f: "In editionibus librorum liturgicorum cura Conferentiarum Episcopalium
parandis, materiam ordinare modo qui ad usum pastoralem aptissimus videatur." It is very
interesting to observe here that the final clause of OE, 21:6, "tamen, ita, ut de materia,
quae in hac editione typica continentur, nihil omittatur" is itself omitted! This omission
suggests that the conferences of bishops may consider some of what is contained in the
Latin editio typica of OI unsuitable for inclusion in the liturgical celebrations of the rite.

alternative texts, particular rituals may add other texts of the same kind."[114] Both numbers 38 and 39, therefore, appear to extend broad authority to the conferences of bishops regarding their competence not only to draw up adaptations but also to be especially attentive to the contemporary needs of individual peoples, their traditions, and their particular cultures.[115] The *praenotanda* conclude with a reminder that the structure of the rite should be adapted to the place and people taking part in the celebration of the rite.[116]

CULTURAL ADAPTATIONS IN THE *PRAENOTANDA* AND IN THE RITE

There are two occasions in the *editio typica* of the *Ordo Unctionis infirmorum* where the type of oil used in the sacrament is mentioned. The first instance occurs in the apostolic constitution which approves and introduces the changes in the rite.[117] Because of the unavailability of olive oil in many parts of the world and in response to the requests of various bishops, the constitution

114. Ibid., no. 39: "Quando Rituale Romanum plures exhibet formulas ad libitum, Ritualia particularia possunt alias formulas eiusdem generis adicere." This is a verbatim repetition of the second sentence of OCM, 1969, no. 13; it is also included in OCM, 1991, no. 41:2.

115. Numbers 40 and 41 conclude the *praenotanda* by specifying the pastoral adaptations allowed to the local minister in the celebration of the rite. The minister, for example, should be sensitive to the circumstances, needs, and wishes of the sick and other members of the faithful and should avail himself of the flexibility provided in the rite. The minister may also curtail the celebration as needed, ask for help from the local Christian community, and encourage the sick who regain their health to give thanks for the favor received in the Eucharist or by some other suitable means.

116. OI, no. 41: "In celebratione proinde structuram ritus servet, *accommodatam* (emphasis added) tamen adiunctis loci et personarum." Some other provisions (within the rites themselves) for adaptations occur in no. 45 (adapting elements of the rite in visits to the sick), no. 59 (a shorter rite for communion to the sick due to large numbers of them), no. 67 (the anointing of a large number of sick by imposition of hands), and no. 83 (celebration of the rite of anointing during mass with a large crowd of people, e.g., pilgrims). It should also be noted again that the Approved text for use in the United States of America of the Pastoral Care of the Sick does not follow the Latin text and its sevenfold chapter division but rather divides the ritual into three parts and eight chapters. As the foreword states: "This edition and *adaptation* (emphasis added) includes original English texts which address pastoral circumstances not foreseen in the Latin edition nor in the provisional English edition of 1973. See OI, trans. by ICEL, 1983, foreword, 9–11 and no. 62 (adapting the visit to the sick to children), no. 132 (for sensitivity to language [especially gender and number] in anointing within Mass), and no. 186 (accommodating the celebration of Viaticum to those present and the nearness of death)."

117. OI, trans., by ICEL, 1983, 9–10: "Cum autem oleum olivarum, quod hucusque ad valorem Sacramenti conficiendi praescribebatur, in nonnullis regionibus deficiat vel

allows a substitution of another kind of oil (provided it is derived from plants and is thus similar to olive oil) in the administration of the sacrament. This provision serves as an excellent example of Paul VI's allowing the rite to be adapted according to the local traditions and customs of a people.[118] The second instance occurs in number 20 of the *praenotanda* repeating this permission granted in the apostolic constitution: "The matter proper for the sacrament is olive oil, or according to circumstances, other oil derived from plants."[119] This twofold insistence on an alternative for olive oil demonstrates that the revised rite is not merely an updating of the older one but rather an attempt to recognize the importance of local cultures and customs.

There are other examples of sacramental revisions that could be studied as a prelude to an analysis of the *Fourth Instruction*. For example, provisional texts for celebrations of the Eucharist, some enjoying more success than others, have been and may still be in use in various cultures and languages.[120]

---

difficultate comparetur, decrevimus, petentibus pluribus Episcopis, ut pro opportunitate, etiam aliud oleum in posterum adhiberi possit, quod tamen e plantis sit expressum, utpote oleo ex oliva similius." Cf. Bugnini, *The Reform of the Liturgy 1948–1975*, 691: "In the past, olive oil has always been the obligatory matter for the anointing of the sick because the Bible sees it as a sacramental symbol of healing and relief (Mark 6:12–13; James 5:14–15). Henceforth, however, it is permissible in case of need to use some other oil, provided it is derived from a plant."

118. See Chupungco, *Liturgies of the Future: The Process and Methods of Inculturation*, 152: "Paul VI himself set an admirable and inspiring example of cultural adaptation in relation to the oil for the sacrament." However, it must also be stated that Chupungco neglects to point out that needs are as much envisaged as traditions, which in this matter, in fact, did not exist.

119. OI, trans. by ICEL, 1983, no. 20. OI, 1972, no. 20: "Materia apta sacramenti est oleum olivarum aut, pro opportunitate, aliud oleum e plantis expressum." Gy notes that the footnote to accompany number 20 specifies the source of authority for the change in the type of oil (*Ordo benedicendi Oleum catechumenorum et infirmorum et conficiendi Chrisma, Praenotanda*, n. 3 Typis Polyglottis Vaticanis 1970). In addition, he raises the interesting question for the future about the eventual admission of animal or mineral oil or perhaps some other material of a medical nature: Gy, "Le nouveau rituel des malades," 40: "Comme on le sait, le rituel de la bénédiction des saintes huiles (1971), par une disposition qui est reprise dans le passage central de la constitution *Sacram Unctionem Infirmorum*, prévoit que l'huile d'olive peut être remplacé, le cas échéant, par une autre huile. Reste ouverte, du point du vue théorique, la question de l'admission d'une huile animale ou minérale, ou éventuellement d'une autre matière sacramentelle ayant le caractère d'un médicament."

120. See, for example, Catholic Bishops' Conference of India. "An Order of the Mass for India." *International Review of Mission* 65 (1976): 168–76; *Misa ng Bayang Filipino* (The Order of Mass for the Philippines), text appears in Tagalog and English in A. Chupungco, *Towards a Filipino Liturgy* (Manila, 1976), 96–139; "Le Missel Romain pour les diocèses du Zaïre," *Notitiae* 24 (1988): 454–72. An English translation of the text appears Nwaka Chris Egbulem, *The Power of Africentric Celebrations: Inspirations from the Zairean Liturgy* (New York: Crossroad, 1996), 141–63.

Before beginning to analyze certain writings of John Paul II as genetic precursors of the *Fourth Instruction,* a brief summary of our examination regarding *Sacrosanctum Concilium* and the revisions it mandated is in order. In the first place, *Sacrosanctum Concilium* commissioned a new edition of the Roman Ritual and also provided general principles for the adaptation of the liturgy. Moreover, in certain places and under the direction of both the conferences of bishops and the Apostolic See, it envisioned an even more profound adaptation of the liturgy. The procedure for such adaptation was not spelled out in great detail in *Sacrosanctum Concilium* but rather envisaged as desirable when the Roman rite came into contact with local cultures.

In the case of the revisions of the sacraments and rites, the Marriage rite deserves special consideration and careful examination. When it mandated the revision of this sacramental ritual, *Sacrosanctum Concilium* used terminology that was different from that used in reference to the revisions of the other sacraments and rites. The liturgical constitution urged that conferences of bishops were not only to revise the Roman ritual of Marriage but even to compose [*exarare ritum*] a new rite (according to the principles stated in the same constitution in 63b) suited to the particular needs, cultural outlook, traditions, and practices of various peoples. Moreover, in the case of the revision of marriage, the rites were not the only things to be adapted; the liturgy and the Christian spirit were to be "adapted" to previously existing rites of long-standing tradition within a culture. These provisions are repeated in both *editiones typicae* of *Ordo celebrandi Matrimonium,* 1969 and 1991, respectively.

Secondly, in the years immediately following the promulgation of *Sacrosanctum Concilium,* three instructions concerning its proper implementation addressed the question of adaptations once again. In these instructions, theological principles, pastoral adaptations, and rubrical directives were specified to curb perceived excesses and to encourage correct implementation of any additional adaptations.

In the two decades that ensued after the publication of the *Third Instruction* in 1970, the work of revision of the sacramental rites and the composition of new *editiones typicae* yielded much fruit. The study groups of the Consilium and later the Sacred Congregation for Divine Worship (which eventually became the Congregation for Divine Worship and the Discipline of the Sacraments) included *praenotanda* or general introductions in the new *editiones typicae*. In the latter, they made provisions for the local conferences of bishops to adapt the Roman ritual to the native character, talents, customs, and traditions of various peoples and regions, to retain previously existing local rites, and to integrate them into the Roman ritual. Finally, the local episcopal conferences were empowered to rearrange, add to, or complete parts of the newly revised rites. The conferences of bishops, in turn, were to submit proposals for adaptations to the Apostolic See for final approval.

Toward the end of the 1980s as the work of revision of the sacraments and rites began to enter into a second phase producing *editiones typicae alterae*, John Paul II, the pontiff who had replaced Paul VI in 1978,[121] began to focus his attention on the encounter between church and culture, in particular on the dynamic involved in the areas of catechesis, evangelization, and worship and their relationships to local culture. Of particular interest to the first pope from Poland was the nature of the interchange when the Church and local cultures attempted to accommodate each other. As he began to write apostolic exhortations, letters, and encyclicals, John Paul II reflected on the end result of such mutual encounters and suggested that the entire process was not a new phenomenon but one that had helped form the life of the Church throughout the centuries. It is with *Sacrosanctum Concilium*, the three instructions on its proper implementation, and the revisions of the sacramental rites in mind that we now turn to some writings of John Paul II which pertain to the area of adaptation and inculturation of the liturgy as genetic precursors of the *Fourth Instruction*.

---

121. John Paul I (Albino Luciano) had a short pontificate. He was elected to the papacy on August 26, 1978 and died shortly thereafter on September 28, 1978. John Paul II (Karol Wojtyla) was elected pope on October 16, 1978.

CHAPTER IV

PERTINENT WRITINGS OF JOHN PAUL II AS GENETIC PRECURSORS OF THE *FOURTH INSTRUCTION*

The twenty-four and one-half years intervening between the publication of *Liturgicae instaurationes* in 1970 and the *Fourth Instruction* in 1994 may be characterized as a period of innovations and changes in the liturgical celebrations of the Roman rite. In the last chapter, we considered the *editiones typicae* of the Rites of Ordination (1968, 1989), the Rite of Marriage (1969, 1991), the Funeral Rites (1969), and the Pastoral Care of the Sick: Rites of Anointing and Viaticum (1972, 1983). At the conclusion of that chapter, we referred the reader to several examples of liturgical adaptations concerning the Eucharist.

It was also during the 1970s and 1980s that a new vocabulary appeared in the scholarly literature dealing with adaptations of the liturgy.[1] The term *inculturation* began to figure prominently in considerations of the relationships between faith and culture, culture and worship, worship in particular churches, and worship in the Church universal.[2] In an attempt to understand

---

1. The references below do not pretend to be a summary of the scholarly literature in the field of inculturation; rather, they serve as one way of substantiating our statement above that the terminology of "inculturation" gained acceptance in the years 1979–1994 in the scholarly literature related to this issue. See for example, Aary A Roest Crollius, SJ, "What is so New About Inculturation? A Concept and Its Implication," *Gregorianum* 59 (1978):721–38. His definition of inculturation highlights the important role of the local church and the relationships among local church, culture, and community as well as how the Church universal is enriched by the process of inculturation: "[Inculturation] is the integration of the Christian experience of the local church into the culture of its people, in such a way that this experience not only expresses itself in elements of this culture, but becomes a force that animates, orientates, and innovates this culture so as to create a new unity and community, not only in the culture in question but also as a enrichment of the Church universal." (Ibid., 735.)

2. See, for example, G. A. Arbuckle, "Inculturation, Not Adaptation: Time to Change Terminology," 517. Arbuckle appropriates a definition of inculturation from M. de C. Azevedo and a significant insight about the encounter of Gospel and culture from M. Amaladoss. For the former, see M. de C. Azevedo, *Inculturation and the Challenges of Modernity* (Rome: Gregorian University, 1982), 11: "Inculturation is the dynamic relation between the Christian message and culture or cultures; an insertion of the Christian life into a culture; an ongoing process of reciprocal and critical interaction between them." For the latter, see M. Amaladoss, "Inculturation and Tasks of Mission," in *Toward a New Age in Mission:*

the meaning and nuances of the term *inculturation* in the years 1970–1994, authors distinguished among the terms *adaptation*, *contextualization, indigenization, acculturation, enculturation*, and finally *inculturation*,[3] and suggested further that the work set out by the Second Vatican Council in the area of adaptation of the liturgy to the temperaments and traditions of various peoples was yet to be done.[4]

In the areas of catechesis and evangelization, missionaries, scholars, international commissions,[5] and popes discussed the context, methodology, and definitions of *inculturation* in their

International Congress of Mission (Manila: IM/ICO, 1981), 3:34: ". . . whenever the Gospel encounters a new or different culture, it arrives as the Gospel already embodied in a particular culture; therefore, the encounter is really between two cultures and not merely between the Gospel and the new culture. The primary agent of inculturation, then, is a living faith community." (Ibid., no. 37.)

3. Cf. Aary A. Roest Crollius, sj, ":What is so New About Inculturation? A Concept and its Imlication," *Gregorianum* 59 (1078):722–29. The definition of each of these terms is found in the pages cited. What is important for our consideration is that *inculturation* is the term that perdured in the ensuing years. For a concise summary of these terms, see, Peter C. Phan, "Contemporary Theology And Inculturation in the United States," in William Cenkner, op, ed., *The Multicultural Church: A New Landscape in U.S. Theology* (New York: The Paulist Press, 1995), 177–78, footnotes 3 and 5. See also Peter Schineller, sj, *A Handbook on Inculturation* (New York: Paulist Press, 1990), Chapter II: "Inculturation and Other Words," 14–27.

4. Cf. Chupungco, *Liturgies of the Future: The Process and Methods of Inculturation*, especially Chapter I, 2 (SC 37–40: Toward A Pluriform Liturgy); and I, 4 (Approaches to Adaptation: Acculturation, Inculturation, and Creativity); Chapter II, 2 (Toward Alternative Forms of the Order of Mass); Chapter III (The Future Shape of Sacramental Celebrations); finally, Chapter IV (The Future Shape of the Liturgical Year). See also idem, *Cultural Adaptation of the Liturgy* (New York: Paulist Press, 1982).

5. Commissio Theologica Internationalis, "Fides et inculturatio," *Gregoranium* 70 (1989): 625–46. The English translation may be found in International Theological Commission, *Faith and Inculturation, Origins* 47 (1989): 800–807. The actual statement was formulated in 1987, approved in 1988, and made available for publication in 1989. This document spans the gap in years between the following two papal encyclicals: Ioannis Pauli PP. II Summi Pontificis, *Epistula Encyclica ad Episcopos, Sacerdotes, Religiosos Omnesque Christifideles: Memoria Recolitur Undecimo Transacto Saeculo, Operis Evangelici Sanctorum Cyrilli et Methodii, Slavorum apostoli* (Vatican City: Typis Polyglottis Vaticanis, 1985), no. 21 [Vatican translation in English: *Encyclical Epistle of His Holiness Pope John Paul II to the Bishops, Priests, and Religious Families and to All the Christian Faithful In Commemoration of the Eleventh Centenary of the Evangelizing Work of Saints Cyril and Methodius,. Slavorum apostoli.* (Boston, MA: The Daughters of St. Paul, 1985)], and idem, *Litterae Encyclicae Redemptoris missio de perenni vi mandati missionalis* (Vatican City: Librería Editrice Vaticana, 1990). [*Encyclical Letter of the Supreme Pontiff John Paul II On the Permanent Validity of the Church's Missionary Mandate, Redemptoris missio* (Washington, DC: USCC, 1990).]

The statement from the commission contains an Introduction, three parts, and a conclusion: (I) Nature, Culture, and Grace; (II) Inculturation in the History of Salvation; and (III) Present Problems of Inculturation. Number 11 of Part I contains a definition of inculturation: "The process of *inculturation* (original emphasis) may be defined as the church's efforts to make the news of Christ penetrate a given sociocultural milieu, calling on the latter to grow writings.[6] In fact, in the years intervening between the first three instructions on the orderly implementation of *Sacrosanctum Concilium* and the publication of the *Fourth Instruction*, John Paul II issued an exhortation, an apostolic letter, and two encyclicals that contained his thoughts about the process of inculturation. In some of these documents, John Paul II formulated definitions of *inculturation*.

The goal of the present chapter is to examine in chronological order the pertinent writings of John Paul II concerning inculturation that appeared during the years 1979–1994 as genetic precursors of the *Fourth Instruction*. In the presentation of the material on inculturation in the writings of John Paul II, this chapter will attempt to highlight the twofold movement from Gospel to culture and from culture to Gospel/life of the Church within the process of inculturation. This double movement in the process of inculturation is an important part of John Paul II's description of the work of evangelization; it will influence his definitions of inculturation that will appear early on in the *Fourth Instruction*.

---

according to all its particular values, as long as these are compatible with the Gospel. The term *inculturation* includes the notion of growth, of the mutual enrichment of persons and groups, rendered possible by the encounter of the Gospel with a social milieu. According to John Paul II in the great apostles of the Slavic peoples, 'an example of that undertaking which today puts before itself the name "of the bringing in of the soul of culture" or of the insertion of the Gospel into autochthonous human cultures—and at the same time, the bringing into the life of the church of that human culture itself'."

["*Inculturationis* (original emphasis) processus tamquam Ecclesiae conatus definiri potest ut Christi nuntium in determinatum socialem et culturalem penetrare faciat ambitum, illum appellans ut secundum omnes suos valores proprios crescat, in quantum ipsi cum Evangelio conciliari possunt. Vox *inculturatio* (original emphasis) ideam includit augmenti, mutuae personarum et coetuum amplificationis propter Evangelii cum ambitu sociali occursum. Secundum Ioannem Paulum II, in magnis slavorum apostolis 'illius rei exemplum invenitur, quae nomen hodie prae se fert "animi culturae inductionis"—nempe insertionis Evangelii in humanum autochthonum cultum—atque simul inductionis in Ecclesiae vitam ipsius illius cultus humani.'"] (Ibid., I: 11, 630).

6. Pauli VI, Summi Pontificis, "Adhortatio Apostolica Ad Episcopos, Sacerdotes et Christifideles totius Catholicae Ecclesiae: de Evangelizatione in mundo huius temporis," *Evangelii nuntiandi: AAS* 68 (1976): 5–76. Although this document does not deal directly with the issue of inculturation, it contributed significantly to the important dialogue concerning the Church's mission of evangelization.

JOHN PAUL II AND INCULTURATION

THE APOSTOLIC EXHORTATION
CATECHESI TRADENDAE[7]

The apostolic exhortation *Catechesi tradendae* contains an introduction, nine chapters, and a conclusion. For the purposes of this
study, number 53 of this exhortation merits examination because
it includes the first mention of the word *inculturation* in an official papal document:[8]

> Now a second question. As we said recently to the members of the
> Biblical Commission: "The term 'acculturation' or 'inculturation'
> may be a neologism, but it expresses very well one factor of the great
> mystery of the Incarnation." We can say of catechesis, as well as of
> evangelization in general, that it has as its purpose to bring the
> power of the Gospel into the intimate ordering of human culture
> and of the forms of this same culture.[9]

The quotation is significant for several reasons. First of all,
since John Paul II is quoting what he himself had said about the
term *inculturation*, it would appear that he is ready to adopt the
term *inculturation* (as well as *acculturation*). Secondly, he also
appears willing to relate both of these terms to the mystery of the
Incarnation, although he does not use the word *incarnation* in

---

7. Ioannis Pauli PP. II, Summi Pontificis, "Adhortatio Apostolica ad Episcopos, Sacerdotes
et Christifideles totius Catholicae Ecclesiae de catechesi nostro tempore tradenda [hereafter
Catechesi tradendae]," AAS 71 (1979): 1277–1340. ["Apostolic Exhortation *Catechesi
tradendae* of His Holiness John Paul II to the Episcopate, the Clergy and the Faithful of
the Entire Catholic Church On Catechesis In Our Time." Washington, DC: USCC, 1979.]

8. Peter Schineller, SJ, *A Handbook on Inculturation* (New York: Paulist Press, 1990), 21–
22. See also Stephen Bevans, SVD, *Models of Contextual Theology*, Faith and Culture Series
(New York: Orbis Books, 1992), 43 and Aylward Shorter, *Toward A Theology of Inculturation*
(Maryknoll, NY: Orbis Books, 1988), 233. Nicholas Standaert, SJ, "L'histoire d'un néologisme:
Le terme *inculturation* dans les documents romains," *Nouvelle Revue Théologique* 110
(1988): 555–70. The latter is more precise about the first papal usage of the term: "Le terme
'acculturation' ou 'inculturation' a beau être un néologisme, il exprime fort bien l'une des
composantes du grand mystère de l'*Incarnation* (emphasis added)." (Ibid., 559). Standaert
cites John Paul II's talk to the Pontifical Biblical Commission, "L'insertion culturelle de
la Révélation," as the actual first "use" of the term by the him as distinct from its first
"appearance in print" as a term in a papal document (see above). See *Documentation
Catholique* 76 (1979): 455.

9. Ioannis Pauli II, *Catechesi tradendae*, no. 53: "Altera nunc est Nobis quaestio aggredienda:
quemadmodum ad sodales Commissionis Biblicae diximus, vocabulum Gallicum
'acculturation' vel '*inculturation* (emphasis added)' est quidem verbum novum, quod tamen
unum ex elementis magni mysterii Incarnationis egregie exprimit." John Paul II continues:
"Asseverare possumus catechesi, perinde ac evangelizationi in universum, propositum esse,
ut vim Evangelii in intimas rationes cultus humani et formarum eiusdem cultus inferat."

the definitions of either *inculturation* or *acculturation*. He asserts that catechesis has the possibility of peoples' recognizing the good elements in their own culture:

> In this way, catechesis leads men and women to recognize from the various forms of human culture the hidden mystery; and, it helps them so that they bring out, from their own living tradition, their unique ways which manifest the Christian life, the celebration of the sacred, and a way of thinking.[10]

John Paul II also maintains that there has always been a constant pattern and interaction between the Gospel and culture since the Gospel message has always been transmitted by means of an apostolic dialogue that inevitably becomes part of a dialogue of cultures.[11]

Number 53 concludes with an affirmation by John Paul II that true catechists renew catechesis in a fitting manner [*Veri enim catecheseos institutores probe noverunt catechesim*] to be inserted into the various forms of human culture or various ways of human living [*in diversas inseri humani cultus formas vel in varias humani convictus rationes*].[12] They are also convinced that true catechesis of this type enriches cultures [*catechesim eiusmodi culturas locupletare*] when it helps cultures overcome the imperfect and also inhuman features in them [*cum eas adiuvet ad superanda illa, quae in iisdem sunt imperfecta atque etiam inhumana*], and when it (i.e., true catechesis) bestows on cultures the fullness of Christ which is already present in them [*et cum bonis, quae in iis legitime insunt, plenitudinem Christi attribuat*].[13] The

---

10. Ibid. "Sic videlicet homines e variis humani cultus formis adducet, ut mysterium absconditum agnoscant, eosque adiuvabit, ut e viva traditione sibi propria depromant singulares rationes, quae christianam vitam, celebrationem sacrorum et cogitandi modum manifestant."

11. Ibid. "Hinc scilicet nuntium evangelicum non posse simpliciter seiungi ab illa cultura, in quam primitus sit insertus . . . neque, since gravi iactura, a culturae formis, in quibus saeculorum decursu traditus sit . . . deinde eum semper transmitti ope dialogi apostolici, qui necessario in quasi quendam dialogum culturarum includatur."

12. Ibid. "Veri enim catecheseos institutores probe noverunt catechesim in diversas inseri humani cultus formas vel in varias humani convictus rationes."

13. Ibid. "Ii enim persuasum sibi habent veram catechesim euismodi culturas locupletare, cum eas adiuvet ad superanda illa, quae in iisdem sunt imperfecta atque etiam inhumana, et cum bonis, que in iis legitime insunt, plenitudinem Christi attribuat." The principles in footnote 12 and the present footnote are adopted by the CDWDS in no. 5 of the *Fourth Instruction* and modified to state: "Inculturatio ita definita suum habet locum et in cultu christiano et in ceteris vitae Ecclesiae ambitibus. Equidem ipsa, cum una ex Evangelii inculturationis rationibus exstet, veram expostulat integrationem, in vita fidei uniuscuiusque populi, valorum permanentium culturae datae magis quam eius manifestationum transeuntium."

terminology that John Paul II uses to describe the role of evangelization [*inseri humani cultus formas*] will be repeated in subsequent writings and eventually applied to the definition(s) of *inculturation* which appear in the *Fourth Instruction*.

THE ENCYCLICAL *SLAVORUM APOSTOLI*[14]

The 1985 encyclical, *Slavorum apostoli*, honors Cyril and Methodius who are remembered by the Church for their great work of evangelization.[15] Throughout the encyclical, John Paul II demonstrates that their work of evangelization was always in relation to the culture of the local people. Reiterating that the work of Cyril and Methodius in territory inhabited by Slav peoples occurs within the wider framework of the Church's mission to evangelize, John Paul II describes the evangelization that they accomplished with the terminology he used above regarding catechesis. Since this is a second instance of his use of such terminology, and since this terminology is also found in the definition(s) of *inculturation* in the *Fourth Instruction*, his description of the work of evangelization merits close attention.[16] Perhaps a table would serve to highlight the terminology used in *Slavorum apostoli*:

Table 1. John Paul II's Description of the Work of Evangelization

Latin	English
In evangelizationis opere	In the work of evangelization
quod—(. . .)—simul illius rei exemplum invenitur	which—(. . .) is at the same time an example of that
quae nomen hodie prae se fert	which today bears the name
"animae culturae inductionis"	of (the) bringing in of the soul (or spirit) of a culture

14. See footnote 5 above for the full reference to the Latin and English texts of *Slavorum apostoli*.

15. Ibid., no. 21: "Slavorum apostoli, sancti Cyrillus et Methodius, eorumque praeclarum evangelizationis opus, quod perfecerunt, in memoria sunt Ecclesiae."

16. Ibid. "In evangelizationis opere, quod—uti praecursores in regione a Slavicis populis habitata exegerunt—simul illius rei exemplum invenitur, quae nomen hodie prae se fert 'animi culturae inductionis'—nempe insertionis Evangelii in humanum autochthonum cultum—atque simul inductionis in Ecclesiae vitam ipsius illius cultus humani."

Table 1. *continued*

Latin	English
—nempe insertionis Evangelii in humanum autochthonum cultum	—namely, of the insertion of the Gospel into autochthonous human culture
atque simul inductionis in Ecclesiae vitam ipsius illius cultus humani.	and, at the same time, bringing that same human culture into the life of the church.

John Paul's description of the work of evangelization is noteworthy for several reasons. The table above reveals that in the work of evangelization there is one purpose, i.e., the entry of the spirit or soul of a culture into the Church and two specific tasks: 1) inserting the Gospel into the culture, respecting its independence and self-sufficiency, and 2) bringing that culture itself into the life of the Church. A quick glance back to the language used by John Paul II in *Catechesi tradendae* to describe a true catechesis reveals that both catechesis and evangelization interact with human cultures by inserting the Gospel values into them. Furthermore, both catechesis and evangelization also elicit from, or illuminate in, a culture what is already present; namely, the fullness of Christ. In this way, once this presence of Christ is elicited or illumined, all that is good within culture is brought into the life of the Church.

John Paul II concludes his reflections in this part of the encyclical in number 22 by acknowledging the role of the paleoslavonic language in the liturgy. He states that in the historical development of the Slavs of the Eastern rite, this language (paleoslavonic) gave unity to the Slav peoples similar to the unity given to the Western world by Latin.[17] John Paul II's thoughts on the relationship between the Gospel and culture did not end with the publication of this encyclical but rather underwent further refinement during the closing years of that decade.

---

17. Ibid., no. 22: "Historica in progressione Slavorum orientalis ritus hic sermo pares partes habuit linguae Latinae in orbe occidentali."

THE APOSTOLIC LETTER *VICESIMUS QUINTUS ANNUS*[18]

Vicesimus quintus annus contains an introduction, six topical headlines, and a conclusion.[19] The twenty-fifth anniversary of the promulgation of *Sacrosanctum Concilium*[20] presented John Paul II an excellent opportunity to reaffirm the importance of the enduring principles of *Sacrosanctum Concilium*, and at the same time, to highlight some new problems occasioned by the rapid changes in the Church and in society.[21] John Paul II also took the occasion in this apostolic letter to mention some difficulties that confronted the liturgical reforms,[22] and to mention some concerns

---

18. Ioannis Pauli PP. II, Summi Pontificis, "Litterae Apostolicae Quinto iam illustro expleto conciliari ab promulgata de Sacra Liturgia Constitutione *Sacrosanctum Concilium*," *Vicesimus quintus annus*, AAS 81 (1989): 897–918. ["Apostolic Letter of His Holiness Pope John Paul II On the Twenty-fifth Anniversary of the Liturgy Constitution." *Vicesimus quintus annus. Origins* 19 (1989): 17–25.]

19. Ibid. "I: Renovatio ad Traditionis Regulam; II: Directoria Constitutionis Principia; III: Directoria Principia ad Liturgicae Vitae Temperandam Renovationem IV: Reformationis Usus; V: Renovationis Futurum; VI: Corpora Ad Quae Renovatio Liturgica Pertinet; Conclusio."

20. Vatican Council II, *Constitution on the Sacred Liturgy, Sacrosanctum Concilium,* [hereafter SC] in Norman P. Tanner, SJ, English ed., *Decrees of the Ecumenical Councils,* vol. 2, *Trent to Vatican II* (London: Sheed and Ward, 1990), 820–49.

21. Cf. ibid., no. 2: "Quarta igitur transacta saeculi parte, per quam et Ecclesia et hominum Societas celeres expertae sunt altasque rerum commutationes, momentus illustrare interest Concilaris hius Constitutionis atque praesentem eius virtutem novis collatam cum quaestionibus exorientibus necnon perpetuam illius principorum efficacitatem." [After a quarter of a century, during which both Church and society have experienced profound and rapid changes, it is a fitting moment to throw light on the importance of the Conciliar Constitution, its relevance in relation to new problems tend the enduring value of its principles.]
In the final number of this letter (23), John Paul II restates that the time has come to renew that spirit which inspired the Church at the time that *Sacrosanctum Concilium* was prepared. [Cf. ibid., no. 23: "Tempus venisse videtur rursus reperiendi vehementum illum afflatum qui Ecclesiam incitavit cum Constitutio *Sacrosanctum Concilium* est praeparata, agitata, decretata, promulgata primisque est adhibita modis."] [The time has come to renew that spirit which inspired the Church at the moment when the Constitution *Sacrosanctum Concilium* was prepared, discussed, voted upon and promulgated, and when the first steps were taken to apply it.]

22. Ibid., no. 11. John Paul II suggests a series of reasons for the difficulties the liturgical reform encountered: "Concedendum quidem est reformationis liturgicae usum in difficultates incidisse praesertim ex condicionibus ortas parum propitiis, quarum propria erat privatus ambitus religiosus, quaedam omnis institutionis recusatio, minor Ecclesiae in societate visio, revocatio fidei personalis in controversiam. Opinari etiam licet transitum a simplici praesentia, desidi interdum muta, ad pleniorem et actuosiorem participationem aliquid nimium forte ab aliquibus postulasse . . . alii novos libros acceperunt quadam cum neglectione vel mutationum causas nec percipere nec significare curantes; alii, quod valde dolendum est, modo solum suo et unico ad antecedentes liturgicas formas se contulerunt. . . . Alii, denique novitates foverunt fallaces, a normis aberrantes auctoritate Apostolicae Sedis praescriptus aut ab Episcopis, unitatem ita Ecclesiae et fidelium pietatem perturbantes, conflictantes quandoque cum ipsis fidei argumentis." [It must be recognized

that had not been addressed but had arisen since the promulgation of the liturgical constitution.[23]

Section V, "The Future of the Renewal," contains very significant guidelines for adaptation of the liturgy and ultimately for liturgical inculturation. In the opening lines of number 16, John Paul II enunciates both the general purpose of and some specific principles for accommodation of the liturgy.[24] He uses some of the exact terminology that appeared three years earlier in the encyclical *Slavorum apostoli* to state this purpose: the large task of inserting the liturgy into certain cultures [*Magnus perstat labor **inserendi** (emphasis added) Liturgiam in quasdam culturas*].[25] The task of inserting the liturgy into culture entails a further movement: accepting from these cultures meanings that can be combined with the true and genuine horizon of the liturgy.[26]

---

that the application of the liturgical reform has met with difficulties due especially to an unfavorable environment marked by a tendency to see religion as a private affair; a rejection of institutions; a decrease in the visibility of the Church in society; by calling personal faith into question; the demand for a shift from passive to active participation in the liturgy; indifference on the part of some to the reformed liturgical books; a turning back to the previous liturgical forms; but finally others have promoted outlandish innovations, departing from the norms issued by the authority of the Apostolic See or the bishops, disrupting the unity of the Church and the piety of the faith, and even on occasion contradicting matters of the faith.]

23. Ibid., no. 17: "Liturgia non est corpore abstracta. His viginti quinque annis novae ortae sunt quaestiones aut novum sumpserunt momentum; quales, verbi gratia, exercitium diaconatus viris concessum matrimonio coniunctis; munera liturgica quae in celebrationibus possunt laicis delegari, viris aut mulieribus; celebrationes liturgicae pro pueris, iuvenibus ac mentis vel corporis immunitione laborantibus; modi textus liturgicos componendi certae definitaeque nationi aptos." [The liturgy is not disincarnate. In these 25 years new problems have arisen or have assumed new importance, for example: the exercise of a diaconate open to married men; liturgical tasks in celebrations which can be entrusted to lay people; liturgical celebrations for children, for young people and the handicapped; the procedures for the composition of liturgical texts appropriate to a particular country.]

24. Ibid., no. 16: "Alia in posterum res magni momenti accommodationem contingit Liturgiae ad diversas culturas." The Latin word *accommodatio* predominates in this section on the future of the liturgical renewal.

25. It is important to note that John Paul II uses *insero* in either a substantive or verbal form in both of the writings previously examined; namely, *Catechesi tradendae*, no. 53: [". . . hinc scilicet nuntium evangelicum non posse simpliciter seiungi ab illa cultura, in quam primitus sit *insertus* (emphasis added)], and in *Slavorum apostoli*, no. 21: [". . . *insertionis* (emphasis added) Evangelii in humanum autochthonum cultum"].

26. Ioannis Pauli II, *Vicesimus quintus annus*, no. 16: "Magnus perstat labor inseendi Liturgiam in quasdam culturas, ex eis illas accipiendo significationes, quae convenire possunt *veris et germanis aspectibus Liturgiae* (original emphasis), susbstantiali servata Ritus Romani unitate, in libris liturgicis expressam." The reference to the mutual interchange appears in SC, nos. 37 and 40. The latter prescription concerning preserving the unity of the Roman rite also appears in SC, no. 38.

John Paul II immediately presents two principles that set limits to the cultural accommodation of the liturgy. He believes that the work of inserting the liturgy into cultures must take place within the Roman rite so as to protect its substantial unity [*substantiala servata Ritus Romani unitate*].[27] He continues to refine the principles for the cultural accommodation of the liturgy by stating that the liturgy has an immutable core [*In accommodatione perficienda . . . oportet in Liturgia, partem immutabliem inesse*], divinely instituted [*utpote divinitus institutam*], of which the Church is the guardian [*cuius Ecclesia est custos*], and parts which can be changed [*et partes quae mutari possunt*].[28] John Paul II then indicates two additional things that must take place for accommodation in the liturgy, especially in the liturgy of the sacraments: 1) the Church has the competency and the duty, now and then, to adjust to the cultures of recently evangelized peoples those parts of the liturgy that can be changed;[29] 2) the cultural adaptation of the liturgy requires a conversion of hearts [*accommodatio ad culturas cordis conversionem exigit*], and if necessary, even a cessation of the practice of some ancestral customs that are incompatible with catholic faith [*si necesse sit, etiam intermissionem consuetudinum avitarum cum fide catholica insociabilium*].[30]

The final section of *Vicesimus quintus annus*, "The Organisms Responsible for Liturgical Renewal," repeats many of John Paul II's concerns regarding the proper authority and channels for any implementation of adaptations of the liturgy. Although the episcopal conferences and diocesan bishops have a right and duty to foster adaptation as the renewal of the liturgy progresses, the task of promoting the renewal of the liturgy pertains in the first place to the Apostolic See. Consequently, John Paul II advocates reviewing provisional translations of liturgical books, composing or approving chants to be used in the liturgy, ensuring respect for

---

27. Although John Paul II does maintain that the process of cultural accommodation of the liturgy is to take place within the limits of the Roman rite so as to preserve its substantial unity, he does not clarify (at least in this instance) what constitutes this essential or substantial unity of the Roman rite.

28. Ioannis Pauli II, *Vicesimus quintus annus*, no. 16: "In accommodatione perficienda consideretur oportet in Liturgia, et praesertim in sacramentorum Liturgia, partem immutabilem inesse, utpote divinitus institutam, cuius Ecclesia est custos . . ." Similar concerns will also appear in *Redemptoris missio*, no. 54

29. Ibid. ". . . et partes quae mutari possunt, quas ipsa potest et interdum debet ad culturas componere populorum recens evangelizatorum."

30. Ibid. "Accommodatio ad culturas cordis conversionem exigit et, si necesse sit, etiam intermissionem consuetudinum avitarum cum fide catholica insociabilium."

and compliance with the approved new texts, and finally, publishing liturgical books in a form that both testifies to the stability achieved and is worthy of the mysteries being celebrated.[31] The concluding sentences of number 20 of this section of the apostolic letter once again reveal both the concern of John Paul II in the important area of translations of liturgical texts and a consistency in his use of terminology regarding adaptation of the liturgy:

> The time has come to evaluate this commission's[32] way of working, both productive and unproductive, and the help and guidance it has received from the episcopal conference regarding its composition and its activity. The task of this commission is much more difficult when the episcopal conference touches upon ways of accommodating [accommodationis] or of the bringing in of higher human culture [vel altioris humani cultus inductionis].[33]

Thus, *Vicesimus quintus annus* occupies an important place in the genesis of the term *inculturation* in papal and magisterial documents and, by extension, in the genesis of the *Fourth Instruction*. Moreover, some of the concerns advanced by John Paul II in

---

31. Ibid., no. 20: "Temporariae necessitates induxerunt interdum ad utendum translationibus ad tempus, quae probatae sunt *ad interim* (original emphasis). Sed iam tandem meditandum est de aliquibus difficultatibus quae deinceps patuerunt; quibusdam medendum indiligentiis et erratis; libri parte tantum rediti, plene sunt convertendi, cantus conficiendi vel probandi in Liturgia adhibendi, de observandis textibus approbatis est providendum, libri liturgici denique edendi statu, qui stabilis habeatur, et specie mysteriis celebratis."

32. Ibid. The commission alluded to is explained in the preceding sentences of number 20: "The episcopal conferences have had the weighty responsibility of preparing the translations of the liturgical books. Immediate need occasionally led to the use of provisional translations, approved *ad interim.* But now the time has come to reflect upon certain difficulties that have subsequently emerged, to remedy certain defects or inaccuracies, to complete partial translations, to compose or approve chants to be used in the liturgy, to ensure respect for the texts approved and lastly to publish liturgical books in a form that both testifies to the stability achieved and is worthy of the mysteries being celebrated.
"For the work of translation, as well as for the wider implications of liturgical renewal for whole countries, each episcopal conference was required to establish a *national commission* (emphasis added) and ensure the collaboration of experts in the various sectors of liturgical science and pastoral practice." This national commission *(huius Commissionis)* is what John Paul II refers to in what follows immediately.

33. Ibid. "Expedit nunc et ratio exquiratur, aut fructuosa aut inanis, huius Commissionis, consilia inquirantur et auxilium quae a Conferentiae accepit in sua compositione ac navitate. Huius Commissionis munus tum difficilius est, cum Conferentia Episcopalis aliquos tractat modos accommodationis vel altioris humani cultus *inductionis* (emphasis added)." The terminology of *inductio* appeared both in *Catechesi tradendae* and in *Slavorum apostoli* when John Paul II referred to catechesis, evangelization, and the in-bringing of the soul or spirit of a culture.

this apostolic letter will be repeated and nuanced both in *Redemptoris missio*[34] and in the *Fourth Instruction.*

THE ENCYCLICAL *REDEMPTORIS MISSIO*

Redemptoris missio reveals not only how John Paul II's frequent journeys to foreign countries motivated him to write the encyclical, it also explains the genesis of the encyclical itself:

> From the beginning of my pontificate, we have chosen to travel to the ends of the earth in order that we might show this missionary concern; and our direct contact with peoples who do not know Christ has convinced us even more of the *urgency of missionary activity* (original emphasis), a subject to which we are devoting the present encyclical.[35]

John Paul II next affirms the missionary nature of the Church and of all Christian life; moreover, he emphasizes that the laity's participation in the work of evangelization has brought a new awareness that missionary activity is for all Christians, for all dioceses and parishes, Church institutions, and associations.[36] Finally, in the concluding section of the introduction, John Paul II clearly states his motive for the publication of the present document:

> Nevertheless, in the "new time" of Christianity there is an undeniable negative tendency, and the present document wishes to help overcome it. Missionary activity specifically directed to the nations is seen to be waning, and this tendency is certainly not in line with the directives of the Council and of subsequent statements of the Magisterium. . . . But we are even more strongly moved to proclaim the urgency of missionary evangelization by the fact that it is the primary service which the Church can render to every individual and to all humanity in the modern world.[37]

---

34. Ioannis Pauli II, *Redemptoris Missio.* See footnote 5 above for the full reference to the Latin and English texts.

35. Ibid., no. 1: "Ab initio Nostri Pontificatus elegimus itinera facere usque ad ultimos terrarum fines, ut hanc missionalem sollicitudinem ostenderemus, et haec quidem proxima congressio cum populis Christum ignorantibus magis Nobis persuasit de *necessitate actionis missionalis,* (original emphasis), cui has Litteras Encyclicas dicamus."

36. Ibid., nos. 1–2: "Concilium Vaticanum II renovare statuit vitam et actionem Ecclesiae pro mundi huius temporis necessitatibus: eius 'indolem missionalem' protulit in lucem . . . laicorum cura evangelizandi vitam novat ecclesiam. . . . Ante omnia nova gliscit conscientia: *missionem* nempe *ad omnes christianos pertinere,* (original emphasis for both) ad omnes dioeceses et paroecias, ad instituta et consociationes ecclesiales."

37. Ibid. "In hoc tamen christianismi 'novo vere' obtegi non potest perniciosa quaedam proclivitas, quam ad cohibendam hoc Documentum conferre vult: missio *ad gentes* (original

In the closing lines of number 2, John Paul II includes a lengthy list of his reasons and aims for the encyclical,[38] calling upon all people everywhere to open the doors to Christ.[39] He brings the introductory section to a conclusion, stating that he senses that the time has come for the Church to commit all of its energies to a new evangelization *ad gentes:*[40] "No believer in Christ, no institution of the Church can avoid this supreme duty: Christ must be proclaimed to all peoples."[41]

In Chapter V, "The Paths of Mission," in a section entitled "The Gospel's embodiment in the cultures of peoples," John Paul II addresses the context and content in the activity of inculturation.[42] Number 52 begins by recalling the Church's missionary relationship to cultures: by missionary work, the Church finds place among many cultures, and so, by its presence, becomes part

---

emphasis) specifica relaxari videtur, non perfecto congruenter praescriptionibus Concilii et subsequenti Magisterio. . . . Ideo autem maxime incitamur ad proclamandam evangelizationis missionalis necessitatem, quia prima haec est opera, quam Ecclesia praebere potest omni homini et universo generi humano in mundo huius temporis."

38. Ibid., no. 2: "Sed aliae causae non desunt nec proposita: multis postulationibus respondere, documentum eiusmodi petentibus: dubitationes expellere et ambiguitates quod missionem *ad gentes* ad confirmandos in suo munere bene meritos filios et filias actioni missionali deditos omnesque, qui eos adiuvant; vocationes missionarias excitare; theologos adhortari ad altius perscrutandas, certoque ordine exponendas varias missionis facies; missionem pro sua significatione refovere, Ecclesiae particulares distringendo, praesertim novellas, ut missionarios mittant et accipiant; non christianis, et imprimis Auctoritate Nationum ad quas dirigitur actio missionalis suadere hanc ad hoc unum spectare, videlicet ad homini serviendum per revelationem amoris Dei, qui est ostensus in Christo." [We [John Paul II] also have other reasons and aims: to respond to the many requests for a document of this kind; to clear up doubts and ambiguities regarding missionary activity *ad gentes* (original emphasis), and to confirm in their commitment those exemplary brothers and sisters dedicated to missionary activity and all those who assist them, to foster missionary vocations; to encourage theologians to explore and expound systematically the various aspects of missionary activity, to give a fresh impulse to missionary activity by fostering the commitment of particular Churches—especially those of recent origin—to send forth and receive missionaries and to assure non-Christians and particularly the authorities of countries to which missionary activity is being directed that all of this had but one purpose: to serve humanity by revealing the love of God made manifest in Jesus Christ.]

39. Ibid., no. 3: "Populi omnes, Christo portas aperite!" (original emphasis).

40. Ibid. "Animadvertimus tempus advenisse omnes adhibendi vires ecclesiales pro nova evangelizatione et missione *ad gentes* (original emphasis)." It is curious that John Paul II chose to use the masculine *vires* and not the more inclusive *homines* to refer to the obligation of all men and women in the church regarding a new evangelization.

41. Ibid. "Nemo in Christum credentium, nullum Ecclesiae institutum potest se subducere de hoc maximo officio: Christum omnibus populis nuntiandi."

42. Ibid., Caput V, "Missionis Viae," nos. 41–60, especially: *Evangelium Concorporare cum Populorum Culturis,* nos. 52–54.

of the process of inculturation [*inculturationis motum*].[43] John Paul II notes that it is as a living reality within culture that the Church effects its missions, and as part of that task, takes on the process of inculturation.

Clarifying that the plan and process of the insertion of the Church into the cultures of people [*ratio et processus inserendae Ecclesiae in populorum culturas*] require a long period of time [*longa exigit temporum intervalla*], John Paul II states that the entire process of inculturation is not one of mere exterior adaptation [*non enim de exteriore sola agitur adaptatione*].[44] Rather, appropriating the definition of *inculturation* from the 1985 Extraordinary Synod of Bishops, he affirms that inculturation [*inculturation*] means the intimate transfiguration of the true goods of human culture through their reception into Christianity and at the same time, the insertion of the name of Christian into various human cultures.[45]

Thus, John Paul II gives official status to the definition of *inculturation* from the 1985 Extraordinary Synod of Bishops. His adoption of this definition from the *Relatio* of the Synod highlights a double movement in the plan and process of inculturation:

---

43. Ibid., no. 52: "Suum persequens missionale opus inter gentes incidit Ecclesia in diversas culturas et ipsa vicissim includitur in talis inculturationis motum. Est ideo haec necessitas quaedam, quae totum eius historiae iter signavit, at hodie praesertim gravis est et urgens."

44. Ibid. "Ratio et processus *inserendae Ecclesiae in populorum culturas* (emphasis added) longa exigit temporum intervalla. Non enim de exteriore sola agitur aptatione quoniam inculturatio . . . ." Once again, John Paul II uses the terminology of *insero* to describe the activity of the Church in the process and plan of cultural adaptations.

45. Ibid. ". . . inculturatio 'intimam significat *transfigurationem* verorum cultus humani bonorum per ipsam eorum receptionem in rem christianam itemque nominis christiani *insertionem* varias in culturas.'" I have emphasized certain word changes in John Paul's quotation of the synodal definition; similarly, I am emphasizing key words in the original definition from the 1985 Synod of Bishops in order to facilitate the discussion of such modifications in the body of this study. The original definition appears in Giovanni Caprille, SJ, *Il sinodo dei vescovi: Seconda assemblea generale straordinaria* [24 novembre—8 dicembre 1985] (Roma: Edizioni "La Civiltà Cattolica," 1986), Ecclesia Sub Verbo Dei Mysteria Christi Celebrans Pro Salute Mundi, *Relatio finalis*, Ab Em.Mo D. Godefrido Card. Danneels, Archiepiscopo Mechliniensi-Bruxellensi, relatore, redacta ad suffragationem patrum submissa, annuente Summo Pontifice publicata, 567–68: "Inculturatio tamen a mera adaptatione externa diversa est, quia intimam *transformationem* authenticorum valorum culturalium per *integrationem* in christianismum et *radicationem* [emphases added to all] christianismi in variis culturis humanis significat [emphases added in all cases]." [The English translation from the USCC which follows allows some of the subtleties of the Latin changes to go unnoticed. Cf. Extraordinary Synod of Bishops, *A Message to the People of God and The Final Report* (Washington, DC: USCC, 1986), II, D:4: "Yet inculturation is different from a simple external adaptation because it means the intimate transformation of authentic cultural values through their integration in Christianity in the various human cultures."]

1) the reception of all that is good in a culture into the Church, and 2) the insertion of the name of Christian into the culture. This comports not only the proclamation of the Gospel but the entire weight and custom of church life. It would appear, then, that in his understanding of the process, John Paul II emphasizes how intimately inculturation affects the very life of the Church.

In addition, John Paul II's appropriation of the original definition of *inculturation* from the Extraordinary Synod of Bishops in 1985 reveals subtle changes in terminology. Perhaps the table below may serve to illustrate the chronological shift in terminology:

Table 2. A Comparison of the Terminology in the Descriptions of Inculturation from *Slavorum apostoli, Redemptoris missio*, and the 1985 Extraordinary Synod of Bishops

June 1985 *Slavorum apostoli:*	December 1985 **Extraordinary Synod of Bishops:**	December 1990 *Redemptoris missio:*
John Paul II's description:	Synodal definition:	John Paul II's definition:
the bringing in of the soul or spirit of a culture	*inculturation*	*inculturation*
insertionis Evangelii *in humanum autochthonum cultum*	*intimam transformationem* authenticorum valorum culturalium per	*intimam transfigurationem verorum cultus humani bonorum*
[of the insertion of the Gospel into autocththonous human culture]	[the intimate transformation of the authentic cultural values by their]	[the intimate transfiguration of the true goods of human culture
		per ipsam eorum receptionem in rem christianam
		[through the reception itself of those goods into Christianity]

Table 2. *continued*

June 1985 *Slavorum apostoli:*	December 1985 **Extraordinary Synod of Bishops:**	December 1990 *Redemptoris missio:*
*atque **inductionis** ipsius illius cultus humani*	***integrationem** in christianismum*	*itemque **nominis christiani insertionem** varias in culturas*
[and at the same time of (the) bringing that same human culture]	[integration into Christianity]	[and likewise, the insertion of the name of Christian into various cultures.]
*in **Ecclesiae vitam***	*et **radicationem** christianismi in variis culturis humanis*	
[into the life of the church]	[the rooting of Christianity in various human cultures]	

The modifications in the definitions merit some attention. For example, the original definition of *inculturation* from the *Relatio finalis* of the Extraordinary Synod of Bishops in 1985 states that inculturation is an innermost *transformationem* of the authentic values of cultures through their *integrationem* into Christianity and Christianity's *radicationem* in various human cultures. The terminology used by John Paul II in *Redemptoris missio* appears to express similar ideas but with a difference in vocabulary. In *Redemptoris missio*, he uses the Latin phrase *transfigurationem verorum cultus humani bonorum* in place of the original *transformationem authenticorum valorum culturalium*. Although the modification above is slightly nuanced, the deliberate shift in terminology may reveal a subtle theological inference on the part of John Paul II. *Transfiguration* is a term that has a particular resonance with the Gospel story of Jesus' transfiguration in both Mark and Matthew (Mark 9:2; Matthew 17:2). Perhaps his use of *transfigurationem* in a definition of *inculturation* in this encyclical indicates his belief that in the process of inculturation, there is a total change of the human person brought about by God's action and the work of the Gospel as the Gospel is inserted into cultures.

Further in the same number, John Paul II elaborates on the importance of the effect of inculturation on the Church. The statement by him represents a second example of the dual movement in the plan and process of inculturation:

> Through inculturation, the church embodies the Gospel in different cultures [*per inculturationem corporat Ecclesia Evangelium diversis in culturis*] and at the same time brings peoples with their own distinctive cultures into its own community [*ac simul gentes cum propriis etiam culturis in eandem suam communitatem*].[46]

John Paul II, however, is not unaware of the dangers involved in inculturation. After enunciating a definition of *inculturation*, he then adds the following qualifying statement:

> The process is thus a profound and all-embracing one, which involves the Christian message and also the Church's reflection and practice. But, at the same time, it is a difficult process, for it must in no way compromise the distinctiveness and integrity of the Christian faith.[47]

The concluding paragraphs of number 52 indicate that John Paul II envisions the actual process of inculturation taking place in local churches. He next presents an ecclesiological perspective regarding inculturation and places the entire process under the careful supervision of the local bishop:

> Thanks to this action within the local Churches, the universal Church herself is enriched with forms of expression and values in the various sectors of Christian life, such as evangelization, worship, theology and charitable works. She comes to know and to express better the mystery of Christ, all the while being motivated to continual renewal.
>
> Inculturation is a slow journey [*progressio lenta*], which accompanies the whole of missionary life. It involves those working in the Church's mission *ad gentes*, the Christian communities as

---

46. Ibid. "Hanc per inculturationem corporat Ecclesia Evangelicum diversis in culturis ac simul gentes cum propriis etiam culturis in eandem suam communitatem inducit."

47. Ibid. "Motus proinde hic altus est et universus, qui simul nuntium christianum complecitur, simul Ecclesiae ipsius ponderationem et consuetudinem. Sed difficilis etiam processus est, cum nullo prorsus pacto in periculum adducere fidei christianae debeat proprietatem nec integritatem." Bevans' comment on John Paul II's insistence on preserving unity and communion is worth noting: "Foremost in the pope's mind, it seems, is the preservation of the unity of the faith; and for him, this can be accomplished only by emphasizing a primary universality of ecclesial communion and doctrinal expression." (Bevans, *Models of Contextual Theology*, 44.)

they develop, and the Bishops, who have the task of providing discernment and encouragement for its implementation.[48]

John Paul II's clarity about who has the responsibility for implementing the process of inculturation, including the liturgy, will be expressed with similar precision in the prescriptions of the *Fourth Instruction*.[49]

Number 53 of this section serves as a bridge between the definition of *inculturation* in the preceding number and the warnings that follow in number 54. Referring to the fact that the work of inculturation requires prudent judgment [*Huius itaque rei gratia, praesertim in elementis inculturationis*], John Paul II urges cooperation among the particular churches of the same province [*particulares Ecclesiae eiusdem provinciae operabuntur inter se concordantes*]. He adds further that this cooperation should also be extended to the universal Church [*et universa cum Ecclesia*], so that in union with it, the particular churches may manifest the treasure of faith with legitimate variety [*et universalis et particularis Ecclesiae . . . ad thesaurum fidei in legitimas eius significationis varietates transferendum*].

The final sentence of number 53 is quite significant. Those who have already been evangelized [*coeuts iam evangelizati*] will look to the "conversion" of the Gospel message [*ad nuntii "evangelici" conversionem*], which is necessary to the evangelization of culture by bearing in mind the various ways in which faith and culture have been intertwined in the past [*utilitates per aetates partas exipsa consortione christiane religionis cum variis culturis*]. In this activity, however, they need to be attentive to the danger of changing the Gospel message itself, and not just its forms [*non tamen periculorum obliviscentes mutationum quae interdum evenerunt*].[50]

---

48. Ibid. "Universalis autem Ecclesia ipsa, per hanc localium Ecclesiarum actionem, sese exprimendi rationibus locupletatur ac bonis in multiplici vitae christianae regione, qualis est evangelizatio, cultus, theologia, caritas; multo melius Christi mysterium percipit et exponit congruentius, dum ad continentem sui renovationem impellitur. Argumenta haec, quae reperiuntur in Concilii documentis ac subsequente Magisterio iterum iterumque Nostris in itineribus pastoralibus ad Ecclesias iuniores agitavimus. Progressio lenta est inculturatio quae totam comitatur missionariam vitam appellatque varios actores illius missionis ad gentes, christianas communitates paulatim procedentes, Pastores obligatos officio discernendi atque hortandi ad eam explendam."

49. See numbers 34–37 of the *De Liturgia Romana et inculturatione*.

50. Ibid., no. 53: "Huius itaque rei gratia, praesertim in elementis inculturationis quae maiorem postulant prudentiam, particulares Ecclesiae eiusdem provinciae operabuntur inter se concordantes et universa cum Ecclesia, sibi nempe persuasum habentes considerationem tantum universalis et particularis Ecclesiae aptas eas esse reddituram ad thesaurum fidei in

In number 54 of this section, John Paul II draws attention to restrictions on the process of inculturation: 1) compatibility with the Gospel [conventiae cum Evangelio] and 2) communion with the universal Church [communionis cum Ecclesia universa].[51] Applied to a broader field, these restrictions are in keeping with those on liturgical inculturation mentioned by John Paul II in Vicesimus quintus annus; namely, the substantial unity of the Roman rite (corresponding to keeping communion within unity) and those parts of the liturgy that are divinely instituted (corresponding to compatibility with the Gospel).

As John Paul II brings the section on incarnating the Gospel into people's cultures to an end, he states that there is a risk of passing uncritically from a form of alienation from culture to an overestimation of culture, since culture is a human creation, marked by sin and in need of healing, ennobling, and perfecting.[52] Furthermore, continuing to insist that the process of inculturation involves the whole people of God, John Paul II clearly asserts that inculturation needs to be guided and encouraged, not forced, lest it give rise to negative reaction among Christians.[53]

---

legitimas eius varietates transferendum. Quam ob rem coetus iam evangelizati argumenta ad nuntii evangelici 'conversionem' subministrabunt neque praetermittent utilitates per aetates partas ex ipsa consortione christianae religionis cum variis culturis, non tamen periculorum obliviscentes mutationum quae interdum evenerunt."

51. Ibid., no. 54. "Hac in re potissima manent quaemodam monita. Duplici enim principio moderanda haec inculturatio suo in recto progressu est: 'convenientiae cum Evangelio et communionis cum Ecclesia universa.'" These specific principles are taken from an earlier Apostolic Exhortation; namely, Familiaris consortio, no. 10: "Duplici defixo principio convenientiae variarum animi culturae formarum cum Evangelio assumptarum et communionis cum Ecclesia universa, . . ." This same number in Familiaris consortio states that it is by means of "inculturation" that one proceeds toward the full restoration of the covenant with the wisdom of God, which is Christ himself. Moreover, John Paul II maintains that the whole Church will be enriched by cultures, although lacking in technology, which abound in human wisdom and are enlivened by profound moral values. ["Per eandem cultus humani inductionem progressus fit plenam ad redintegrationem foederis cum Dei Sapientia, quae cupletabitur omnis Ecclesia, quae, licet technologia careant, humana tamen sapientia abundant praestantibusque bonis moralibus vivificantur."] For the exact reference from Familiaris consortio, see Ioannis Pauli Pp. II, Summi Pontificis, Adhortatio Apostolica ad Episcopos, Sacerdotes et Christifideles totius Catholicae Ecclesiae: de Familiae Christianae Muneribus in mundo huius temporis, Familaris consortio (Vatican City: Typis Polyglottis Vaticanis, 1981), no. 10 (p. 12). ["Apostolic Exhortation of His Holiness Pope John Paul II to the Episcopate, to the Clergy, and to the Whole Catholic Church regarding the Role of the Christian Family in the Modern World," On the Family (Washington, DC: USCC, 1981).]

52. Ioannis Pauli II, Redemptoris missio, no. 54: ". . . periculum enim existat ne ab aliqua alienationis culturalis forma sine ullo solido iudicio ad nimiam transeatur culturae aestimationem, quae hominis nempe institutum proinde peccato signata est. Haec ideo etiam necesse est 'sanetur, elevetur et consummetur.'"

53. Ibid. "Inculturatio denique totum Dei popouli implicare debet. . . . Inculturatio profecto regenda erit, immo excitanda, at minime imponenda, ne contraria in christianis

Before beginning an analysis of the *Fourth Instruction* in the next chapter, it may be well to summarize what we have come to understand thus far regarding inculturation and its implication for liturgy. Inculturation first occurred when the Gospel was implanted in the Palestinian milieu; hence, inculturation is a basic principle of the life of faith.[54] Moreover, the terms *adaptation* and *inculturation* were introduced more formally into theological discussion in the years following the promulgation of the documents of the Second Vatican Council. Subsequently, the term *inculturation* gradually became associated with the process of making adaptations or adjustments to the liturgy suited to the native character, customs, and traditions of various regions and peoples. The vocabulary of "liturgical inculturation" began to replace the terminology of "adaptations of the liturgy" referred to in *Sacrosanctum Concilium*, numbers 37–40.[55]

Beginning with *Catechesi tradendae* in 1979 and continuing throughout his pontificate, John Paul II made the encounter between faith and culture, especially the insertion of the Gospel message into autochthonous human cultures in the work of catechesis and evangelization, an integral part of his description of inculturation in two encyclicals. He also maintained that the unity of the Roman rite and the communion of local churches with the Apostolic See (especially in liturgical celebrations) pertained to the very nature of the Church and her liturgy.

One also notices that John Paul II placed considerable emphasis on the encounter between faith and culture in his writings. He maintained in his 1990 encyclical *Redemptoris missio* that in this exchange, the Church, although respectful of the receiving culture, must take care lest the true message of the Gospel be tainted by elements in the local culture not yet purified and possibly incompatible with the Gospel.

Moreover, the above survey of some of John Paul II's important writings related to inculturation revealed his conviction that in the process of inculturation, there is a double movement. First, the Church encounters local cultures and inserts the Gospel into

---

pariatur adfectio: significatio enim esse debet vitae communitatis, id est, intra communitatem ipsam maturescere, non fructus modo eruditarum investigationum. Bona quidem tradita tueri est ipsum effectus fidei maturae."

54. Edward J. Kilmartin, SJ, "Inculturation of the Liturgy," in *Canadian Studies in Liturgy* 5 "Culture of the Praying Church: The Particular Liturgy of the Individual Church" (Ottawa, Ontario: Canadian Conference of Catholic Bishops, 1990): 55.

55. See Anscar Chupungco, OSB, *Liturgical Inculturation: Sacramentals, Religiosity, and Catechesis* (Collegeville, MN: The Liturgical Press, 1992), 28–30.

them. Second, the Church purifies, transforms, or eliminates those elements in the local cultures incompatible with Christianity; simultaneously, the Church not only allows but even welcomes elements from local cultures (which are compatible with the Gospel) into the life of the Church. Thus, in much the same way that local cultures are enriched by their encounter with the Gospel, both the proclamation of the Gospel and the life of the Church are transformed in the process of inculturation by bringing into the Church's life all that is good from local cultures.

Finally, John Paul II acknowledged that the process of inculturation ultimately leads to an encounter between the local culture and worship. However, in any adaptations of the Roman rite to the local churches, he insisted that those who wish to make adaptations of the Roman liturgy according to the native character and traditions of various regions and peoples must submit themselves to the guidance and authority of the diocesan bishop. The latter, in turn, consults with the local episcopal conference. The local conference of bishops submits all experimentations and adaptations to the Apostolic See for revision and final approval.[56] In short, for John Paul II, liturgical inculturation must occur within a clearly defined context and must conform to an explicit procedure. As the following chapter will show, the areas for adaptation/inculturation of the Roman rite and the procedures to be followed are spelled out in Part IV of the *Fourth Instruction.*

---

56. It is interesting to notice that the *Fourth Instruction* was issued very shortly prior to the opening of special session of the Synod of Bishops for Africa (April 10–May 8, 1994). The topic of inculturation in evangelization and in liturgy was expected to be discussed. [Cf. *Origins,* 24 (1994): 1–13.] The relationship between the timing of the release of the *Fourth Instruction* and the subsequent Synod of Bishops for Africa is itself matter for further study. See, for example, Nathan Mitchell, "The Amen Corner: Liturgy Encounters Culture— Again," *Worship* 68 (1994), 370; and Power, "Liturgy and Culture Revisited," pp. 371–72. Mitchell quotes Peter Hebblethwaite from the *National Catholic Reporter* 30:26 (29 April 1994). Hebblewaithe formulates a hypothesis, which claims that the timing of the release of the *Fourth Instruction* was deliberative, and a "preemptive strike" against those (in Zaire, for instance) who have worked for decades to encourage the evolution of distinctively African families of rites. However, he offers no concrete proof to support his claims.

CHAPTER V

AN ANALYSIS OF THE
FOURTH INSTRUCTION

The *Fourth Instruction for the Right Application of the Conciliar Constitution on the Liturgy (Nos. 37–40): On the Roman Liturgy and Inculturation* begins with an Introduction subdivided into two headings: a) the Nature of this Instruction[1] (nos. 1–3), and b) Preliminary observations[2] (nos. 4–8). The instruction is then further subdivided into four parts and a conclusion: Part I: The Process of Inculturation throughout the History of Salvation (nos. 9–20);[3] Part II: Requirements and Preliminary Conditions for Liturgical Inculturation (nos. 21–32);[4] Part III: Principles and Practical Norms for Inculturation of the Roman Rite (nos. 33–51);[5] Part IV: Areas of Adaptation in the Roman Rite (nos. 52–69);[6] and finally, a Conclusion (no. 70).

Since an analysis of the contents of the entire instruction would exceed the scope of this work, the goal of the present chapter is to examine five particular areas in the *Fourth Instruction:* 1) the definitions of inculturation it contains; 2) the significant vocabulary distinctions concerning adaptation of the liturgy with regard to the revision of the sacraments and rites it prescribes; 3) the important role that language occupies in liturgical adaptation and inculturation; 4) the principles and practical norms for the inculturation of the Roman rite it enunciates; and finally, 5) the areas of adaptation in the Roman rite it specifies.

With this in mind, this chapter will first present the definitions of inculturation contained in the *Fourth Instruction,* noting, in particular, the influence of John Paul II on such definitions.

---

1. CDWDS, *De Liturgia Romana et inculturatione,* 80–81: "Prooemium. . . . (a) De natura huius Instructionis." See Chapter I, footnote 1 for the official Latin and English texts.

2. Ibid., 82: "Notae praeviae."

3. Ibid., 85: "Inculturationis Processus in Historia Salutis."

4. Ibid., 91: "Liturgicae Inculturationis Exigentiae et Condiciones Praeviae."

5. Ibid., 98: "Principia et Agendi Rationes ad Ritum Romanum Inculturandum."

6. Ibid., 106: "Aptationum Ambitus in Ritu Romano."

Secondly, significant vocabulary distinctions concerning the adaptation of the liturgy which appear in the *Fourth Instruction* will be examined in order to compare the provisions of the instruction with the revisions of the sacraments and rites. Chapter V will also consider the important role of language in the work of adaptation and inculturation of the liturgy. Some of the principles and practical norms for inculturation of the Roman rite contained in Part III of the instruction will then be exposed and analyzed. In addition, this chapter will compare the procedures for revisions of the sacraments and rites stated in Part IV: "Areas of Adaptation of the Roman rite," of the *Fourth Instruction,* numbers 52–69, with those in the *editiones typicae [alterae]*. The chapter will conclude with a brief summary of the analysis presented herein.

DEFINITIONS OF *INCULTURATION* IN THE *FOURTH INSTRUCTION*

In the previous chapter, I pointed out that three definitions of *inculturation,* taken from *Slavorum apostoli,*[7] *Redemptoris missio,*[8] and the *Relatio finalis* of the Extraordinary Synod of Bishops in 1985,[9] respectively, would appear in the *Fourth Instruction.* The fourth number of the instruction presents two definitions of *inculturation* and three results envisioned in the process.

Number 4 begins with a historical reference to the different forms of liturgical adaptation *[aptatione]* contained in *Sacrosanctum Concilium.*[10] Having introduced the notion of *aptatio,* number 4 proceeds to explain that subsequent to the publication of the liturgical constitution, the *magisterium* has used the term *inculturatio* to indicate more precisely the insertion "of the Gospel into autochthonous human cultures, and at the same time, bring-

---

7. Ioannis Pauli II, *Slavorum apostoli,* no. 21: "In evangelizationis opere quod uti praecursores in regione a Slavicis populis habitata exegerunt—simul illius rei exemplum invenitur, quae nomen hodie se fert 'animi culturae *inductionis* (emphasis added)'—nempe *insertionis* (emphasis added) Evangelii in humanum autochthonum cultum—atque simul *inductionis* (emphasis added) in Ecclesiae vitam ipsius illius cultus humani."

8. Id., *Redemptoris missio,* no. 42: "Inculturatio intimam significat transfigurationem verorum cultus humani bonorum per ipsam eorum receptionem in rem christianam itemque nominis christiani insertionem varias in culturas."

9. Coetus Generalis, *Relatio finalis,* II, D:4: "Propterea inculturatio intimam transformationem authenticorum valorum culturalium per integrationem in christianismum et radicationem christianismi in variis culturis humanis significat."

10. CDWDS, *De Liturgia Romana et inculturatione,* no. 4: "Constitutio *Sacrosanctum Concilium* de liturgica *aptatione* (emphasis added) tractavit indicans quaedam eius genera."

ing that same human culture into the life of the church."[11] Number 4 of the instruction immediately gives another definition of *inculturation* from John Paul II:

> Inculturation means the intimate transformation of the authentic values of cultures through their integration into Christianity and the rooting of Christianity into various human cultures.[12]

However, the simultaneous actions of inserting the Gospel into culture and bringing these same cultures into the life of the Church, along with the transformation of human values, their integration, and implantation into Christianity, need to be interpreted in light of what was stated previously in *Gaudium et Spes*. This pastoral constitution highlighted a similar dual exchange in the preaching of the Gospel, the Good News of Christ, in the work of evangelization.[13] As the Gospel penetrates a given sociocultural milieu, it ceaselessly purifies and enhances it. As if from

---

11. Ibid. "Ecclesiaeque deinceps magisterium vocabulum 'inculturatio' adhibuit ad pressius indicandam insertionem "Evangelii in humanum autochthonum cultum atque simul inductionem in Ecclesiae vitam ipsius illius cultus humani." We have already observed in chapter IV that this definition occurs in the statement from the International Theological Commissions, *Fides et inculturatio*, section I: "Natura, Cultura et Gratia," no. 11. Number 4 in the *Fourth Instruction* repeats the description of the task of bringing in the soul or spirit of culture from John Paul II's 1985 encyclical *Slavorum apostoli*, no. 21. [However, a minor change appears in the description as it is restated in no. 4 of the *Fourth Instruction*; the modification is required by the syntax of each text respectively: *insertionis* and *inductionis* occur in the accusative case (*insertionem and inductionem*) in the text of *Fourth Instruction* and not in the genitive singular as in *Slavorum apostoli*.] It is improbable that the insertion of John Paul's "definition" so early in the instruction is an accident. Finally, it should be noted that the Vatican's English text confuses *autochthonous* (native, indigenous) and *autonomous* (independent), using the latter where the official Latin text of the *Fourth Instruction* and the original source (*Slavorum apostoli*, no. 21) clearly have *autochthonum*.

12. Ibid. "Propterea inculturatio intimam transformationem authenticorum valorum culturalium per integrationem in christianismum et radicationem christianismi in variis culturis humanis significat." As footnote 45 in Chapter IV indicated, in both the English and Latin texts of the *Fourth Instruction*, this quotation is a not a verbatim repetition of the first sentence in *Redemptoris missio*, no. 52, paragraph 3. Instead, it is the verbatim repetition of the definition from the 1985 Extraordinary Synod of Bishops, *Relatio Finalis*. What is interesting here is that the Congregation for Divine Worship and the Discipline of the Sacraments has chosen to include the original definition from the *Relatio Finalis* in the body of the *Fourth Instruction*. Neither the Latin nor the English text indicates the original source. Rather, both incorrectly attribute the definition to John Paul II and *Redemptoris missio*, no. 52.

13. There are numerous examples in *Gaudium et Spes* of the double movement between the Church and history, the Church and humanity, the Church and culture, and so on. Perhaps one of the more pertinent references for our purposes in this study occurs in no. 44: "Ipsa enim, inde ab initio suae historiae (i.e., historiae Ecclesiae), nuntium Christi, ope conceptuum et linguarum diversorum populorum exprimere didicit, eumdemque sapientia insuper philosophorum illustrare conata est: in hunc finem nempe ut evangelium tum omnium captui tum sapientium exigentiis, in quantum par erat, *aptaret* (emphasis added). Quae quidem verbi revelati *accommodata* (emphasis added) praedicatio lex omnis

---

the inside, it enriches with heavenly resources, strengthens, completes, and restores in Christ the spiritual endowments and talents of every people and age, thereby contributing to human and social culture. Thus, the Church, in fulfilling her task, thereby encourages and contributes to human and social culture, and by its activity, including the liturgy, leads people to inner freedom.[14]

Similarly, the Church has lived throughout history under various conditions. The Church has also used the resources of various cultures to disseminate and to explain the message of Christ in her preaching to all nations, to examine and understand it more deeply, and to express it more perfectly in liturgical celebration and in the life of the multiform community of the faithful.[15] It would appear that a mutual interchange between church and culture is envisioned in the above statement from *Gaudium et Spes*. Thus, the Church recognizes that there are elements within local cultures (e.g., the resources to disseminate and explain the message of Christ) which are compatible with the Gospel. Such elements are then incorporated into the life of the Church as it catechizes, evangelizes, and ultimately worships. It is with these ideas from *Gaudium et Spes* in mind that we continue our consideration of number 4 of the *Fourth Instruction*.

The second paragraph in number 4 of the instruction offers specific reasons for the shift in terminology from *aptatio* to *inculturatio* even in the liturgical sphere. The term *aptatio*, borrowed originally from missionary terminology, could possibly be understood as referring to changes of a transitory and external nature.[16] The Congregation for Divine Worship and the Discipline of the Sacraments wished to dispel the notion of liturgical changes as merely external and passing; rather, the Congregation

---

evangelizationis permanere debet. Ita enim in omni natione facultas nuntium Christi suo modo exprimendi excitatur simulque vivum commercium inter ecclesiam et diversas populorum culturas promovetur (Cf. *Lumen Gentium*, cap. II, n. 13)."

14. GS, no. 58: "Mores populorum indesinenter purificat et elevat. Animi ornamenta dotesque cuiuscumque populi vel aetatis supernis divitiis vel ab intra fecundat, communit, complet, atque in Christo restaurat. Sic ecclesia, proprium implendo munus, iam eo ipso ad humanum civilemque cultum impellit atque confert, et actione sua, etiam liturgica, hominem ad interiorem libertatem educat" (Tanner, 1109).

15. Ibid. "Pariter ecclesia, decursu temporum variis in condicionibus vivens, diversarum culturarum inventa adhibuit, ut nuntium Christi in sua praedicatione ad omnes gentes diffundat et explicet, illud investiget et altius intelligat, in celebratione liturgica atque in vita multiformis communitatis fidelium melius exprimat."

16. CDWDS, *De Liturgia Romana et inculturatione*, no. 4: "Lexicum cur sit mutatum facile intellegitur, etiam in ambitu liturgico. Verbum 'aptatio,' a sermone missionali mutuatum, insinuare poterat mutationes spectare praesertim quaedam tantum et exteriora capita."

claimed that the term *inculturatio* may serve better to designate the double movement presented in the previous definitions. Number 4 proceeds to express what the Congregation believes to be the result of the process of inculturation: 1) the Church gives the Gospel body in different cultures and at the same time leads peoples, together with their own cultures, into its own community;[17] 2) the entrance of the Gospel into a given social and cultural context gives fruitfulness to the spiritual qualities and gifts proper to each people, strengthens these qualities, and restores them in Christ.[18] Finally, 3) the Church assimilates these values when they are compatible with the Gospel in order to deepen the understanding of the announcement of Christ and give it more effective expression in liturgical celebration and in the many different aspects of the life of the community of believers. In short, the definitions, descriptions, and expectations concerning inculturation contained in number 4 of the present instruction both repeat what the Second Vatican Council espoused in *Gaudium et Spes* and restate what I have already noted concerning John Paul II's views regarding inculturation of the liturgy. Inculturation so defined has a place both in Christian worship and in other areas of the life of the Church.[19]

SIGNIFICANT VOCABULARY DISTINCTIONS IN THE *FOURTH INSTRUCTION: APTATIO, ACCOMMODATIO, AND INCULTURATIO*

THE MEANINGS OF *APTATIO* AND *ACCOMMODATIO*

Although there are several areas of linguistic comparison between the *Fourth Instruction* and the *editiones typicae* examined in the third chapter, for the present I shall limit my consideration of such comparisons to three terms that pertain to the issue of adaptation of the liturgy: *aptatio, accommodatio,* and *inculturatio.* The first distinction, between *aptatio* and *accommodatio,* was considered at the conclusion of Chapter I of the present study. These two

---

17. Ibid. "Hanc per inculturationem corporat Ecclesia Evangelium diversis in culturis ac simul gentes cum propriis etiam culturis in eandem suam communitatem inducit."

18. Ibid. "Ex una enim parte, Evangelii ingressus in quendam contextum socialem et culturalem 'animi ornamenta dotesque cuiuscumque populi (. . .) velut ab intra fecundat, communit, complet atque in Christo restaurat.'"

19. Ibid., no. 5: "Inculturatio ita definita suum habet locum et in cultu christiano et in ceteris vitae Ecclesiae ambitibus."

Latin words frequently appeared in English translation as "adaptation(s)." As I also noted in the first chapter of this study, Chupungco observed that *aptatio* and *accommodatio* are often interchanged quite indiscriminately in *Sacrosanctum Concilium*.[20]

However, the context and frequency of their respective occurrences in the *Fourth Instruction* suggest that the English translation needs to be more nuanced.[21] *Aptatio* appears to occur in the *Fourth Instruction* when the context for "adaptation" refers to structural changes within the rites themselves; i.e., the ordering of the parts of the ritual celebration, the completion of the ritual celebration by the addition of new material, the omission of parts of the ritual celebration, and finally the composition of new ritual celebrations. Number 52 of the *Fourth Instruction*, for example, reiterates that *Sacrosanctum Concilium* had inculturation of the Roman rite in mind [*Constitutio **Sacrosanctum Concilium** (original emphasis) quandam Ritus romani inculturationem prospiciebat*] when it provided norms for the "adaptation" of the liturgy to the native character and traditions of different peoples [***Normas** (original emphasis) statueret ad Liturgiam ingenio et traditionibus differentium populorum aptandam*], and when it provided for inserting adaptations in the liturgical books [*provideretque aptationibus in libris liturgicis inserendis (cf. infra nn. 53–56)*]. The liturgical constitution similarly envisioned the possibility of more profound adaptations in some circumstances, especially in mission lands [*necnon denique aptationibus profundioribus, quibusdam in casibus praesertim in Missionum finibus*].[22] Similarly, when numbers 54–57 of the *Fourth Instruction* specify the areas for liturgical adaptation of the Roman rite in the liturgical books (i.e., the *editiones typicae* for the sacraments, sacramentals, and other ritual celebrations), the vocabulary of *aptatio* predominates.[23]

---

20. See Chapter I, footnote 41.

21. It would be far beyond the scope of this study to give a detailed listing of all the uses of *aptatio* or *accommodatio* in the entire *Fourth Instruction*. The following examples of instances of *aptatio* and *accommodatio* represent what appears to be a pattern of usage in the *Fourth Instruction*.

22. CDWDS, *De Liturgia Romana et inculturatione*, no. 52: "Constitutio *Sacrosanctum Concilium* quandam Ritus romani inculturationem prospiciebat *Normas* (original emphasis) statueret ad Liturgiam ingenio et traditionibus differentium populorum *aptandam* (emphasis added) provideretque *aptationibus* (emphasis added) in libris liturgicis inserendis (cf. infra nn. 53–61) necnon denique *aptationibus* (emphasis added) profundioribus, quibusdam in casibus praesertim in Missionum finibus."

23. Ibid., no 54: "Ad celebrationem eucharisticam quod attinet, Missale Romanum, etsi legitimas varietates et *aptationes* (emphasis added) asciscit de praescripto Concilii Vaticanii

Accommodatio should perhaps be translated into English as "accommodation(s)," or "adjustment(s)" to the liturgical celebration of the sacraments and rites that do not affect the structure of the ritual celebration.[24] While one form or another of *accommodatio* occurs intermittently throughout the *Fourth Instruction*, the context in which *accommodatio* appears is usually

  a) in a repetition of a mandate from *Sacrosanctum Concilium*,[25]

  b) in a repetition from the introduction to a section of the *praenotanda* (in the liturgical books) which specify the adaptations pertaining to the conferences of bishops, or[26]

  c) in the same context as *aptatio* where *aptatio* stands in contrast to *accommodatio*.[27]

II, . . ."; no. 55: "Quoad cetera sacramenta et sacramentalia, editio typica latina uniuscuiusque Ordinis indicat *aptationes* (emphasis added) . . ."; no. 57: "Multis in locis Matrimonii Rituale *aptationem* (emphasis added) quam maximam exigit ne a soicalibus moribus sit alienum." It is interesting to note an occurrence of *accommodatio* in number 56: "Ad ritus initiationis christianae. . . 'in terris Missionum, (. . .) iudicare an elementa initiationis, quae apud aliquos populos in usu esse reperiuntur, ritui Baptismatis christiani *accommodari* (emphasis added) possint.'" The citation in which the word *accommodari* occurs, however, is itself a verbatim repetition of number 30:2 of *Rituale Romanum* ex decreto Sacrosancti Oecumenici Concilii Vaticani II instauratum auctoritate Pauli Pp. VI promulgatum. *Ordo initiationis christianae adultorum*, editio typica (Vatican City: Typis Polyglottis Vaticanis, 1972) and *Rituale Romanum* ex decreto Sacrosancti Oecumenici Concilii Vaticani II instauratum auctoritate Pauli Pp. VI promulgatum, *Ordo Baptismi parvulorum*, editio typica (Vatican City: Typis Polyglottis Vaticanis, 1969), "Praenotanda Generalia" in Kaczynski, 1:563, no. 1806.

24. For example, the fact that in the 1991 *Ordo celebrandi Matrimonium* a delegated layperson in the name of the Church may properly ask for, witness, and receive the exchange of consent of the couple about to be married, accommodates (i.e., adjusts) the liturgical celebration for those areas where priests or deacons, the ordinary witnesses in the name of the Church at marriage rituals, are lacking. The "matter" of the sacramental celebration; i.e., the asking for, the exchange of, and acceptance of consent and the imparting of the nuptial blessing remain unchanged. Although the *praenotanda* allow that the conferences of bishops may adjust (or omit) such things as the questions before the consent or the crowning and/or veiling of the bride and the groom [*ordo partium accommodari*] in the ritual celebration of the marriage rite, the essential elements of the ritual (asking for, exchange of, acceptance of consent and the nuptial blessing) and their ritual formulas may only be adapted or completed [*formulae Ritualis Romani aptari possunt vel, si casus fert, compleri*].

25. CDWDS, *De Liturgia Romana et inculturatione*, no. 35. In proposing some general principles and practical norms for inculturation of the Roman rite in part III of the *Fourth Instruction*, the CDWDS states that the rites need to be adapted to the capacity of the faithful and not require much explanation for them to be understood. ["Oportet insuper ut ritus 'sint fidelium captui accommodati, neque generatim multis indigeant explanationibus' ut intellegantur."] The occurrence of the verbal form *accommodati* is itself a direct citation from *Sacrosanctum Concilium*, no. 34:2, which calls for the revised rites to radiate a rich simplicity and avoid needless repetition.

26. Cf. OCM 1991, IV (De Aptationibus Conferentiarum Episcoporum Cura Parandis), no. 39: "Conferentiis Episcoporum, competit . . . hoc Rituale Romanum, . . . accommodare."

27. CDWDS, *De Liturgia Romana et inculturatione*, no. 3: ". . . bonum visum est Dicasterio Episcopis Conferentiisque Episcoporum auxilium suppeditare, ut facilius

Number 37 (footnote 82) of the *Fourth Instruction* appears to support the opinion that *aptatio* and *accommodatio* had, by the time of the publication of the present instruction, acquired carefully nuanced meanings. The context of the prescriptions contained in number 37 of the present instruction is the descending hierarchy of competency and jurisdictional authority of various organs in the Church concerning the approval of any adaptations of the liturgy: the Apostolic See, the Congregation for Divine Worship and the Discipline of the Sacraments, episcopal conferences, and the diocesan bishop. Number 37 reiterates further the prohibition of *Sacrosanctum Concilium,* number 22: "No other person, not even if he is a priest, may on his own initiative add, remove, or change anything in the liturgy."[28] The final sentence of number 37 is a reminder that inculturation (of the liturgy) is not to be left to the personal initiative of celebrants or to the collective initiative of an assembly.[29] The footnote immediately following the final sentence is a statement on the part of the Congregation for Divine Worship and the Discipline of the Sacraments, clarifying what may or may not be "adapted" by a presider in a liturgical celebration. The text of the footnote contains important information regarding the options available to a presider in a liturgical celebration. Since the presider's choices "accommodate" the liturgical celebration, the entire text of footnote 82 in the *Fourth Instruction* is included here for the convenience of the reader:

> The situation is different when, in the liturgical books published after the constitution (i.e., *Sacrosanctum Concilium*) the introductions and rubrics envisaged adaptations [*accommodationes*] leaving a choice to the pastoral sensitivity of the one presiding, for example, when it says, "if it is opportune," "in these or similar terms," "also," "according to circumstances," "either. . . or," '"if convenient," "normally," "the most suitable form can be chosen." In making a choice, the presider should seek the good of the assembly, taking into account the spiritual preparation and mentality of the participants rather than his own preferences or the easiest solution. In celebrations for particular groups, other possibilities are available. Nonetheless, prudence and discretion are always called for

considerent vel ad effectum adducant, ad normam iuris, *aptationes* (emphasis added) in libris liturgicis statutas, *accommodationes* (emphasis added) iam forte concessas critico examine subiciant. . . ."

28. SC, no. 22:3: "Quapropter nemo omnino alius, etiamsi sit sacerdos, quidquam proprio marte in liturgia addat, demat, aut mutet."

29. CDWDS, *De Liturgia Romana et inculturatione,* no. 37: "Inculturatio igitur neque relinquitur celebrantium personalibus consiliis, neque cuiusdam coetus communibus inceptis."

in order to avoid the breaking up of the local church into little "churches" closed in upon themselves.[30]

The footnote above is significant for several reasons. In the first place, the use of *accommodationes* to refer to the "adaptations" envisaged by the *praenotanda* and rubrics of the liturgical books (e.g., *editiones typicae*) published after the Council appears to confirm the opinion expressed above that *accommodationes* are external adjustments to the liturgical celebrations of the rites that may serve to enhance full, active, and conscious participation of those celebrating them. The fact that *aptationes* does not occur in this direct statement from the Congregation would lend credence to the opinion that when this term is used in the *Fourth Instruction*, it refers to changes in either the formulae or the ordering of the parts of the liturgical celebrations of the rites.

Secondly, the statement from the Congregation (albeit in the footnote cited above) appears to express a concern that the work of inculturation ought to take place in the context of the Roman rite. The closing sentence of the statement by the Congregation (in footnote 82) and the concern expressed therein regarding the possible breakup of local churches into smaller groups bear witness to this fact.

Finally, it would appear that this statement supposes that the choices or options that a presider[31] may choose are not limited to those found in the liturgical books. During liturgical celebrations, the presider is directed to address the assembly with either a text supplied for his use or in "these or similar words" [*his vel*

---

30. Ibid., footnote 82: "Situatio diversa est cum in obris liturgicis, editis post Constitutionem de sacra Liturgia Concilii Vaticani II, Praenotanda et rubricae praevident *accommodationes* (emphasis added) et selectiones opportunas quae iudicio pastorali celebrantis vel praesidentis relinquuntur et ideo in illis dicitur, v. gr.: 'si. . . convenit,' 'pro opportunitate,' 'his vel similibus verbis,' 'potest quoque,' 'sive. . . sive,' 'laudabiliter,' 'de more,' 'forma aptior seligatur.' In seligendis partibus, textibus, formis ille qui praeest attendet in primis commune bonum spirituale coetus, respiciens ad participantium formationem spiritalem ac ingenium potius quam ad suum proprium vel ad faciliores et expeditiores formas celebrationis. In celebrationibus pro coetibus particularibus quaedam ulteriores facultates electionis dantur. Prudentia tamen et discrimen necessaria sunt ad vitandam frequentem divisionem. Ecclesiae localis in sic dictis 'ecclesiolis,' quae quodammodo in seipsis clausae manent."

31. The phrase "ille qui praeest" appears to be inconsistent with the phraseology of the *editiones typicae* examined earlier. For example, in OCM 1991, no. 42, the official witness of the Church is referred to as "assistens." Thus, this term may refer to a priest, a deacon, a lay man or a lay woman. Moreover, the terminology of OCM 1991 changed that of OCM 1969, no. 17, "sacerdos assistens." Perhaps in its place the CDWDS could use *praeses, -idis* to refer to the person presiding, since clear provision is made for delegated lay presiders in some of the rites. Such terminology would be more consistent with the language used in OCM 1991.

similibus verbis]. However, the overall tone of the statement from the Congregation (in footnote 82) suggests that the options already available in the liturgical books suffice.

Thus, although Chupungco maintains that the difference in meaning between *aptatio* and *accommodatio* is negligible in *Sacrosanctum Concilium*,[32] and that in postconciliar documents there developed the neat distinction between *aptatio* as the competence of the conferences of bishops and *accommodatio* as the competence of the minister,[33] it would appear from our examination of this terminology that there is a nuanced difference between these two terms when they are used to refer to the adaptations of sacramental and other ritual celebrations, especially in the work of inculturation of the liturgy. This difference becomes more noticeable when *aptatio* and *accommodatio* are used in contrast to *inculturatio*.

THE SHIFT FROM *APTATIO/ACCOMMODATIO* TO *INCULTURATIO*

A second linguistic element in the *Fourth Instruction* that is related to the interpretation of the meanings of *aptatio* and *accommodatio* is the use of the term *inculturatio*. Since the title of the *Fourth Instruction* [*De Liturgia Romana et inculturatione*] indicates that the document will examine the Roman liturgy and *inculturation*, it would appear reasonable to expect that the language of *inculturatio*[34] would remain rather consistent throughout

---

32. See Chapter I, footnote 4.

33. Cf. Chupungco, *Liturgies of the Future: The Process and Methods of Inculturation*, 23–25.

34. CDWDS, *De Liturgia Romana et inculturatione*, no. 4: "Lexicum cur sit mutatum facile intellegitur, etiam in ambitu liturgico. Verbum 'aptatio,' a sermone missionali mutuatum, insinuare poterat mutationes spectare praesertim quaedam tantum et exteriora capita." It must be noted, however, that in *De Liturgia Romana et inculturatione*, number 3, *accommodatio* and *aptatio* are used in the same sentence: "Dum enim principia theologica relate ad quaestiones de fide et inculturatione altius adhuc investiganda sunt, bonum visum est Dicasterio Episcopis Conferentiisque Episcoporum auxilium suppeditare, ut facilius considerent vel ad effectum adducant, ad normam iuris, *aptationes* (emphasis added) in libris liturgicis statutas, *accommodationes* (emphasis added) iam forte concessas critico examine subiciant. . . ." [Cf. *Fourth Instruction*, no. 3 of the Vatican's English text: "Since the theological principles relating to the questions of faith and inculturation have still to be examined in depth, this congregation wishes to help bishops and episcopal conferences consider or put into effect, according to the law such *adaptations* (emphasis added) as are already foreseen in the liturgical books; to re-examine critically *arrangements* (emphasis added) that have already been made. . . ."] *Aptationes* are those adaptations that are found in the liturgical books; *accommodationes* are adaptations that are conceded but are not in the liturgical books but are rather the *aptationes* that are foreseen in *Sacrosanctum*

the *Fourth Instruction*. In fact, this is not the case. After the first two sections of the *Fourth Instruction* present the background and development of inculturation throughout salvation history and specify the requirements and preliminary conditions for liturgical inculturation using the language of *inculturatio*, a noticeable shift in terminology occurs in the remainder of the instruction. About midway through the instruction, the terminology of *aptatio* begins to predominate over that of *inculturatio*. In this regard, David Power notes:

> Given the opening choice of vocabulary (*inculturatio*), it is curious that throughout the instruction the word *aptatio* is constantly used. The word apparently suits the desire to have the whole process of inculturation in non-Eurocentered cultures take place "within the unity of the Roman Rite," or "within the context of the Roman Rite."[35]

Power's observation should not be taken lightly. Although his reflection is more directly concerned with the entire process of inculturation in the *Fourth Instruction,* Power calls attention to an important aspect of adaptations of the liturgy that was observed in the revisions of the rites; namely, that adaptations of the rites usually occur within the context of the Roman rite and do not necessarily envision the creation of new rites even in those countries receiving the Gospel for the first time (the marriage rite notwithstanding). As we saw previously, this crucial question of the possibility of creating new rites in the work of liturgical inculturation is, in fact, specifically ruled out in number 36 of the *Fourth Instruction:*

> The work on inculturation does not foresee the creation of new families of rites; inculturation responds to the needs of a particular culture and leads to *adaptations* which still remain a part of the Roman rite [*quae semper pars manent Ritus romani*].[36]

Concilium, no. 40. Thus, *accommodationes* most likely refers to those matters such as music, art, etc. The terminology used later in the *Fourth Instruction* appears to bear witness to this distinction. (See, for example, *De Liturgia Romana et inculturatione,* no. 40: "*Musica et cantus* . . . 'Cum in regionibus . . . huic musicae aestimatio debita necnon locus. . . quam in cultu ad earum indolem *accommodando* [emphasis added].'" Nevertheless, the *Fourth Instruction* continues to prefer the terminology of *aptatio* to *accommodatio.* The latter occurs, in one form or another, fewer than 10 times; the former occurs in one of its forms at least 30 or more times.

35. Power, "Liturgy and Culture Revisited," 226.

36. CDWDS, *De Liturgia Romana et inculturatione,* no. 36: "Inculturationis inquisitio non contendit ad novas familias rituales creandas; consulens autem culturae datae exigentiis, aptationes inducit, quae semper pars manent Ritus romani." This is a restatement of what John Paul II had said to the plenary session of the Congregation for Divine Worship and

While the deliberate switch in terminology from *inculturatio* to *aptatio* may indicate that liturgical inculturation (as defined and limited by the *Fourth Instruction*) does not entail the creation of new rites or families of rites, the use of *aptatio* in the present instruction may imply further that in the future, the "more profound adaptations" envisioned by *Sacrosanctum Concilium* numbers 37–40 are to be interpreted in a similar manner. Thus, number 63 of the present instruction concludes:

> Moreover, adaptations of this kind (i.e., "more profound adaptation of the liturgy") do not envisage a transformation of the Roman Rite but are made within the context of the Roman Rite.[37]

In this regard, it is very important to recognize the name given to the liturgical adaptation of the *Ordo missae* for Zaire: "The *Roman* (emphasis added) Missal for the Dioceses of Zaire" (Le Missel *Romain* [emphasis added] pour les diocèses du Zaïre).[38] Thus, although the title of the instruction [*De Liturgia Romana et inculturatione*] suggests that the instruction would treat the topic of inculturation of the liturgy in the context of the Roman liturgy, the examination of the different uses of *aptatio, accommodatio,* and *inculturatio* reveals that the instruction itself mixes the vocabulary of *aptatio* and *inculturatio,* appearing to prefer the former to the latter when treating liturgical "adaptations" of sacramental and ritual celebrations in local cultures.

---

the Discipline of the Sacraments on January 29, 1991. [Cf. AAS, 83 (1991): 940: "Il senso di tale indicazione non è di proporre alle Chiese particolari l'inizio di un nuovo lavoro, successivo all'applicazione della riforma liturgica, che sarebbe l'adattamento o l'inculturazione. E neppure è da intendersi l'inculturazione come creazione di riti alternativi. (. . .) Si tratta, pertanto, di collaborare affinché il rito romano, pur mantenendo la propria identità possa accogliere gli opportuni adattamenti."]

37. Ibid., no. 63: "Huiusmodi quoque aptationes minime tendunt ad Ritum romanum transformandum, sed potius intra ipsum suum obtinent locum."

38. For a brief discussion of the cultural form adapted in the Roman Missal for the Dioceses of Zaïre, see Chupungco, *Liturgies of the Future: The Process and Methods of Inculturation,* 89–92. On page 92, Chupungco concludes: "The mass for Zaïre and the twelve points concerning the order of mass for India are two pioneering models of cultural adaptation. They not only opened new horizons but also gave concrete example of how the passage from the Roman order of mass to new alternative forms can be achieved. In both models, we observe that the Roman form was the *terminus a quo* of the long and arduous process. We observe, too, that they have faithfully guarded the theological and spiritual treasures of tradition and have even enriched this tradition with new textual and ritual forms derived from the culture and customs of the people. (. . .) Surely the appearance of these new orders of mass is a major step forward in liturgical tradition, a legitimate progress based on sound tradition."

THE ROLE OF LANGUAGE IN LITURGICAL ADAPTATION

THE VERNACULAR IN EVANGELIZATION AS A PRELIMINARY CONDITION FOR LITURGICAL INCULTURATION

Careful attention to the role that the vernacular language occupies in the work of adaptation and inculturation of the liturgy is a prerequisite for understanding the principles, practical norms, and areas for inculturation of the Roman rite. In fact, in the closing numbers of Part II of the *Fourth Instruction*, "Requirements and Preliminary Conditions for Liturgical Inculturation" [*Liturgicae inculturationis exigentiae et condiciones praeviae*], the Congregation for Divine Worship and the Discipline of the Sacraments stresses the importance of the vernacular of a given people and culture as one of the "preliminary conditions for inculturation of the Liturgy."[39] In the first place, language and liturgy are directly related to the initial evangelization of a people. Number 28 of the *Fourth Instruction*, for example, states that since it is the mother tongue that conveys the mentality and culture of a people, the vernacular language of a people plays an important role in their evangelization. By using the vernacular, one may attain the spirit or mindset of a people, teach or form it according to the Christian spirit, and enable a deeper sharing in the prayer of the Church.[40] In fact, the first apostles of a country were often those who wrote down languages that up till then had only been oral.[41] Moreover, the proclamation in the vernacular of the word of God to the newly evangelized and the translation into their native language of the Bible or at least of biblical texts used in the liturgy are viewed by the Congregation as necessary steps in the process of inculturation of the liturgy.[42]

---

39. CDWDS, *De Liturgia Romana et inculturatione*, no. 95: "Condiciones praeviae inculturationis Liturgiae."

40. Ibid., no. 28: "Traditio missionalis Ecclesiae semper curavit ut homines sua quaque lingua evangelizarentur. . . et iure quidem, nam lingua nativa, quae est mentis habitus et culturae vehiculum, populi animum sinit attingere, spiritu christiano instruere, altius ut paticipet Ecclesiae orationem fovere."

41. Ibid. "Saepius vero contigit up primi apostoli in quadam natione scripto mandarent linguas antea tatummodo voce prolatas."

42. Ibid. "Prima evangelizatione peracta, proclamatio verbi Dei vulgari nationis sermone maxime populo prodest in celebrationibus liturgicis. Versio Biblorum Sacrorum vel saltem textuum biblicorum, qui in Liturgia adhibentur, necessario igitur ut primum ponitur momentum cuiusdam verae inculturationis progressus in ambitu Liturgiae."

In addition, the difficulties and challenges posed by those situations wherein the Church encounters a region where the population uses several different languages is mentioned in number 29 of the *Fourth Instruction*.[43] Finally, the Congregation clarifies that the work of inculturation of the liturgy requires the assistance of *periti* who are both competent in the liturgical tradition of the Roman rite and knowledgeable about the values of local cultures.[44] The *Fourth Instruction* urges further that preliminary studies of a historical, anthropological, exegetical, and theological nature are necessary; the results of such studies should be examined in light of the pastoral experience of the local clergy, especially those native to the country.[45] In this regard, the advice of wise people whose human wisdom is enriched by the light of the Gospel would also aid in the work of liturgical inculturation.[46] Finally, liturgical inculturation should also strive to satisfy the needs of traditional culture, and at the same time, take into account the needs of those affected by an urban and industrial culture.[47]

THE NATURE AND QUALITIES OF LITURGICAL LANGUAGE

After establishing the important role that language plays in the work of inculturation of the liturgy, the Congregation for Worship and the Discipline of the Sacraments includes some important guidelines in the *Fourth Instruction* regarding the nature and

---

43. Ibid., no. 29: "Complexior autem condicio inveniri potest ubi populi plurlismo culturae ac linguae fruuntur." The CDWDS also distinguished between the situation of countries that were evangelized centuries ago and where the Christian faith continues to influence the culture from those countries that were evangelized more recently or where the Gospel has not penetrated deeply into cultural values. ["Condicionum ecclesialium diversitas non parum confert ad perpendendum requisitum inculturationis liturgiae gradum Etenim alia est condicio regionum, quae a saeculis Evangelium receperunt et ubi fides christiana in cultura adstare permanet, alia vero illarum regionum, ubi evangelizatio nuper facta est vel res culturales altius non penetravit" (Ibid.)]

44. Ibid., no. 30: "Ad rituum inculturationem apparandam Conferentiae Episcoporum compellent oportet peritos, tam in Ritus romani traditione liturgica inquirenda quam in localibus valoribus culturalibus perpendendis."

45. Ibid. "Necessaria ergo evadunt studia praevia historica, anthropologica, exegetica et theologica, quae tamen comparentur oportet cum experientia pastorali cleri localis, potissimum autochthonis."

46. Ibid. "Magni quoque erit momenti sententia 'sapientum' nationis, quorum humana sapientia evangelica luce collustrata."

47. Ibid. "Pariter inculturatio liturgica sataget ut culturae traditae exigentiis satifaciat, ratione habita populorum, cultura urbana et industriali signatum."

qualities that liturgical language should possess. However, since texts are composed of words, and words are constitutive of language, where the *Fourth Instruction* refers to what is required for texts, I have taken the liberty to apply some of these requirements to the broader area of the nature and quality suggested for liturgical language. Thus, what is posited below concerning "liturgical language" represents an attempt to express the important role of language and its relation to liturgy and culture:

1. Liturgical language should clearly express the holy things signified so that the Christian people, as far as possible, may be able to understand them (i.e., both the language and the things signified) with ease and participate fully and actively in the ritual celebrations of the community.[48]

2. Liturgical language should be adapted to the capacity of the faithful so that the entire liturgical action may be understood without additional explanations.[49]

3. Liturgical language should announce to the faithful the good news of salvation and express the Church's prayer to the Lord. For this reason, it must always express, along with the truth of the faith, the grandeur and holiness of the mysteries being celebrated.[50]

4. Liturgical language should be expressed in a variety of genres used in the liturgy: biblical texts, presidential prayers, psalmody, acclamations, refrains, responsories, hymns, and litanies.[51]

5. In those countries where many languages are in use, liturgical language should respect the individual rights of small language

---

48. Cf. ibid., no. 35. This principle is a repetition of SC, no. 21: "Textus et ritus ita ordinari oportet, ut sancta, quae significant, clarius exprimant, eaque populus christianus, in quantum fieri potest, facile percipere atque plena, actuosa, et communitatis propria celebratione participare possit."

49. Cf. ibid.: "Oportet insuper ut ritus 'sint fidelium captui *accommodati* (emphasis added) neque generatim multis indigeant explanationibus,' ut intellegantur, attentis vero natura ipsa Liturgiae necnon notis biblicis et traditis eius structurae ac peculari sese exprimendi ratione, ut supra [nn. 12–17] exponuntur." This principle borrows heavily from SC, no 34: "Ritus nobili simplicitate fulgeant, sint brevitate perspicui et repetitiones inutiles evitent, sint fidelium captui *accommodati* (emphasis added) neque generatim multis indigeant explanationibus."

50. Cf. ibid., no. 39: "*Sermo vivus* (original emphasis) quatenus praecipuum hominibus exstat instrumentum mutuae communicationis, in celebrationibus liturgicis finem habet proclamandi fidelibus bonum nuntium salutis et Ecclesiae orationem ad Dominum dirigendi. Igitur manifestet semper, oportet, una cum fidei veritate, maiestatem ac sanctitatem mysteriorum, quae celebrantur."

51. Cf. ibid.: "Pariter spectare expedit diversa litterarum genera in Liturgia adhibita, uti sunt lectiones biblicae, quae proclamantur, orationes praesidentiales, psalmodia acclamationes, responsoria, responsa, versus, hymni et oratio litanica."

groups so that they are not excluded from full, active, and conscious participation in the liturgical action.[52]

6. Liturgical language should express the relationship between the text and the liturgical action.[53]

Since liturgical language occurs within the ritual texts of the Roman rite in the various celebrations of the liturgy, the composition of new texts and translations into the vernacular such as Lectionaries, Sacramentaries, pontificals, the *editiones typicae* of the various rituals, the Liturgy of the Hours, and books containing blessings, all of which comprise the Roman rite, will necessarily be governed by certain principles and practical norms.

PRINCIPLES AND PRACTICAL NORMS FOR INCULTURATION OF THE ROMAN RITE

Before examining Part III of the *Fourth Instruction*, it is necessary to recall the specific nature and purpose of the present instruction stated by the Congregation for Divine Worship and the Discipline of the Sacraments in the introductory section. Number 3 clarifies the nature of the *Fourth Instruction* and affirms that it was by order of the Supreme Pontiff (John Paul II) that the Congregation for Divine Worship and the Discipline of the Sacraments prepared this instruction [*Congregatio de Cultu Divino et Disciplina Sacramentorum de mandato Summi Pontificis hanc Instructionem paravit*]. In the instruction the norms for the adaptation of the liturgy to the native character and traditions of the people that were given in *Sacrosanctum Concilium*, numbers 37–40 [in qua **Normae ad aptationem ingenio et traditionibus populorum perficiendam,** *sub nn. 37–40 in Constitutione* **Sacrosanctum Concilium** *latae*] are defined more clearly [*clarius definiuntur*]; certain principles are expressed in more general terms in those articles [*nonnulla principia, in iisdem articulis verbis generalioirbus expressa*]; are explained more precisely [*pressius explicantur*]; and

---

52. Cf. ibid., no. 50: "Nonnumquam in eadem regione plures vulgate sunt linguae, quarum quaeque propria est parvi personarum coetus vel unius tribus. Tunc aequilibrium quoddam inveniendam est, ut iura peculiaria horum coetuum vel tribuum observentur, remoto quidem periculo liturgicas celebrationes ratione quam maxime particulari peragendi. Neque pariter neglegatur quod interdum in quadam natione evolutio fieri possit unam versus linguam principalem."

53. Cf. no. 53: "Ceterum interpretes mentem ponant oportet in textus necessitudinem cum actione liturgica, in communicationis verbalis exigentias necnon in populi sermonis viventis qualitates litterarias."

finally, the prescriptions and order of procedure (for adaptation) are set out in a more appropriate way [*praescripta declarantur ac denique rationes servandae in iisdem exsequendis determinantur*]. These prescriptions and procedures are explained so that in the future, the norms and guidelines stated here will be put into practice [*ita ut in posterum haec materia secundum eadem in praxim deducatur*].[54]

Although number 3 also states that the congregation wishes to help bishops and episcopal conferences consider or put into effect, according to the law, such adaptations as are already foreseen in the liturgical books [*bonum visum est Dicasterio Episcopis Conferentiisque Episcoporum auxilium suppeditare, ut facilius considerent vel ad effectum, adducant, ad normam iuris, **apta-tiones** (emphasis added) in libris liturgicis statutas. . . *][55] and critically re-examine adaptations that have already been made, [*accommodationes iam forte concessas critico examine subiciant*][56] and finally, in certain cultures where pastoral necessity requires a more profound and at the same time a more difficult adaptation of the liturgy, regulate more suitably the process of adaptation in use and in practice according to the law [*ac denique, si in nonnullis culturis pastoralis necessitas illa **aptationis** (emphasis added) Liturgiae forma urgeat, quae eadem Constitutione vocatur 'profundior' ac simul tamquam 'difficilior' indicatur, aptius in usu et praxi secundum ius ordinetur*],[57] the limitation for liturgical inculturation enunciated from the beginning of the Fourth Instruction is that any adaptation is to be put into effect

---

54. Ibid., no. 3: "Congregatio de Cultu Divino et Disciplina Sacramentorum de mandato Summi Pontificis hanc Instructionem paravit, in qua *Normae ad aptationem ingenio et traditionibus populorum perficiendam*, sub nn. 37–40 in Constitutione *Sacrosanctum Concilium* latae, clarius definiuntur, nonnulla principia, in iisdem articulis verbis generalioribus expressa, pressius explicantur, praescripa declarantur ac denique rationes servandae in iis exsequendis determinantur, ita ut in posterum haec materia secundum eadem in praxim deducatur."

55. Ibid. ". . . bonum visum est Dicasterio Episcopis Conferentiisque Episcoporum auxilium suppeditare, ut facilius considerent vel ad effectum, adducant, ad normam iuris, *aptationes* (emphasis added) in libris liturgicis statutas. . . ."

56. Ibid. "accommodationes iam forte concessas critico examine subiciant." The Vatican's English text in *Origins* 23 (April 14, 1994): 747 translates *accommodationes* as "arrangements."

57. Ibid. "ac denique, si in nonnullis culturis pastoralis necessitas illa *aptationis* (emphasis added) Liturgiae forma urgeat, quae eadem Constitutione vocatur 'profundior' ac simul tamquam 'difficilior' indicatur, aptius in usu et praxi secundum ius ordinetur."

according to the law [*ius ordinetur*]. It is in light of these statements that the both the principles and practical norms for inculturation of the Roman rite as well as those areas of adaptation in the Roman rite are examined below.

Part III of the *Fourth Instruction* discloses the principles and practical norms for inculturation of the Roman rite. It is subdivided into three sections: a) General Principles;[58] b) Adaptations Which Can Be Made;[59] and c) Necessary Prudence.[60] There are three general principles that are presented in the third part of the instruction.[61] These principles form the basis for the practical norms which appear later in the *Fourth Instruction*.

The first principle in number 35, quoting from *Sacrosanctum Concilium* (number 21), identifies the goal of liturgical inculturation: "The texts and rites must be so organized [*textus et ritus ita ordinari oportet*] so that they express more clearly the holy things which they represent [*ut sancta, quae significant, clarius exprimant*] and so that insofar as it is possible, the Christian people [*eaque populus christianus*] may be able to understand easily and participate in [*facile percipere atque. . . participare possit*] a full, active, and proper celebration of the community [*plena, acutosa, et communitatis propria celebratione*]."[62]

The second principle enunciated in the *Fourth Instruction* in number 36 is a repetition of *Sacrosanctum Concilium* (number 38) concerning the substantial unity of the Roman rite [*servata substantiali unitate ritus romani*] with an interesting addition: the work (or investigation) of inculturation [*inculturationis inquisitio*] does not foresee the creation of new families of rites [*non*

---

58. Ibid., 98: "Principia generalia."

59. Ibid., 100: "Quid aptari possit."

60. Ibid., 104: "Prudentia necessaria."

61. Ibid., no. 34: "Ad Ritus romani inculturationem inquirendam atque perficiendam ratio est habenda: (1) de finalitate operi inculturationis inhaerente; (2) de substantiali unitate Ritus romani; (3) de competenti auctoritate."

62. Ibid., no. 35: "*Finalitas* (original emphasis), quae Ritus romani inculturationem moderari debet, non alia est ac Concilium Vaticanum II posuit instaurationtis generalis fundamentum: 'Textus et ritus ita ordinari oportet, ut sancta, quae significant, clarius exprimant, eaque populus christianus, in quantum fieri potest, facile percipere atque plena, actuosa, et communitatis propria celebratione possit.'" Cf. Geraldo Agnelo, "Liturgia Romana e inculturazione," *Notitiae* 30 (1994): 74: "Sono da tener presenti, simultaneamente, tre principi generali. Il primo concerne la finalità dell'inculturazione, cioè: permettere al popolo di cogliere facilmente il sensi dei riti, di parteciparvi maggiormente e di vivere meglio il mistero cristiano (n. 35)."

contendit ad novas familias rituales creandas];[63] rather, taking into account the exigencies of a given culture, it (inculturation) brings in adaptations that remain part of the Roman rite [*aptationes inducit, quae pars manent Ritus romani*].[64]

The third principle (in number 37) states that adaptations of the Roman rite [*Ritus romani aptationes*], even in the area of inculturation [*etiam in ambitu inculturationis*], depend solely on the authority of the Church [*unice pendent ab Ecclesiae* **auctoritate**] (original emphasis).[65] Number 37 next reiterates the prohibition of *Sacrosanctum Concilium*, number 22:3; namely, that absolutely no other one [*nemo omnino alius*], i.e., other than the competent ecclesiastical authorities outlined in SC, 22:1 and 22:2, not even if he be a priest, should, of one's own initiative, add, remove, or change anything in the liturgy.[66] It is interesting to note that the Congregation for Divine Worship and the Discipline of the Sacraments included the original prohibition from the liturgical constitution and not John Paul II's modification of it from *Vicesimus quintus annus*, number 10. The following table illustrates similarities and differences in both prohibitions:

---

63. CDWDS, *De Liturgia Romana et inculturatione*, no. 36: "Inculturationis processus perficiendus est Ritus romani *unitate substantiali servata* (original emphasis). Unitas haec hisce nostris temporibus invenitur in libris liturgicis typicis ex auctoritate Summi Pontificis editis et in libris liturgicis illis respondentibus, a Conferentiis Episcoporum probatis et suis respectivis dicionibus atque a Sede Apostolica confirmatis. Inculturationis inquisitio no contendit ad novas familias rituales creandas; consuelens autem culturae datae exigentiis, aptationes inducit, quae semper pars manet Ritus romani." Cf. Agnelo, 74–75: "Il secondo principio è indicato dalla Costituzione liturgica, precisamente quando tratta di adattamento: l'art. 36 (corrected from the original which had incorrectly noted art. 38) domanda de rispettare 'l'unità sostanziale del Rito romano.' Questo significa che la ricerca di inculturazione non si propone la creazione di nuove famiglie rituali, ma che gli adattamenti si iscrivano nel quadro del Rito romano."

64. However, Agnelo admits that the liturgical reform restored a certain flexibility and openness which was already known in the past, when the Roman liturgy was in contact with the customs and the mentality of the French and Germanic peoples: "La riforma liturgica gli ha restituito una flessibilità ed apertura già conosciute in passato, quando la liturgia romana si era incontrata coni costumi e la mentalità dei popoli franchi e germanici" (Ibid., 75).

65. CDWDS, *De Liturgia Romana et inculturatione*, no. 37: "Ritus romani aptationes, etiam in ambitu inculturationis, unice pendent ab Ecclesiae *auctoritate* (original emphasis), quae Sedis est Apostolicae, eam exercentis per Congregationem de Cultu Divino et Disciplina Sacramentorum; est quoque, intra limites iure statutos, Conferentiae Episcoporum atque Episcopi dioecesani."

66. Ibid. "'Nemo omnino alius, etiamsi sit sacerdos, quidquam proprio marte in Liturgia addat, demat, aut mutet.'" Cf. Agnelo, 75: "Il terzo principio è un'avvertenza: l'ambito dell'inculturazione liturgica non è lasciato alla scelta dei celebranti o delle 'comunità' o movimenti di vario genere; per essere veramente della Chiesa, l'inculturazione richiede un'autorità responsabile (n. 37). Anche qui l'Istruzione non dice altro di diverso dalla Costituzione (art. 22)."

Table 3. A Comparison of the Prohibitions in *Sacrosanctum Concilium*, *Vicesimus quintus annus*, and the *Fourth Instruction* with respect to Adding, Subtracting, Changing, or Turning around Anything in the Liturgy

Sacrosanctum Concilium	Vicesimus Quintus annus	The Fourth Instruction
Quapropter nemo omnino alius	*Qua de causa non licet cuipiam*	*Nemo omnino alius*
[Wherefore, absolutely no other one]	[For this reason, it is not permitted to anyone]	[Wherefore, absolutely no other one]
etiamsi sit sacerdos	*ne sacerdoti quidem neque cuilibet fidelium numero*	*etiamsi sit sacerdos*
[even if he be a priest]	[neither to a priest nor indeed to anyone numbering among the faithful]	[even if he be a priest]
quidquam propria marte	*quidquam proprio iudicio*	*quidquam propria marte*
[by (or on) one's own initiative]	[by one's own judgment]	[by (or on) one's own initiative]
in Liturgia addat, demat, aut mutet	*addere inibi demere aut invertere*	*in Liturgia addat, demat, aut mutet*
[that he/she add, remove or change anything in the liturgy]	[to add, to remove, or to turn over (or around) anything in that matter]	[that he/she add, remove or change anything in the liturgy]

The peculiarities of the terminology reveal that the original prohibition in *Sacrosanctum Concilium* and the restatement found in the *Fourth Instruction* are more generic prohibitions, applicable even to priests. The terminology used by John Paul II in *Vicesimus Quintus annus* extends the generic prohibition in *Sacrosanctum Concilium* so as to preclude making changes in the liturgy by anyone, be they clergy or members of the laity. Furthermore, the deliberate change in terminology from *mutet* to *invertere* must be interpreted in light of the words *quidquam* and *inibi*. The fact that this prohibition is repeated in several documents indicates that the liturgy belongs most properly to the Church and not to any one individual or group.

The *Fourth Instruction* next mentions some specific areas of inculturation in the liturgy; namely, language, music, singing, gesture, posture, art and images of Christ, the Virgin Mary, and the saints.[67] In each of these respective areas, the instruction encourages that in adaptations of the liturgy, attention be paid to what can properly be brought into the liturgical celebration from local cultures.[68]

AREAS OF ADAPTATION IN THE ROMAN RITE[69]

Part IV of the *Fourth Instruction* comprises two main sections: a) Adaptations in the Liturgical Books;[70] and b) Adaptations Envisaged by Number 40 of the *Conciliar Constitution on the Liturgy*.[71] Each section has an additional subheading for the "procedure" to be followed in the implementation of the respective adaptations.[72]

---

67. CDWDS, *De Liturgia Romana et inculturatione*, nos. 39–45. Cf. Agnelo, ibid., 75: "Quali elementi possono essere oggetto d'inculturazione?. . . sono tutti I seguenti mezzi di espressione e di comunicazione ad essere in gioco: innanzitutto il linguaggio, quale sistema di espressione del pensiero e di comunicazione, ma anche la musica e il canto, i gesti e gli atteggiamenti del corpo, l'arte e l'iconografia (nn. 38–45)." It is interesting to note that the Latin text of number 44 in the instruction refers to *sacras imagines Christi Iesu, Virginis Mariae et Sanctorum venerationi fidelium proponendi*. It is Agnelo who introduces the term *iconografia*.

68. Cf. ibid., no. 39: "Quamobrem magna cum cura attendendum erit quaenam uniuscuiusque populi sermonis elementa convenienter introduci possint in celebrationes liturgicas. . . ."; no. 40: " 'Cum in regionibus quibusdam, praesertim Missionum, gentes inveniantur quibus propria est traditio musica, magnum momentum in earum vita religiosa ac sociali habens, huic musicae aestimatio debita necnon locus congruus praebeatur, tam in fingendo earum sensum religioso, quam in cultu ad earum indolem accommodando' " (this is a verbatim repetition of SC, no. 119); no. 41: " Ex humo culturali uniuscuiusque nationis seligendi erunt gestus et corporis habitus, qui hominis coram Deo condicionem exprimant, significationem christianam eis conferendo, ut, quantum fieri potest, cum gentibus et corporis habitibus consonent, qui e Sacra Scriptura originem ducunt"; no. 42: "Apud eos tales formae expressionis corporeae locum habere possunt in actione liturgica. . . "; no. 43: "Qua de re (i.e., contributio artis) in Ecclesia omnium gentium et regionum, ars liberum exercitium habeat, dummodo conferat ad sacrarum aedium et rituum liturgicorum pulchritudinem adipiscendam, servatis autem reverentia et honore, quae eis debentur."

69. Ibid., 106: "Aptationum Ambitus in Ritu Romano," nos. 52–69.

70. Ibid. "Aptationes a libris liturgicis praevisae," nos. 53–61.

71. Ibid., 111: "Aptatio ad normam art. 40 Constitutionis Concilii Vaticanii II de sacra Liturgia," nos. 63–64.

72. Ibid. "Ratio procedendi quoad aptationes in libris liturgicis praevisas," no. 62, "Ratio procedendi ad art. 40 Constitutionis Concilii Vaticani II de sacra Liturgia perficiendum," nos. 65–69.

Two levels of adaptations and the procedure to be used in any implementation of adaptation are envisioned.[73] The first level concerns the adaptations already foreseen in the liturgical books; i.e., the role exercised by episcopal conferences in the translations and revisions of the Roman Missal, Roman Ritual, and other liturgical books. This level is open to a vast application of inculturation.[74]

The second level concerns more profound adaptations that were not foreseen in the liturgical books.[75] Since this subdivision of the instruction concerns the concrete implementation of the general principles stated in Part III of the *Fourth Instruction*,[76] the norms mentioned here are straightforward. Moreover, the fourth part of the instruction does not open the way for any liturgical revolution nor any drifting away from the Roman rite. The prescriptions in the fourth part of the instruction are a serious reflection upon the principles, the placement, and the limits and conditions for a true inculturation of the liturgy, particularly in the lives of young churches.[77]

AREAS OF ADAPTATION IN THE ROMAN RITE ENUNCIATED BY THE *FOURTH INSTRUCTION*

The fourth and final part of the *Fourth Instruction* concerns the adaptations envisioned in the liturgical books and the adaptations envisaged by number 40 of *Sacrosanctum Concilium*.[78] Each of

---

73. Cf. Agnelo, "Liturgia Romana e inculturazione," 76: "L'ambito degli adattamenti nel rito romano comprende due livelli: l'Istruzione ha cura di distinguerli e di precisare per ciascuno la procedura da seguire."

74. Cf. Ibid. "Il primo livello concerne gli adattamenti già previsti nei libri liturgici (Cf. SC, 39). L'Istruzione raccoglie tutte le possibilità già offerte alle Conferenze episcopali nel Messale, nel Rituale e negli altri libri liturgici. La semplice lettura basta a mostrare come a questo livello sia già vasto il campo di applicazione per un inculturazione."

75. Cf. Ibid. "Il secondo livello riguarda gli adattamenti più profondi, non previsti nei libri liturgici (Cf. SC, 40)."

76. Cf. Ibid. "E soprattutto a questo livello che acquistano importanza i principi generali esposti nella terza parte dell'Istruzione."

77. Cf. Ibid. "Questa quarta Istruzione per una corretta applicazione della Costituzione Sacrosanctum Concilium non apre la strada ad un'imprecisata rivoluzione, né tanto meno ad un progressivo andare alla deriva del Rito Romano. Essa intende chiarire quanto esposto negli articoli 37-40 della Costituzione conciliare e portare ad un riflessione circa i principi, le poste in gioco, i limiti e le condizione di una vera inculturazione della liturgia, principalmente nelle giovani Chiese."

78. CDWDS, *De Liturgia Romana et inculturatione*, 106; 111. "Aptationum Ambitus in Ritu Romano: (A) Aptationes a libris liturgicis praecisae; and (B) Aptatio ad normam art. 40 Constitutionis Concilii Vaticani II de sacra Liturgia."

the preceding subdivisions contains a section regarding specific procedures to be followed in any implementation of liturgical inculturation.

Number 52 of the present instruction gives a general introduction to the subdivisions mentioned above. In essence, number 52 states that when *Sacrosanctum Concilium* established norms for the adaptation of the liturgy to the temperament and needs of different peoples, the intention expressed by these norms is tantamount to liturgical inculturation of the liturgy. Furthermore, the *Constitution on the Sacred Liturgy* also provided for a "degree of adaptation" in the liturgical books when it envisaged the possibility of more profound adaptations in some circumstances within mission lands.[79] Perhaps the following table may help to schematize and summarize the main points in this section:

Table 4. Adaptations in the Liturgical Books[80]

Area for adaptation	Reasons for adaptation	Special considerations
I. Translation of liturgical books into the language of the people: First significant measure of inculturation:	A. All peoples, even the most primitive, have a religious language, which is suitable for expressing prayer.	A. Completion and revision of translation (where necessary) should be effected according to the directives given by the Holy See on the subject.
	B. Liturgical language has its own special characteristics: (i) deeply impregnated by the Bible; (ii) certain words in current Latin use [*memoria, sacramentum*] took on a new meaning in the Christian faith;	B. Different literary genres are to be respected.

---

79. Ibid., no. 52: "Constitutio *Sacrosanctum Concilium* quandum Ritus romani inculturationem prospiciebat cum Normas statueret ad Liturgiam ingenio et traditionibus differentium populorum *aptandam* (emphasis added), provideretque *aptationibus* (emphasis added) in libris inserendis (cf. infra, nn. 53–61), necnon denique *aptationibus* (emphasis added) profundioribus, quibusdam in casibus praesertim in Missionum finibus (cf. infra, nn. 63–64)."

80. Table 4 represents a summary of numbers 53–61 in the *Fourth Instruction.*

Table 4. *continued*

Area for adaptation	Reasons for adaptation	Special considerations
	(iii) certain Christian expressions can be translated from one language to another, as has happened in the past; e.g., *ecclesia, evangelium, baptisma, eucharistia.*	C. Contents of Latin typical edition are to be preserved.
		D. Translations must be (i) understandable to participant (ii) suitable for proclamation and singing, with (a) appropriate responses, and (b) acclamations by the assembly.
II. The celebration of the Eucharist	A. Allowance is made for (i) legitimate differences (ii) adaptations according to the prescriptions of the Second Vatican Council.	A. The Roman Missal must remain a sign and instrument of unity of the Roman rite within the diversity of languages.
		B. In accordance with the constitution on the liturgy, each conference of bishops has the power to (i) lay down norms for its own territory that are suited to the traditions and characters of (a) peoples (b) regions (c) different communities.

Table 4. *continued*

Area for adaptation	Reasons for adaptation	Special considerations
		C. The same applies to (i) gestures and postures (ii) veneration of the altar and the Book of the Gospels (iii) the song at preparation of the gifts (iv) the communion song (v) the rite of peace (vi) conditions regulating Communion with the chalice (vii) the materials for construction of the altar and liturgical furniture (viii) the material and form of sacred vessels (ix) liturgical vestments.
		E. Episcopal conferences can also determine the manner of distributing Communion.
III. Other sacraments and sacramentals		A. The Latin typical edition of each ritual indicates the adaptations which (i) pertain to the episcopal conferences or (ii) pertain to individual bishops in particular circumstances.
		B. These adaptations concern (i) texts (ii) gestures (iii) the ordering of the rite (sometimes).

Table 4. *continued*

Area for adaptation	Reasons for adaptation	Special considerations
		C. *When the typical edition gives alternate formulas, conferences of bishops can add other formulas of the same kind.* (emphasis added)
IV. Rites of Christian initiation	A. Episcopal conferences are (i) to examine with care and prudence what can properly be admitted from (a) the traditions (b) the character of each people (ii) to judge (in mission countries) whether initiation ceremonies practiced among the people can be adapted into the rite of Christian initiation (iii) to decide whether or not (ii) may be used.	A. It is necessary to remember that the term *initiation* does not have the same meaning or designate the same reality when (i) it is used of societal rites of initiation among certain peoples, or (ii) it is contrary to the process of Christian initiation, which leads through the rites of the catechumenate to incorporation into Christ in the Church by means of the sacraments of Baptism, Confirmation, and Eucharist.
V. The marriage rite	A. In many places this is the rite that calls for the greatest degree of adaptation so as not to be foreign to social customs.	A. Each episcopal conference has the faculty to prepare its own marriage rite which must always conform to the law requiring the ordained minister or *the assisting layperson* (emphasis added), according to the case: (i) to ask for, and (ii) to obtain the consent of the contracting parties (iii) to give them the nuptial blessing.

Table 4. *continued*

Area for adaptation	Reasons for adaptation	Special considerations
		B. This proper rite must obviously (i) bring out clearly the Christian meaning of marriage (ii) emphasize the grace of the sacrament, and (iii) underline the duties of the spouses.
VI. Funeral rites	A. Among all peoples, funerals are always surrounded with special rites, often of great expressive value.	A. Episcopal conferences must choose those which correspond best to local customs.
	B. To answer to the needs of different countries, the Roman Ritual offers several forms of funerals.	B. Episcopal conferences will wish (i) to preserve all that is good in family traditions and local customs; (ii) to ensure that funeral rites manifest (a) the Christian faith in the Resurrection, and (b) a witness of the true values of the Gospel.
		C. It is in this perspective that funeral rituals can incorporate the (i) customs of different cultures, and (ii) respond as best they can to the needs and traditions of each region.

Table 4. *continued*

Area for adaptation	Reasons for adaptation	Special considerations
VII. Blessings VIII. The liturgical year IX. The Liturgy of the Hours	A. The blessing of (i) persons (ii) places (iii) things.	A. Episcopal conferences will (i) be able to employ the foreseen dispositions, and (ii) be attentive to the needs of the country.
	B. Touches the everyday life of the faithful for (i) maintaining local customs, and (ii) admitting popular usage.	A. Each particular church and religious family adds its own celebrations to those of the universal Church, after approval by the Apostolic See.
	A. The Liturgy of the Hours has as its goal (i) the praise of God, and (ii) the sanctification by prayer of (a) the day (b) all human activity.	B. Episcopal conferences can also, with the prior approval of the episcopal See, (i) suppress the obligation of certain feasts (ii) transfer them (the observance and the obligation) to a Sunday.
		C. Episcopal conferences also decide the time and manner of celebrating: (i) rogationtide, and (ii) ember days.
		A. Episcopal conferences can make adaptations in (i) the second reading of the office of readings (ii) hymns (iii) intercessions (iv) final Marian antiphons.

The disproportion among the three columns of Table 4 merits some attention. First of all, in *Sacrosanctum Concilium*, the previous three instructions, and in the *editiones typicae*, we noted a continued and persistent emphasis on the role of the Apostolic See and its right to approve adaptations of the liturgy presented by the various episcopal conferences. The present section of the instruction is no exception to that pattern; rather, it continues to mandate the same. In the second place, a most curious "special consideration" occurs in III: C, concerning the special considerations regarding the adaptations of the sacraments and sacramentals. This prescription appears to allow the Conference of Bishops to add other formulas of the same kind when the *editio typica* gives alternatives. Indeed, the same terminology that appeared in some of the *ordines* examined in Chapter III occurs in number 55. One example of this similarity in terminology between number 55 of the *Fourth Instruction*[81] and that of an *ordo* occurs in the *Ordo celebrandi Matrimonium* 1991 (number 41:2),[82] concerning episcopal conferences and their competency to adapt the liturgical celebration of the marriage ritual. Aside from some minor changes in the choice of vocabulary,[83] the prescriptions remain essentially unchanged.[84]

Before concluding this section, it is necessary to single out two numbers in the *Fourth Instruction* that deserve special attention; namely, number 57 dealing with the marriage rite and number 58 concerning the funeral rites. The former[85] uses the same

---

81. CDWDS, *De Liturgia Romana et inculturatione*, no. 55: ". . . Si editio typica plures formulas ad libitum exhibeat, Conferentiae *Episcoporum alias formulas eiusdem generis addere possunt* (emphasis added)."

82. OCM, 1991, no. 41:2: "Quando Rituale Romanum plures exhibet formulas ad libitum, alias formulas eiusdem generis adicere licet."

83. It would appear that the subjunctive form *exhibeat*, used in the *Fourth Instruction*, allows for the *editiones typicae* which are or will be in the process of revision in the future. The difference in usage between *adicere licet* in OCM 1991 and *addere possunt* in 1994 may reflect a subtle change in tone and content, i.e., from a more pastoral approach to adaptation reflected in the *editiones typicae* of the rites to a more juridical approach in the *Fourth Instruction* to the process of adaptation/inculturation of the liturgy.

84. However, it is worth noting that number 62 of the *Fourth Instruction* reiterates what we have seen consistently throughout the documents we have examined; namely, that it is only after recognition by the Apostolic See according to the law that the episcopal conferences may promulgate the decree and determine the date when the new liturgical book (i.e., *editio typica* for a conference or region) may be used. [Cf. Latin text of no. 62: "Post recognitionem Apostolicae Sedis ad normam iuris, Conferentia Episcoporum procedet ad decretum promulgationis, tempus indicans a quo liber approbatus vigere incipiat."]

85. CDWDS, *De Liturgia Romana et inculturatione*, no. 57. Cf. OCM 1991, no. 42: "Praeterea unaquaeque Conferentia Episcoporum facultatem habet exarandi ritum proprium

terminology that appeared in *Ordo celebrandi Matrimonium* 1969 and 1991 to state that each episcopal conference has the power to prepare its own proper marriage rite [*Conferentia Episcoporum quaeque facultatem habet exarandi ritum proprium Matrimonii*] suitable to the customs of regions and peoples [*usibus locorum et populorum congruentem*], which must always conform to the law requiring that the ordained minister or the assisting layperson, according to the circumstances, [*firma tamen lege, que statuit ut Matrimonio, assistens, sive clericus sive laicus, prout, casus fert*] must, in the name of the Church, ask for and receive the consent of the contracting parties [*exquirat manifestationem contrahentium consensus eamque nomine Ecclesiae recipiat*] and impart to them the nuptial blessing [*atque super nupturientes orationem benedictionis nuptialis proferat*].

The latter, (i.e., number 58)[86] echoing the terminology used in the *editio typica* for the funeral rites, states that as an answer to the needs of different countries, the Roman Ritual offers several forms of funerals [*Ad diversarum regionum condicionibus respondendum, Rituale romanum plures typos praebet pro exsequiis*]. In addition, episcopal conferences must choose those rites that correspond best to local customs [*inter se distinctos, ex quibus Conferentiis Episcoporum competit eum seligere, qui usibus localibus melius aptetur*]. Similarly, episcopal conferences will

---

Matrimonii, ad normam Constitutionis de sacra Liturgia (n. 63b), locorum et populorum usibus congruentem, actis ab Apostolica Sede probatis, firma lege ut assistens requirat excipiatque contrahentium consensum et benedictio nuptialis impertiatur."

86. Ibid., no. 58: "Ad diversarum regionum condicionibus respondendum, Rituale romanum plures typos praebet pro exsequiis, inter se distinctos, ex quibus Conferentiis Episcoporum competit eum seligere, qui usibus localibus melius aptetur. Libenter servantes quodquod in traditionibus familiaribus et moribus locorum bonum inveniatur, sane invigilabunt, ut exsequiae fidem paschalem manifestent reveraque evangelicum spiritum testifidentur. Hac servata ratione exsequiarum Ritualia usus diversarum culturarum assumere possunt atque uniuscuiusque regionis rerum adiunctis et traditionibus aptius respondere." Cf., OE, no. 4: "Ut omnium regionum condiciones perspectae quodammodo habeantur, Ordo exsequiarum pro adultis hic propositus iuxta tres typos distinguitur. . . ."; no. 9: "ideo Conferentia Episcopalis, attentis necessitatibus particularibus, opportune providebit"; no. 21:1: "Aptationes definire, intra limites in hoc titulo statutos"; no. 21:3: "Propria autem Ritualium particularium iam exstantium elementa, si quae habeantur, retinere, dummodo cum Constitutione sacra Liturgia et necessitatibus hodiernis componi possint, vel ea aptare."; and finally, no. 2: "Sive ergo de familiarum traditionibus agitur, sive de locorum consuetudinibus, sive de societatibus ad funera curanda constitutis, quidquid bonum invenerint, libenter probent, quidquid vero Evangelio contradicere videatur, ita transformare nitantur, que quae exsequiae pro christianis celebrentur, et fidem paschalem ostendant et evangelicum spiritum vere demonstrent."

wish to preserve all that is good in family traditions and local customs [*Libenter servantes quodquod in traditionibus familiaribus et moribus locorum bonum inveniatur sane invigilabunt*],
and ensure that the funeral rites manifest the Christian faith in
the Resurrection and bear witness to the true values of the
Gospel [*ut exsequiae fidem paschalem manifestent reveraque
evangelicum spiritum testifidentur*]. It is in this perspective that
funeral rituals can incorporate the customs of different cultures
and respond as best they can to the needs and traditions of each
region [*hac servata ratione exsequiarum Ritualia usus diversarum culturarum assumere possunt atque uniuscuiusque regionis rerum adiunctis et traditionibus aptius respondere*].

The second subdivision of Part IV, "Adaptations Envisaged
by number 40 of the Conciliar *Constitution on the Liturgy*,"[87] is
followed by a section entitled "Procedures."[88] Number 63 in the
former contains one of the most forceful statements regarding
the limitations of adaptations of the liturgy and recalls a principle stated in *Sacrosanctum Concilium*, number 40. The principle
provides for "an even more profound adaptation of the liturgy
[*profundior Liturgiae aptatio*] in some places and circumstances,
and this entails greater difficulties."[89] Number 63 of the *Fourth
Instruction* first repeats the principle from *Sacrosanctum Concilium* and next explains the *Liturgiae aptatio* (SC, 40) as more
than the sort of adaptations envisaged by the previous three
instructions on the liturgical constitution and the *praenotanda*
of the liturgical books [*Hic non amplius de aptationibus agitur
quae Institutionibus generalibus et Praenotandis librorum liturgicorum continentur*].[90]

Two important presuppositions regarding "an even more
profound adaptation of the liturgy" are mentioned next: 1) an
episcopal conference has exhausted all the possibilities of adaptation offered by the liturgical books;[91] and 2) that the episcopal

---

87. Ibid., 111: "Aptatio ad normam art. 40 Constitutionis Concilii Vaticani II de sacra Liturgia."

88. Ibid., "Ratio procedendi ad art. 40 Constitutionis Concilii Vaticanii II de sacra Liturgia perficiendum."

89. SC, no. 40. Cf. Tanner, 828–29: " . . . variis in locis et adiunctis, *profundior Liturgiae aptatio* (emphasis added) urgeat, et ideo difficilior evadat."

90. CDWDS, *De Liturgia Romana et inculturatione*, no. 63: "Hic non amplius de aptationibus agitur, quae Institutionibus generalibus et Praenotandis librorum liturgicorum continentur."

91. Ibid. "Id postulat Conferentiam Episcoporum, antequam altioris aptationis inceptum iniret, omnes opportunitates imprimis adhibuisse, libris liturgicis praebitas."

conference has made an evaluation of the adaptations already introduced and may be revised before proceeding to more far-reaching adaptations.[92]

The final paragraph of number 63 in the instruction mentions the limitations of liturgical adaptation by stating that changes may be made in one of the areas considered in numbers 53–61 of the instruction without implying the need for changes in other areas mentioned therein.[93] The last sentence echoes number 36 of the present instruction and states quite clearly that adaptations of this kind (i.e., even more radical) do not envisage a transformation of the Roman rite, but are made within the context of the Roman rite.[94] This subsection ends in number 64 in which the role of the episcopal conferences in the process of inculturation is redefined.[95]

The final subsection of Part IV, "Procedure," numbers 65–69 specifies the procedure to be followed in the area of an "even more profound adaptation of the liturgy" and defines the roles of the participants in such a task. Perhaps the table that follows may serve as a summary of the difference in roles and responsibilities between the episcopal conferences and the Congregation for Divine Worship and the Discipline of the Sacraments (CDWDS):

---

92. Ibid. ". . . aptationum iam introductarum exitum perpendisse easdemque forte retractavisse."

93. Ibid. "Utilitas vel necessitas talis aptationis manifestari potest circa quandam materiam supra indicatam (cf. supra, nn. 53–61), ceteris imutatis."

94. Ibid. "Huiusmodi quoque aptationes minime tendunt ad Ritum romanum transformandum, se potius intra ipsum suum obtinent locum."

95. Although number 64 of the *Fourth Instruction* does not relate directly to the cultural adaptations of the liturgy but rather to areas where there are still problems concerning the participation of the faithful in liturgical celebrations, it nevertheless includes an interesting nuance about the role of episcopal conferences in the whole process of liturgical inculturation: "It is the function of episcopal conferences *to propose* (emphasis added) to the Apostolic See modifications it wishes to adopt following the procedure set out below (i.e., in nos. 65–69)." ["Episcoporum Conferentiae deinde competit aptationes, quas statuere exoptat, iuxta modum procedendi infra decretum, Sedi Apostolicae *proponere* (emphasis added)."] The closing paragraph clarifies that the episcopal conferences are subject to the authority of the Congregation for Divine Worship and the Discipline of the Sacraments in the area of liturgical adaptation. ["Congregatio de Cultu Divino et Disciplina Sacramentorum praesto adest ad Conferentiarum Episcoporum propositiones recipiendas easdemque examini subiciendas, prae oculis habito bono Ecclesiarum localium, quarum interest, necnon bono communi universae Ecclesiae, atque ad inculturationis processum sedulo adiuvandum, ubi utile vel necessarium videatur, secundum principia et rationes hac in Instructione exposita (cf. supra, nn. 33–51), animo semper parato ad cooperationem confidenter prasestandam ac mutuam officii conscientiam participandam."] The question of proper jurisdiction in adaptations will be considered again in Chapter VI of this work.

Table 5. Procedures to be Followed in "more profound adaptations"[96]

Episcopal Conferences	Congregation for Divine Worship and the Discipline of the Sacraments
A. Examines [*examini ea subiciet*] what had to be modified in liturgical celebrations because of the traditions and native character of peoples.	A. Examines the proposals carried out together by the episcopal conference and the CDWDS [*Incepti examine expleto, a Conferentia Episcoporum et a Congregatione simul peracto*].
B. Asks [*studium harum aptationum committet Commissioni nationali vel regionali de Liturgia*] the national or regional liturgical commission to study the matter and examine the different aspects of the elements of local culture [*ad culturae localis diversos elementorum aspectus examinandos*] and their eventual inclusion in the liturgical celebrations [*num eadem, si casus ferat, in celebrationes liturgicas inseri possint*].	B. Grants the episcopal conference a faculty to make an experiment for a definite period of time where this is appropriate [*ipsi Conferentiae a Congregatione facultas tribuetur, si casus fert, experimentum per determinatum tempus peragendi*].
C. Collaborates with the episcopal conferences of neighboring countries or with the same culture [*Examen hoc praevium fiet cooperantibus, si casus fert, Conferentiae Episcoporum regionum propinquarum vel eiusdem culturae*].	C. Examines the dossier (containing the material sent from the episcopal conference) [*Documentationis examine peracto, Congregatio approbationis*].
D. Presents proposals to the CDWDS before any experimentation takes place [*Antequam quodcumque propositum hac in re experiatur, Conferentiae Episcoporum proprium	D. Issues a decree giving its consent, possibly with some qualifications [*Congregatio approbationis decretum edere poterit*], so that the changes can be introduced [*animadversionibus

---

96. Table 5 represents a summary of numbers 65–69 of the *Fourth Instruction*.

Table 5. *continued*

Episcopal Conferences	Congregation for Divine Worship and the Discipline of the Sacraments
consilium Congregationi scripto et dilucide exponet]. This presentation should include i) a description of the innovations proposed, ii) the reasons for their adoptions, iii) the criteria used, iv) the times and places chosen for a preliminary experiment and an indication which groups will make it, and v) the acts of the discussion and the vote of the conference.	*forte additis]* into the territory covered by the episcopal conference [*ut variationes seu mutationes, quae exquirebantur, in territorio, Conferentiae Episcoporum iurisdictioni subiecto, admittantur].*

E. Supervises the process or experimentation, normally with the help of the national or regional liturgical commission [*Conferentia Episcoporum invigilabit ut experimentum bene evolvatur*].

F. Ensures that the experimentation does not exceed the limits of time and place that were fixed [*Insuper vigilibat ne experimentum limites statutos locorum ac temporum praetergrediatur*].

G. Ensures that pastors and the faithful know about the limited and provisional nature of the experiment [*ut pastores et fideles edoceantur de eius natura ad tempus et circumscripta*].

H. Does not publicize the experiment in a way that could have an effect on the liturgical practice of the country [*demum ne ita divulgetur ut vitam liturgicam nationis ultro afficere possit*].

Table 5. *continued*

Episcopal Conferences	Congregation for Divine Worship and the Discipline of the Sacraments
I. Decides (at the end of the period of experimentation) whether it matches up to the goal that was proposed or whether it needs revisions [*Tempore experimenti exacto, Conferentia Episcoporum diiudicabit utrum propositum finalitati inquisitae respondeat an retractandum sit circa quaedam elementa*].	
J. Communicates its conclusions to the CDWDS with full information about the experiment [*et deliberationem una cum documentationis fasciculo, in quo propositi experimenta describuntur, Congregatione deferet*].	

Table 5 reveals some interesting phraseology regarding the respective roles of the episcopal conferences and the Congregation for Divine Worship and the Discipline of the Sacraments. In the first place, it is obvious that it falls to the various episcopal conferences to bear the greater burden in the overall work of "even more profound adaptations" of the liturgy. The conferences of bishops take the initiative, order and oversee the research concerning liturgical inculturation, make proposals, and after receiving proper permission, implement and adjudicate their success. Their work further includes not only setting limitations of time, place, geographical collaboration, and so on for any proposed adaptation of the liturgy, but also informing both pastors and laity about the temporary and provisional nature of any proposed experimentation. For its part, the Congregation for Divine Worship and the Discipline of the Sacraments, exercising collaborative authority with the episcopal conferences, grants them the faculty to proceed with experiments and gives its consent to what is proposed by the episcopal conferences.[97]

Number 70 of the *Fourth Instruction* (where *inculturatio* reappears), ends the Fourth Instruction by stating,

> The Congregation for Divine Worship and the Discipline of the Sacraments presents these rules to the episcopal conferences to govern the work of liturgical inculturation envisaged by the Second Vatican Council as a response to the pastoral needs of people of different cultures.[98]

The concluding number of the instruction also recalls the opening lines of the *Fourth Instruction:* Legitimate differences in the Roman rite were allowed (especially in mission lands) and foreseen by the *Constitution on the Sacred Liturgy;*[99] the diversity of forms and of liturgical families in the universal Church bears witness to the Church's unwillingness to impose, even on the liturgy, a rigid uniformity in matters that do not affect the faith or the good of the whole community.[100] In short, the *Fourth Instruction* begins with a declaration that diversity in liturgy does not harm the unity of the Church and proposes that such diversity be further developed;[101] it ends with a hope that diversity in certain elements of liturgical celebrations may be a source of enrichment for particular churches, especially for churches of a younger age, provided that the substantial unity of the Roman rite, the unity of the whole Church, and the integrity of the faith are respected.[102]

---

97. Cf. CDWDS, *De Liturgia Romana et inculturatione,* nos. 66 and 68.

98. Ibid., no. 70: "Congregatio de Cultu Divino et Disciplina Sacramentorum Conferentiis Episcoporum has rationes exhibet, quae opus inculturationis Ritus romani, a Concilio Vaticano II provisum, moderari debent, ad necessitatibus a pastoralibus populorum, cultura diversorum, satisfaciendum."

99. Ibid., no. 1: "Varietates legitimae in Ritum romanum temporibus praeteritis introductae sunt atque ut novae introducerentur, praesertim in Missionibus, praevidit Concilium Vaticanum II per Constitutionem *Sacrosanctum Concilium.*"

100. Ibid. "Etenim, 'Ecclesia, in iis quae ad fidem aut bonum totius communitatis non tangunt, rigidam unius tenoris formam ne in Liturgia quidem imponere cupit,' quippe quae formarum familiarumque liturgicarum diversitatem agnoverit et adhuc agnoscat."

101. Ibid. ". . . ita ut huiusmodi varietetem nedum suae ipsius nocere unitati, eam potius fovere protenus censeat."

102. Ibid., no. 70: "Congregatio autem confidit unamquamque Ecclesiam particularem, praesertim Ecclesias quae sunt recentioris aetatis, experii posse quomodo diversitas, quoad elementa quaedam, celebrationis fons locupletationis prorsus esse valeat, Ritus romani substantiali unitate servata, item totius Ecclesiae unitate atque integritate semel traditae sanctis fidei (cf. Iud. 3)."

CONCLUSION

The examination of the genetic roots of the *Fourth Instruction* in *Sacrosanctum Concilium*, the three previous instructions, and the revisions of the sacraments and other rites, disclosed certain similarities and dissimilarities in their respective descriptions of the task of adapting the liturgy to the native character, customs, and traditions of various regions and peoples. The *Fourth Instruction* repeats many of the principles and norms contained in the documents and *editiones typicae [alterae]* examined in the first four chapters of this work. In particular, the language of *aptatio* and *accommodatio*, which is so prevalent in *Sacrosanctum Concilium*, especially in numbers 37–40, occurs again, slightly nuanced in meaning, in the *Fourth Instruction*. However, the language of adaptation used in the *Fourth Instruction* also presents some differences from that used in the documents and *editiones typicae [alterae]* examined earlier in this study. Our brief linguistic examination revealed that in the *Fourth Instruction*, the terminology of *aptatio* rather than that of *accommodatio* pervades the prescriptions contained therein.[103]

In addition, the present instruction repeats, in a language similar to what appears in *Sacrosanctum Concilium*, the three former instructions, and the revisions of the rites examined in Chapter III of the present study, a concern for adapting the rites to the traditions and/or customs and native character of peoples, regions, and different communities [*traditiones, ingenium populorum, regionum et diversorum coetuum*]. Finally, in a manner

---

103. The word *accommodatio* in any of its forms does not occur with the frequency of *aptatio*. The former appears to occur significantly some five times, in CDWDS, *De Liturgia Romana et inculturatione*, no. 3: " . . . Bonum visum est Dicasterio Episcopis Conferentiisque Episcoporum auxilium suppeditare. . . accommodationes iam forte concessas critico examine subiciant"; in ibid., no. 35 (which is a verbatim inclusion of SC, no. 34): opportet insuper ut ritus "sint fidelium captui accommodati, neque generatim multis indigeant explanationibus"; in CDWDS, *De Liturgia Romana et inculturatione*, no. 37, footnote 82 (see footnote 30 in this chapter); in CDWDS, De Liturgia Romana et inculturatione, no. 40 (a verbatim inclusion of SC, no. 119): "Musica et cantus (original emphasis), quae populi animum manifestant, locum eminentem in Liturgia obtinent. (. . .) Cum in regionibus quibusdam, praesertim Missionum, gentes inveniantur quibus propria est traditio musica, magnum momentum in earum vita religiosa ac sociali habens, huic musicae aestimatio debita necnon locus congruus praebeatur tam in fingendo earum sensu religioso, quam in cultu ad earum indolem accommodando"; and finally in ibid., no. 56 (a verbatim inclusion of no. 30:2 of Ordo initiationis christianae adultorum, *Ordo Baptismi parvulorum*, Praenotanda generalia, no. 30:2): ". . . et in 'terris Missionum, (. . .) iudicare an elementa initiationis, quae apud aliquod populos in usu esse reperiuntur, ritui Baptismatis christiani accommodari possint, et decernere an sint in eo admittenda.' "

reminiscent of *Sacrosanctum Concilium* (no. 40), the three previous instructions, and the *editiones typicae* of the rites examined in Chapter III, the *Fourth Instruction* highlights the important and central role that episcopal conferences play in carefully and prudently considering what elements may be taken from the traditions and cultures of individual peoples and may properly be admitted into divine worship [*sedulo et prudenter consideretur quid ex traditionibus ingenioque singulorum populorum opportune in cultum divinum admitti possit*].

Another linguistic element of our study dealt with the definitions of *inculturation* included in the *Fourth Instruction*. With the pertinent writings of John Paul II regarding inculturation in mind, we observed that his descriptions and definition(s) of *inculturation* were included, albeit in a slightly modified manner, in the instruction. He described *inculturation* in the terminology of a twofold movement: a) the intimate transfiguration of the true goods of human culture [*intimam. . . transfigurationem verorum cultus humani bonorum*] through their reception itself of those goods into Christianity [*per ipsam eorum receptionem in rem christianam*], and b) likewise, the insertion of the Christian name into various cultures [*itemque nominis christiani insertionem varias in culturas*]. The *Fourth Instruction* repeated these observations of John Paul II and expanded on the ideas contained therein in the first two parts of the instruction. In particular, his emphasis on the dual movement in the exchange between church and culture as a process of mutual growth and enrichment appeared in the first half of the instruction. However, some of his reservations about the dangers to the liturgy which the process of inculturation forebodes appeared to influence the prescriptions of the second half of the instruction dealing with principles and areas for adaptation of the liturgy.

A final linguistic consideration centered upon the role of language in the work of evangelization and inculturation. Our study of the role of the vernacular in liturgical inculturation revealed that in many instances, it was the early missionaries who were responsible for the first appearance in written form of a people's mother tongue. In addition, biblical and liturgical texts in the vernacular allowed peoples to share more deeply in the worship of the Church. Finally, the *Fourth Instruction* advocates that the liturgical language that appears in the composition and revision of ritual texts of the liturgy needs to be clear, precise, inclusive, and unencumbered as it expresses the liturgical action and the mysteries being celebrated therein. In short, the *Fourth Instruction* proposes that liturgical language reflect what previous documents and the *editiones typicae* of the liturgical rites referred to as the *ingenium* and *traditiones* of peoples.

Our examination of the *Fourth Instruction* in chapters I–V focused on the genetic roots of the present instruction in *Sacrosanctum Concilium*, in the three previous instructions, in the revisions of the sacraments and other rituals, and finally in some pertinent writings of John Paul II. With this is mind, Chapter VI will offer an assessment of the *Fourth Instruction.*

CHAPTER VI

ASSESSMENT OF THE
FOURTH INSTRUCTION

The first four chapters of this study considered the background for the *Fourth Instruction for the Right Application of the Conciliar Constitution on the Liturgy (Nos. 37–40)*. Beginning with *Sacrosanctum Concilium*, and continuing with the first three instructions concerning the proper implementation of the liturgical constitution, we observed that the reform and the renewal of the Roman liturgy decreed by the Second Vatican Council mandated the revision of the *Roman Ritual*, in particular, the sacramental rites contained therein. The new *editiones typicae* that were published in subsequent years contained progressively expansive introductions *(praenotanda)*, which included both theological principles and pastoral adaptations for the rites they introduced.

In the years intervening between the first three instructions and the publication of the *Fourth Instruction*, i.e., from 1964 to 1994, a paradigm shift also occurred. An older terminology regarding adaptations of the liturgy was gradually replaced by the vocabulary of inculturation. This term was borrowed from the experiences of missionaries in their work of catechesis and evangelization in largely unchristianized lands.

In addition, during this same period of time, both Paul VI and John Paul II published several important apostolic exhortations, letters, and encyclicals concerning the interaction between church and culture. Upon the death of one of his predecessors, John Paul II began to focus his attention more directly on this interchange. He undertook frequent foreign journeys which gave him the opportunity to observe firsthand both how the message of the Gospel had taken root in mission territories as well as how that Gospel faith was actualized and ritualized in the worship of local churches. As a result of these trips, John Paul II became increasingly aware of the dangers that these encounters between faith and culture forebode for the liturgical celebrations of the newly inculturated faith in local worship. In the opinion of John Paul II, the substantial unity of the Roman rite, the authentic spirit of the liturgy, and finally the union with and among particular churches and the universal Church were not to be compromised in any adaptation or inculturation of the liturgy.[1]

Convinced that the liturgy must always and everywhere be an expression of the living faith of the Church and its traditions, John Paul II mandated that the Congregation for Divine Worship and the Discipline of the Sacraments prepare a fourth instruction on the correct implementation of the mandates of the *Constitution on the Sacred Liturgy*, concerning the native character [*ingenium*] and the traditions of peoples [*traditiones populorum*] (SC, numbers 37–39) and the "more profound adaptations" envisioned in number 40 of the Constitution. The *Fourth Instruction* was issued

---

1. Cf. Ioannis Pauli, Summi Pontificis, "Allocutio ad quosdam Brasiliae episcopos limina Apostolorum visitantes," AAS 88 (1996): 550–559, especially, 556: "Com referência ao 'espírito da Liturgia' . . . Este 'espírito' não deriva das formas exteriores, que na maior parte, são provenientes das culturas nas quais o Cristianismo se difundia, mas e subjacente a eias como aquilo que lhes confere o ser, como instrumento e manifestação exterior de convergência de ação de Cristo e de sua Igreja a nível de graça invisível."; and 557:
"O Concilio Vaticano II, usando a expressão *servata substantiali unitate Ritus romani*, queria sublinhar que a inculturação, que está em causa, reentra, quanto à parte normativa, naquilo que se refere só ao Rito romano, e que dele deveria continuar a fazer parte cada nova forma adaptada e inculturada segundo o direito e com a aprovação de Se Apostolica. (. . .)
A necessidade e a exigência de unidade, que é uma das notas da Igreja, deve continuar a ser ainda mais presente hoje, no âmbito do Rito romano, para sustentar a interna vida da Igreja e sua relação com o mundo a evangelizar." [John Paul II, "Address to the Bishops from Brazil on the occasion of their *ad limina* visit," (title corrected), in Bishops' Committee on the Liturgy, *Newsletter* 32 (April, 1996):13–14: "The spirit of the liturgy does not come from the external forms which come mainly from cultures in which Christianity has spread but underlies them as that which gives them their being as an instrument and an external expression of the convergence of the action of Christ and his Church at the level of invisible grace. (. . .) The Second Vatican Council, using the expression *'servata substantiali unitate Ritus romani'* (*Sacrosanctum Concilium*, no. 38) wishes to underline the fact that the normative part of this inculturation pertains to what refers to the Roman Rite, and that the latter must continue to be part of any new adapted and inculturated form in accordance with the law and with the approval of the Apostolic See. (. . .) The need or demand for unity which is a feature of the Church must continue to be more and more present today, in the context of the Roman Rite, to sustain the whole life of the Church and her relationship with the world to be evangelized."]
Unfortunately, the BCL *Newsletter* cited above designates September 5, 1995 as the date on which John Paul II addressed the issue of inculturation and the Roman liturgy on the occasion of the *ad limina* visit of the bishops from Northeastern Brazil. This information is incorrect and the editors have confused two texts. The September 5, 1995 Portuguese text of John Paul II addresses the issue of ecumenism to the bishops from Northeastern Brazil, regions 1 and 4. His address in Portuguese concerning *On The Roman Liturgy and Inculturation* was delivered on September 29, 1995, on the occasion of the *ad limina* visit of the Brazilian bishops from the two ecclesiastical provinces of Bahia and Aracajú (Sergipe), region 3. The latter first appeared in Portuguese in *L'Osservatore Romano* (Vatican City), 7 de Ottobre de 1995, 6–8.

to clarify previous misunderstandings regarding possible adaptations of the liturgy to the character and traditions of various peoples and cultures and to define the correct procedure to be followed in any future process of liturgical inculturation.[2]

In Chapter V of the present study, the genetic examination and analysis of the *Fourth Instruction* reveals that it contains many quotations from pertinent writings of John Paul II concerning the process of inculturation. The inclusion in the *Fourth Instruction* of his definitions of *inculturation* and his reflections on the procedures for inculturation influenced the overall tone of the document. Considering these inclusions and the liturgical documents and rites that preceded the appearance of the instruction, the question of the consistency both of the *Fourth Instruction* with the prescriptions of the three previous instructions, and its consistency with the revisions of the sacramental rites, and/or its inner consistency must be discussed. Thus, this final chapter will offer an assessment of the *Fourth Instruction* in light of the three areas mentioned above.

CONSISTENCY OF THE *FOURTH INSTRUCTION* WITH THE THREE PREVIOUS INSTRUCTIONS

The *Fourth Instruction* has been labeled both "a milestone in liturgical renewal in its own rite"[3] and a document that is schizophrenic, "appearing to affirm a principle while later rescinding it."[4]

---

2. Ibid., 557–558: "Em conformidade com o Concilio, na Carta Apostolica *Vicesimus quintus annus* retomei aquele texto agregando a referência aos livros liturgicos. Em seguida, a Instrução sobre 'A Liturgia romana e a inculturação,' retomou o tema e oportunamente indicou como a atenção à unidade do Rito romano entra, com pleno direito, entre os 'Principia generalia' (original emphasis) que devem guiar cada investigação e cada acção de inculturar o Rito romano, junto com a finalidade mesma da inculturação e da relação com a autoridade de competente." ["In conformity with the Council, in the Apostolic Letter *Vicesimus quintus annus* (no. 16), I have used that text and added the reference to the liturgical books. The Instruction 'On The Roman Liturgy and Inculturation' then took up the theme (i.e., inculturation and the substantial unity of the Roman rite) and appropriately indicated how attention to the substantial unity of the Roman Rite should belong with full right to the 'Principia generalia' (original emphasis)" that must guide any research and any action directed to inculturating the Roman rite, with the very purpose of inculturation and the relationship with the competent authority (Cf. Instruction *Varietates legitimae*, nos. 34–36 and 70)."

3. Anscar J. Chupungco, OSB, "Remarks on 'The Roman Liturgy and Inculturation,'" *Ecclesia Orans* 11 (1994): 277.

4. Nathan Mitchell, "The Amen Corner: Liturgy Encounters Culture—Again," *Worship* 68 (1994): 375.

Other authors maintain that the present instruction elicits more questions than it answers.[5] Perhaps all three assessments of the *Fourth Instruction* reveal part of the complexity of this document.

The title of the present instruction, *The Fourth Instruction on the Right Application of the Conciliar Constitution on the Liturgy (Nos. 37–40): On the Roman Liturgy and Inculturation,* reminds both the reader and the would-be critic that the *Fourth Instruction* is the fourth of its kind in a series.[6] The series of instructions, in turn, are related to the *Constitution on the Sacred Liturgy*. The mandate to revise the texts and sacramental rites contained in *Sacrosanctum Concilium* did not advocate a mere cosmetic application of culture on the liturgy; rather, the conciliar constitution declared that the Church cultivates and encourages the gifts and endowments of mind and heart possessed by various races and peoples and allows elements from peoples' cultures into the liturgy, provided these elements are not tainted by superstitions or false beliefs.[7] The liturgical constitution also mandated adaptations in the administration of the sacraments, sacramentals, processions, liturgical language, art, and music of worship within certain defined limits with their ultimate approval subject to the judgment of the competent authority in these matters.[8]

In general, there appears to be a historical and a progressive consistency between the first three instructions and the *Fourth Instruction*. The prescriptions for adaptation of the liturgy it contains represent another major step on the route to inculturation of the Roman liturgy. Although the first instruction, *Inter oecumenici* (1964), was a very important document in the initial

---

5. Pierre Jounel, "Une étape majeure sur le chemin de l'inculturation liturgique," *Notitiae* 30 (1994): 277: "L'analyse succincte de l'Instruction *Varietates Legitimae* a-t-elle laissé deviner en elle une étape majeure de l'inculturation de la liturgie romaine?"

6. Ibid., 269: "En se présentant comme la 'IVè Instruction pour une juste application de la Constitution conciliaire sur la liturgie,' elle s'insère dans une série."

7. SC, no. 37: "Ecclesia . . . variarum gentium populorumque animi ornamenta ac dotes colit et provehit; quidquid vero in populorum moribus indissolubili vinculo superstitionibus erroribusque non adstipulatur, benevole perpendit, ac, si potest, sartum tectumque servat, immo quandoque in ipsam liturgiam admittit, dummodo cum rationibus veri et authentici spiritus liturgici congruat." Cf. Chupungco, "Remarks on 'The Roman Liturgy and Inculturation,' " 270. Chupungco's choice of *incarnation* as the term used in *Sacrosanctum Concilium* to refer to the liturgical celebrations in particular churches is puzzling since the constitution does not appear to use the term *incarnatio* in reference to the liturgy.

8. Ibid., no. 39: "Intra limites in editionibus typicis librorum liturgicorum statutos, erit competentis auctoritatis ecclesiasticae territorialis, de qua in art. 22, 2 aptationes definire, praesertim quoad administrationem sacramentorum, quoad sacramentalia, processiones, linguam liturgicam, musicam sacram et artes, iuxta tamen normas fundamentales quae hac in constitutione habentur."

momentum of the liturgical reform, it did not contain a word about the adaptation of the liturgy to the temperament of different peoples; this issue required some time before it would come to maturation.[9] In addition, the second and third instructions had as their purpose the continuation of the progressive application of the principles enunciated in *Sacrosanctum Concilium* and *Inter oecumenici*, especially regarding the celebration of the Eucharist.[10] Thus, in a manner similar to that of its predecessors, the *Fourth Instruction* continues to advocate the renewal, reform, and adaptation of the liturgy.

In continuity with both *Sacrosanctum Concilium* (nos. 21–40) and consistent with the prescriptions of its three predecessors, the *Fourth Instruction* also envisions a continuation of the work of revising texts and rites.[11] Similarly, it acknowledges that an examination of the theological principles behind the questions of faith and inculturation still remain to be examined in depth.[12] In a manner that is consistent with that of its predecessors but which also uses more precise terminology, the *Fourth Instruction* restates the procedures to be followed[13] for the approval of the decrees of the competent territorial authority.[14] Numbers 36, 62, and 66 of the present instruction maintain that episcopal conferences decide upon the translations and the adaptations that are envisioned by the law.[15] These prescriptions reaffirm the procedures stated pre-

---

9. Cf. Jounel, "Une étape majeure sur le chemin de l'inculturation liturgique," 269: "Ce (i.e., Ière Instruction) fut la plus importante car, en parcourant l'ensemble de la Constitution conciliaire, elle dégagea tout ce qui pouvait en être mis en application sans plus tarder. Le chapitre qu'elle consacrait à l'emménagement des lieux du culte allait exercer une influence immédiate. Mais il convient de noter que, volontairement, elle ne dit mot des normes pour l'adaptation de la liturgie au génie des différents peuples (SC 37–40), parce que la question demandait un long mûrissement."

10. Ibid., 269–270. "Les deux autres instructions avaient pur but de continuer la mise en application progressive de la Constitution spécialement dans la célébration de l'Eucharistie."

11. See CDWDS, *De Liturgia Romana et inculturatione*, no. 3.

12. Ibid. "Dum enim principia theologica relate ad quaestiones de fide et inculturatione altius adhuc investiganda sunt. . . ."

13. These prescriptions are firmly grounded in *Sacrosanctum Concilium*, nos. 22, 39, 40 and in CIC., canons 477–450 and 838.3.

14. Others may not agree with this judgment. See, for example, Nathan Mitchell, "The Amen Corner: Liturgy Encounters Culture—Again," 372–73.

15. CDWDS, *De Liturgia Romana et inculturatione*, no. 62: "In editione propria librorum liturgicorum apparanda, Conferentiae Episcoporum est iudicium ferre de versione seu interpretatione textuum necnon de aptationibus praevisis, ad normam iuris." This is essentially an expansion of the prescription contained in *Tres abhinc annos*, no. 28 and *Liturgiae instaurationes*, nos. 11 and 12.

viously in *Tres abhinc annos*, number 28, and *Liturgiae instaura-tiones*, numbers 11 and 12.

When similar procedures are restated in the *Fourth Instruction*, there is a very specific clarification regarding the channels to be used when such changes are submitted for consideration. For example, rather than paraphrasing the terminology used previously both in *Sacrosanctum Concilium* and in the three previous instructions about the role of the diocesan bishop and episcopal conferences (in adaptations of the liturgy),[16] numbers 65–68 of the *Fourth Instruction* clarify the specific procedure that, from this time on, diocesan bishops and episcopal conferences are to follow for proposed adaptations of the liturgy. The corporate body within the "Apostolic See" that will receive such proposed adaptations is named specifically: the Congregation for Divine Worship and the Discipline of the Sacraments.[17] While it is true that the Congregation has the right to examine the proposal of the episcopal conference and to grant the conference a faculty to conduct an

---

16. Cf. SC, no. 22:2: "Ex potestate a iure concessa, rei liturgicae moderatio inter limites statutos pertinet quoque ad competentes varii generis territoriales episcoporum coetus legitime constitutos"; SC, no. 39: "Intra limites in editionibus typicis librorum liturgicorum statutos, erit competentis auctoritatis ecclesiasticae territorialis, de qua in art. 22, 2, sedulo et prudenter consideretur qui, hoc in negotio, ex traditionibus ingenioque singulorum populorum opportune in cultum divinum admitti possit. *Aptationes definire* (emphasis added), quae utiles vel necessariae existimantur, apostolicae sedi proponantur, de ipsius consensu introducendae."

17. CDWDS, *De Liturgia Romana et inculturatione*, no. 66: "Antequam quodcumque propositum hac in re experiatur, Conferentia Episcoporum proprium consilium Congregationi scripto et dilucide exponet. Haec presentatio complecti debet descriptionem innovationum, quae proponuntur, eas admittendi rationes." It is also interesting to note that in number 37, footnote 78 of the *Fourth Instruction*, we are referred to (among other references) *Vicesimus quintus annus*, no. 19. In that number, Pope John Paul II lists those who are responsible for the task of promoting the liturgical renewal. He also links the work of the Sacred Congregation for Rites (under its various forms and names) from the Council of Trent to Vatican II. It is clear from the context of number 19 that at least since the sixteenth century, the organ within the Apostolic See which has regulated the liturgy was relegated to the SRC, the SCCD, and to the CDF working in tandem with the CDWDS. Cf. *Vicesimus quintus annus*, no. 19: "Officium provehendi renovationem Liturgiae spectat imprimis ad Apostolicam Sedem. Quadrigenti anni hoc explentur anno, ex quo Xystus V Sacram Rituum Congregationem instituit, cui munus delegavit cultus divini pertractationi invigilandi, qui est postea a Concilio Tridentino reformatus. (. . .) Secundum novam Curiae Romanae structuram, Constitutione *Pastor bonus* ratam, totus sacrae Liturgiae campus in unum redigitur uni Dicasterio obnoxius, videlicet Congregationi pro Cultu Divino et Disciplina Sacramentorum. Huius est, Congregationis pro Doctrina Fidei salva competentia, Liturgiam moderari et promovere, cuius parts praecipua sacramenta sunt, actioni pastorali liturgicae favendo, varias Consociationes sustinendo quae apostolatui liturgico student, musicae, cantui, et arti sacrae, et disciplinae sacramentali vigilando."

experiment for a definite period of time,[18] according to the *Fourth Instruction* (nos. 65–69), episcopal conferences nevertheless will

1. examine what has to be modified in liturgical celebrations because of the traditions and native character of peoples;[19]
2. ask the national or regional liturgical commission to study the matter and examine the different aspects of the elements of local culture and their eventual inclusion in the liturgical celebrations;[20]
3. present the proposal to the congregation (CDWDS) before any experimentation takes place;[21]
4. supervise the process of experimentation approved (by the congregation);[22]
5. ensure that the experimentation does not exceed the limits of time and place that were fixed (by the congregation);[23]
6. ensure that pastors and the faithful know about the limited and provisional nature of the experiment;[24]
7. not give it (the experiment) a publicity of a sort which could have an effect on the liturgical practice of the country;[25]
8. decide whether it (i.e., the experiment) matches up to the goal that was proposed or whether it needs revisions;[26]
9. communicate its conclusions to the congregation along with full information about the experiment;[27]

---

18. Ibid., no. 66: "Incepti examine expleto, a Conferentia Episcoporum et a Congregatione simul peracto, ipsi Conferentiae a Congregatione facultas tribuetur, si casus fert, experimentum per determinatum tempus peragendi."

19. Ibid., no. 65: "Conferentia Episcoporum examini ea subiciet, quae in celebrationibus liturgicis mutari debent attentis populi traditionibus atque ingenio."

20. Ibid. "Studium harum aptationum committet Commissioni nationali vel regionali de Liturgia, quae cooperationem peritorum exquirat ad culturae localis diversos elementorum aspectus examinandos, num eadem, si casus ferat, in celebrationes liturgicas inseri possint."

21. Ibid., no. 66: "Antequam quodcumque propositum hac in re experiatur, Conferentia Episcoporum proprium consilium Congregationi scripto et dilucide exponet."

22. Ibid., no. 67: "Conferentia Episcoporum invigilabit ut experimentum bene evolvatur."

23. Ibid. "Insuper invigilabit ne experimentum limites statutos locorum ac temporum praetergrediatur."

24. Ibid. "ut pastores et fideles edoceantur de eius natura ad tempus et circumscripta."

25. Ibid. "demum ne ita divulgetur ut vitam liturgicam nationis ultro afficere possit."

26. Ibid. "Tempore experimenti exacto, Conferentia Episcoporum diiudicabit utrum propositum finalitati inquisitae respondeat an retractandum sit circa quaedam elementa."

27. Ibid. "et deliberationem una cum documentationis fasciculo, ion quo propositi experimenta describuntur, Congregationi deferet."

10. introduce the changes into the territory covered by the episcopal conference.[28]

The list above highlights the considerable role that the *Fourth Instruction* imparts to the episcopal conferences in the work of adaptation and inculturation of the liturgy.[29] However, it must be recognized that the *Fourth Instruction* also states that the Congregation for Divine Worship and the Discipline of the Sacraments may reject such proposals, deeming them undesirable or unnecessary.[30]

Thus, the procedures to be followed in adaptations of the Roman rite stated in the present instruction appear consistent with what was stated in *Sacrosanctum Concilium* (number 40:1, 2) regarding the competency of the local church authority concerning adaptation of the liturgy. Moreover, it is clear that although the Congregation for Worship and the Discipline of the Sacraments grants the faculty to allow experimentation and issues a decree of consent allowing the experiment to take place during a certain period of time,[31] the episcopal conferences exercise a crucial role in the process of adaptation and inculturation of the liturgy when they take the initiative to set the entire process in motion.

---

28. Cf. Ibid., no. 69: "Executio statutorum fiet iuxta rerum adiuncta, transitionis quodam tempore, pro opportunitate, disposito (cf. *supra*, n. 46)."

29. Some authors do not consider the role of the episcopal conferences to be significant. Instead, they maintain that the *Fourth Instruction* has diminished the role of the episcopal conferences and relegated them to a position of inferiority vis-a-vis the Congregation for Divine Worship and the Discipline of the Sacraments. See, for example, Mitchell, "The Amen Corner: Liturgy Encounters Culture-Again," 372–73. Mitchell maintains that the *Fourth Instruction* is "out of step" with its three predecessors. In the first place, he contrasts number 29 of *Inter oecumenici* with what he calls the *Fourth Instruction's* "tightening up (indeed, bureaucratizing)" of the process by which episcopal conferences do their work. Citing the translation found in the *Documents on the Liturgy*, Mitchell underscores the former instruction speaking "simply of episcopal conferences submitting to Rome 'for approval, that is *confirmation* (original emphasis)' the *acta* of their decisions about translations and adaptations." However, Mitchell conveniently avoids mention of number 31 of the *First Instruction*: "The decrees of the territorial authority needing the *approval* (emphasis added), that is *confirmation* (emphasis added) of the Holy See shall be promulgated and implemented only when they have received such approval, that is, confirmation." (Ibid.) [Cf. *Inter oecumenici*, no. 31: "Decreta auctoritatis territorialis quae Apostolicae Sedis probatione seu confirmatione indigent, tunc tantum promulgentur et in praxim deducabantur cum ab Apostolica Sede probata seu confirmata fuerint."]

30. CDWDS, *De Liturgia Romana et inculturatione*, no. 68: "Documentationis examine peracto, Congregatio approbationis decretum edere poterit, animadversionibus forte additis, ut variationes seu mutationes, quae exquirebantur, in territorio, Conferentiae Episcoporum iurisdictioni subiecto, admittantur."

31. Ibid., no. 66: "Conferentiae a Congregatione facultas tribuetur"; and no. 68: "Congregatio approbationis decretum edere poterit."

CONSISTENCY OF THE *FOURTH INSTRUCTION* WITH THE REVISIONS OF CERTAIN SACRAMENTS AND RITES

An exhaustive examination of the *Fourth Instruction* for its consistency with the prescriptions found in the *editiones typicae* [*alterae*] (and typical editions with adaptations approved for use in particular dioceses of an episcopal conference) would form the subject of another lengthy study. Thus, our consideration of this area will limit itself to the consistency of the *Fourth Instruction* with the prescriptions expressed either in the *praenotanda* of the second typical edition (i.e., *editio typica altera*) that we considered in Chapter III of the present study or to the prescriptions that are mentioned specifically in the present instruction.[32]

It would appear that the *Fourth Instruction* is consistent with the revisions of the sacramental rites proposed in the *praenotanda* of the *editio typica altera* of *De Ordinatione Episcopi, presbyterorum et diaconorum* (although this rite is not specifically mentioned in the instruction) and *Ordo celebrandi Matrimonium, 1991*. In the *editio typica altera* of the ordination rites, number 11, in section III entitled "Adaptations for different regions and circumstances," states that it belongs to the conferences of bishops to adapt the rites of ordination of the bishop, presbyters, and deacons to the needs of the particular regions. Similarly, it is equally apparent that the rites may be used in a particular region *after the Apostolic See has reviewed the decisions of a conference of bishops* (emphasis added).[33] This same procedure appears in the *Fourth Instruction* in numbers 62–68.

A similar statement also occurs in *Ordo celebrandi Matrimonium, 1991:* In virtue of the *Constitution on the Liturgy,* the conferences of bishops have the right to adapt this Roman Ritual to the customs and needs of the particular regions for use in their region, *once the* **acta** *have been reviewed by the Apostolic*

---

32. The ICEL translation of OCM, 1991 is under study by the bishops of the member and associate members of ICEL. The rites of Christian initiation are mentioned in the *Fourth Instruction*, no. 56; the marriage rite is mentioned in no. 57; the funeral rites are mentioned in no. 57.

33. *De Ordinatione Episcopi, presbyterorum et diaconorum*, no. 11: ". . . Conferentiis Episcoporum competit, ritus Ordinationum Episcopi, presbyterorum et diaconorum accommodare singularum regionum necessitatibus, ut *actis ab Apostolica Sede recognitis,* (emphasis added) in regionibus ad quas pertinet, adhibeatur. Qua in re Conferentiae Episcoporum, attentis locorum et rerum adiunctis necnon ingenio et traditionibus populorum, possunt: . . ."

See (emphasis added).[34] The prescriptions of number 57 in the *Fourth Instruction* state that in the adaptation of the marriage rite, the episcopal conference must always include provisions that the ordained minister or assisting layperson ask for and receive the consent of the contracting parties and give them the nuptial blessing.[35] This same number also repeats the mandate of *Sacrosanctum Concilium* (number 77), to revise the Rite of Marriage so that it will express the grace of the sacrament more clearly and emphasize the duties of wife and husband.[36] It would appear that the prescriptions of the present instruction are consistent regarding both the manner in which the marriage rite was to be revised and the procedure to be followed in the revision. Since the Latin *editio typica altera* of both the rites of ordination and the Rite of Marriage encourage and allow adaptations to the customs and needs (or temperament) of particular regions, the subsequent publication of these rites in their vernacular editions will reveal more specifically the manner in which the Latin *editio typica altera* is to be celebrated in the regional worship of the various episcopal conferences throughout the world.

Number 58 of the *Fourth Instruction* mentions the importance of the expressive values in the rite of funerals, noting that the Roman Ritual offers several forms of celebrating funerals.[37] The *Ordo exsequiarum* allows for the liturgical celebration of the funeral rites in the home of the deceased, in the church, and at the cemetery.[38] It would appear that the *Fourth Instruction* is very consistent with what is expressed in the *praenotanda* of the *Ordo*

34. OCM, 1991, no. 39: "Conferentiis Episcoporum competit, vi Constitutionis de sacra Liturgia (nn. 37–40 et 63b), hoc Rituale Romanum, singularum regionum consuetudinis et necessitatibus accommodare, ut, *actis ab Apostolica Sede recognitis*, (emphasis added) in regionibus ad quas pertinet, adhibeatur." Numbers 40 and 41 in OCM 1991 specify the responsibilities of and the adaptations pertinent to the conferences of bishops.

35. CDWDS, *De Liturgia Romana et inculturatione*, no. 57: ". . . Conferentia Episcoporum quaeque facultatem habet exarandi ritum proprium Matrimonii, usibus locorum et populorum, congruentem, firma tamen lege, quae statuit ut Matrimonio assistens, sive clericus sive laicus, prout casus fert exquirat manifestationem contrahentium consensus eamque nomine Ecclesiae recipiat atque super nupturientes orationem benedictionis nuptialis proferat. . . ."

36. Cf. Ibid. and SC, no. 77.

37. CDWDS, *De Liturgia Romana et inculturatione*, no. 58: "Omni tempore et apud omnes populos exequiae insignitatae sunt ritibus peculiaribus, saepe magne significandi virtute ditatis." The funeral rites may also be celebrated in a small chapel of the cemetery and at the tomb, or simply in the home of the deceased. See footnote 38 below.

38. OE., nos. 3 and 4, respectively: "Potiora autem momenta, iuxta locorum consuetudines, haec numerari possunt. . . ." [3]; "Ut omnium regionum condiciones perspectae quodammodo habeantur, Ordo exsequiarum pro adultis hic propositus iuxta tres typos distinguitur, quorum: (a) Primus typus tres stationes praevidet, nempe in domo defuncti, in ecclesia, et in coementerio; (b) secundus typus duas tantum stationes considerat, idest in sacello

exsequiarum, since it also repeats the provisions of number 9 of the *praenotanda* concerning the obligation of the episcopal conferences: 1) to choose the form of celebration of the funeral rites that correspond best to local customs;[39] 2) to preserve all that is good in family traditions and local customs;[40] and 3) to ensure that the funeral rites manifest the Christian faith in the Resurrection and bear witness to the true values of the Gospel.[41] As was the case with the sacrament of Matrimony noted above, the consistency of the *Fourth Instruction* with the revisions of the rite is also in accord with the mandate of *Sacrosanctum Concilium*, numbers 81 and 82.

INNER CONSISTENCY OF THE *FOURTH INSTRUCTION*

As noted in Chapter V, the *Fourth Instruction* consists of an introduction, four parts, and a conclusion. It begins with a positive affirmation that the Church has known and still knows many different forms and liturgical families and also believes that this diversity enhances ecclesial unity.[42] This line of thinking pervades the first part of the *Fourth Instruction*. The instruction recognizes the importance of salvation history and the history of the development of the Church and its worship as a component of modern day efforts to find a more contemporary cultural shape for liturgical worship.[43] The cultural shape of the liturgical wor-

---

coementerii et ad sepulcrum; (c) tertius typus unicam stationem habet, et quidem in ipsa domo defuncti."

39. Ibid., no. 9: ". . . Ideo Conferentia Episcopalis, attentis necessitatibus particularibus, opportune providebit." Cf. CDWDS, *De Liturgia Romana et inculturatione*, no. 58: ". . . Rituale romanum plures typos praebet pro exsequiis celebrandis, inter se distinctos, ex quibus Conferentiis Episcoporum competit eum seligere qui usibus localibus melius aptetur."

40. Ibid., no. "In fratrum suorum exsequiis celebrandis. . . Sive ergo de familiarum traditionibus agitur, sive de locorum consuetudinibus. . . ." Cf. CDWDS, *De Liturgia Romana et inculturatione*, no. 58: "Libenter servantes quodquod in traditionibus familiaribus et moribus locorum bonum inveniantur. . . ."

41. Ibid., no. 2: ". . . ut, quae exsequiae pro chistianis celebrentur, et fidem paschalem ostendant et evangelicum spiritum vere demostrent." Cf. CDWDS, *De Liturgia Romana et inculturatione*, no. 58: ". . . ut exsequiae fidem paschalem manifestent reveraque evangelicum spiritum testificentur."

42. Cf. CDWDS, *De Liturgia Romana et inculturatione*, no. 1. In this regard, see Mitchell, "The Amen Corner: Liturgy Encounters Culture—Again," 374.

43. CDWDS, *De Liturgia Romana et inculturatione*, no. 9: "Quaestiones, quae hodie ponuntur ad Ritus romani inculturationem exsequendam, invenire possunt quandam explanationem in ipsa historia salutis, in qua inculturationis processus operatus est diversis sub formis."

ship of the Roman Catholic Church, in its turn, reflects certain theological and cultural principles. While these principles need to be examined in depth in the future,[44] we do find several important affirmations concerning the nature of the liturgy enunciated in the second part of the *Fourth Instruction:*

1. The liturgy is at once the action of Christ the priest and the action of his body the church for the purpose of glorifying God and sanctifying humankind;[45]

2. The liturgy is universal in nature. . . . thus, the Church is called to gather all peoples to speak all languages, to penetrate all cultures;[46]

3. The Church is nourished on the Word of God written in the Old and New Testament. . . . That is why sacred scriptures must not be replaced by any other text, no matter how venerable it may be;[47]

4. Since the Church is the fruit of Christ's sacrifice, the liturgy is always the celebration of the Paschal Mystery of Christ;[48]

5. The liturgical life of the community gravitates around the Eucharist and the other sacraments;[49]

6. The liturgical assembly signifies and makes present the Church of Christ in a given place and in a given time;[50]

7. In the liturgy the Church expresses its life of faith in a symbolic and communitarian form. Hence the need for laws which respect the ordering of its universal worship, the composition of texts [*textus exarandos*], and the work of completing the rites [*ritus peragendos*]. The reason for this type of juridical legislation is that throughout the centuries and even today the orthodoxy of worship is to be assured, not only to avoid errors, but also to pass

---

44. Ibid., no. 3.

45. Ibid., no. 21: "Liturgia insimul actio est Christi Sacerdotis et actio eius corporis Ecclesiae, quia ad implemendum suum opus Deum glorificandi et homines sanctificandi. . . ."

46. Ibid., no. 22: "Ecclesia, cum sit catholica (original emphasis) . . . Quapropter ipsa vocatur omnes homines ad congregandos, omnibus linguis ad loquendum, omnes culturas ad penetrandas."

47. Ibid., no. 23: "Ecclesia verbo Dei alitur scripto in Veteris et Novi Testamenti libris tradito. . . . Igitur Dei Verbum quam maximum habet momentum in celebratione liturgica, ita ut lectiones biblicae commutari nequeant cum aliis lectionibus, quae tales non sint, etsi venerabiles."

48. Ibid., no. 24: "Ut Ecclesia fructus est Christi sacrificii, ita Liturgia semper est celebratio mysterii paschalis Christi."

49. Ibid., no. 25: "Universa igitur vita liturgica volvitur circa sacrificium eucharisticum in primis et circa cetera sacramenta a Christo Ecclesiae commendata."

50. Ibid., no. 26: "Christi Ecclesia praesens fit et significatur, dato in loco et tempore, per Ecclesias locales seu particulares, quae in celebratione liturgica eius manifestant germanam naturam."

on the faith in its integrity so that the rule of praying may correspond to the *rule of believing* (original emphasis).[51]

In much the same way that John Paul II stressed the double movement in the process of inculturation, the *Fourth Instruction* exhibits a twofold dynamic in the area of inner consistency. Numbers 1, 4, and 18 of the instruction, for example, highlight how a diversity in forms and liturgical families have contributed to the life of the Church.[52] The diversity was also reaffirmed by the Second Vatican Council and described in terms of the double movement between the Church and local cultures. Thus, the Church assumes the resources and customs of each people, purifies, strengthens, and ennobles whatever good lies latent within them; local cultures, transformed and cleansed of elements not compatible with the Gospel, enter into and enrich the life of the Church.[53] The attitude expressed in these numbers appears to be one of openness, respect, and mutuality regarding the interchange between the Church and culture in the process of inculturation. However, it must be remembered that the *Fourth Instruction* also maintains that the "more profound adaptations of the liturgy" referred to in *Sacrosanctum Concilium*, number 40, presuppose that the Conference of Bishops has tried all other possibilities for adaptation offered in the liturgical books before it undertakes adaptations of this nature.[54]

---

51. Ibid., no. 27: "Cum in Liturgia Ecclesia fidem suam exprimat sub forma symbolica et communitaria patet opus esse legibus, quae respiciant ad universum cultum ordinandum, textus exarandos, ritus peragendos. Propterea stilo imperativo huiusmodi legislativo iure usa est saeculorum decursu et etiamnunc utitur ad cultus orthodoxiam asservandam, non solum videlicet ad errores vitandos, verum etiam ad fidei integritatem tradendam, quia Ecclesiae *lex orandi* eius *lex credendi* respondet (original emphases)." It is interesting to note the subtle shift in terminology from OCM 1991 to the present instruction. The former used the terminology of the right of the conferences of bishops composing their own marriage rites [*exarandi ritum proprium Matrimonii*]; the latter refers rather to *textus exarandos*. Cf. OCM 1991, no. 42.

52. Cf. ibid., no. 1.

53. Cf. ibid., nos. 1, 4 and 18; also, *Lumen Gentium,* nos. 13 and 17.

54. Chupungco, "Remarks on 'The Roman Liturgy and Inculturation,' " 273. Cf. Power, "Liturgy and Culture Revisited," 226: "There are, however, several indicators in the instruction itself that set the limits of this ordinance (i.e., dealing with no. 40 of SC concerning 'more profound adaptations of the liturgy'). In no. 41, in allowing some change in gestures and postures, the instruction stipulates that these cannot include the 'essential rites of the sacraments required for validity.' It then immediately refers to the role of the priest in presiding over the assembly in the person of Christ and to what is found in the typical editions of the liturgical books. There are references at this point to canon 841 of the Code of Canon Law that reserves the right to determine what is essential to sacraments to the supreme authority of the Church, and to canon 899.2, on the role of the priest in presiding over the liturgical assembly in the person of Christ. [This in turn is taken from

A similar attitude is expressed in the practical norms concerning language, music, singing, gesture and posture, liturgical arts, the use of sacred images, popular religiosity, and multicultural communities. Concerning these areas of cultural heritage and diversity, in number 49 of the *Fourth Instruction*, the conferences of bishops are reminded to respect the riches of each culture and those who advance their cause [*Conferentiae Episcoporum, cum singillatim concretam condicionem attente considerare satagant, uniuscuiusque culturae divitias earumque defensores observabunt*]. Furthermore, they should neither ignore nor neglect a minority culture or one with which they are not familiar [*neque ignorabunt vel neglegent eam culturam quam minor sequitur pars, vel quae ipsis familaris non est*].[55]

Nevertheless, one may simultaneously observe a certain inconsistency in the overall tone of the *Fourth Instruction*. This change in tone may perhaps be due to a noticeable shift in terminology about midway through the document. As stated above, the first two parts of the instruction are devoted to a short history of and preconditions for inculturation. The term *inculturatio* is used repeatedly throughout the first half of the *Fourth Instruction*.

Beginning with Part III of the instruction and continuing consistently to the end, the term *inculturatio* yields more and more to the term *aptatio*.[56] Paralleling this change in terminology, a concomitant shift occurs regarding the prescriptions for the principles and procedures in adaptations of the liturgy. Parts III and IV of the *Fourth Instruction* present not only the areas, principles, and procedures for adaptations of the liturgy but also the dangers to the Church involved in this process as worship encounters local cultures.[57] Furthermore, the aspect of mutual enrichment between the Church and culture in the process of

---

Sacrosanctum Concilium, no. 33.] No theological principles are, however, given to help understand the notion of essential validity. Despite the mention of action in the person of Christ, the restriction on developing new rites is couched primary in juridical terms and is not very helpful to understanding changes that have taken place in the history of sacraments."

55. CDWDS, *De Liturgia Romana et inculturatione*, no. 49: "Conferentiae Episcoporum, cum singillatim concretam condicionem attente considerare satagant, uniuscuiusque culturae divitias earumque defensores observabunt, neque ignorabunt vel neglegent eam culturam quam minor sequitur pars, vel quae ipsis familaris non est." Cf. Chupungco, "Remarks on 'The Roman Liturgy and Inculturation,' " 275.

56. For shifts in terminology (e.g., *inculturatio* to *aptatio*), see Power, "Liturgy and Culture Revisited," 226–27; also, Mitchell, "The Amen Corner: Liturgy Encounters Culture—Again," 374.

57. Cf. CDWDS, *De Liturgia Romana et inculturatione*, nos. 46–50.

inculturation seems to fade into the background in the second half of the instruction. In contrast to the open and welcoming attitude of numbers 1, 4, and 18, numbers 46, 47, and 48, respectively, sternly warn against the dangers of religious syncretism, of rites or gestures suggesting a Christianizing of pagan festivals or holy places, of the acceptance of magic rites, superstition, spiritism, vengeance or rites with a sexual connotation, of excessive separatism on the part of a Christian community, and finally of the use of inculturation for political ends.[58]

A similar shift in attitude occurs in number 67 regarding the responsibilities of episcopal conferences to supervise the process of experimentation in adaptations of the liturgy.[59] It would appear that in number 67, the Congregation for Divine Worship and Discipline of the Sacraments ignores the existence and the importance of modern mass media, thus minimizing the importance of an across-the-board involvement of the ecclesial community where liturgical inculturation is concerned.[60]

Perhaps as a final example of a possible inner inconsistency, numbers 36 and 63 of the *Fourth Instruction*[61] insist that the more profound adaptations envisaged in *Sacrosanctum Concilium*, number 40, do not envision a transformation of the Roman rite but

---

58. Ibid., no. 47: "Cum Liturgia manifestatio sit fidei ac vitae christianae attendendum est ne eius inculturatio, licet tantum specie, syncretismo religioso signetur. Quod evenire poterit si aedes sacrae, cultus supellex vestes liturgicae, gestus et habitus inducant ad cogitandum in celebrationibus christianis nonnullorum rituum significationem non aliam esse ac ante evangelizationis processum"; no. 48: "Idem valet, exempli gratia, ad paganorum festa vel loca sacra, christiana forte reddenda, ad auctoritatis insignia sacerdoti tribuenda. . . . Semper autem oportet quamlibet caveant ambiguitatem. Immo, exqusisitioribus rationibus, Liturgia christiana nullo prorsus pacto assumere potest ritus magiae, superstitionis, spiritismi, vindictae vel sexualis notationis"; no. 49: "pericula insuper perpendant oportet ne communitates christianae segregatae maneant neve inculturatio liturgica ad scopum politicum adhibeatur."

59. Ibid., no. 67: "Conferentia Episcoporum invigilibat ut experimentum bene evlovatur. Commissione nationali vel regionali de Liturgia de more adiuvante. Insuper invigilabit ne exeprimentum limites statutos locorum ac temporum praetegrediatur, ut pastores et fideles edoceantur de eius natura ad tempus et circumscripta, demum ne ita divulgetur ut vitam liturgicam nationis ultro afficere possit."

60. Chupungco, "Remarks on 'The Roman Liturgy and Inculturation,'" 276.

61. Number 36 of the *Fourth Instruction* states that the process of inculturation should maintain the substantial unity of the Roman rite. ["Inculturationis processus perficiendus est Ritus romani *unitate substantiali* (original emphasis) servata."] In addition, it specifies that the work of inculturation does not foresee the creation of new families of rites. ["Inculturationis inquisitio non contendit ad novas familias rituales creandas."] Similarly, number 63 emphasizes the importance of unity since even "even more profound adaptations" do not envision a transformation of the Roman rite but are made within its context. ["Huiusmodi quoque aptationes minime tendunt ad Ritum romanum transformandum, sed potius intra ipsum suum obtinent locum."]

rather are made within its context.[62] These two numbers stand in stark opposition to numbers 1 and 17, which affirm the inherent dignity and value of the diversity of liturgical families within the Church.[63] The tension between these two points of view is not resolved within the parameters of the *Fourth Instruction*. It would also appear from what is stated in other parts of the instruction[64] that the diversity of liturgical families already in existence in the churches in union and communion with Rome suffices. New families of rites and their accompanying life of liturgical worship do not seem to be on the horizon in those regions of the world already "inculturated" into the Roman rite.[65]

CONCLUDING OBSERVATIONS

It would appear that despite some inner inconsistencies regarding the *modus operandi* of the Church as it interacts with culture, the *Fourth Instruction* seems to be consistent with the prescriptions and vision of *Sacrosanctum Concilium* and the first three instructions on the proper implementation of the liturgical constitution, with the revisions of the sacraments and rites, and

---

62. Cf. Mitchell, "The Amen Corner: Liturgy Encounters Culture—Again," 374.

63. Number 1 of the *Fourth Instruction* ends with a statement that the Church has known and still knows many different forms and liturgical families. ["Etenim Ecclesia. . . quippe quae formarum familiarumque liturgicarum diversitatem agnoverit. . . ."] Number 17 acknowledges the creation and development of new forms of Christian celebration and the birth of distinct liturgical families of the churches of the West and of the East. ["Celebrationis christianae formae ortae et progressae sunt gradatim iuxta locales condiciones, intra magnas areas culturales, ubi Bonus Nuntius diffusus est. Ita familiae liturgicae diversae in Occidente et Oriente christiano principium habuerunt, quarum dives patrimonium plenitudinem traditionis christianae fideliter custodit."]

64. CDWDS, *De Liturgia Romana et inculturatione*, especially nos. 33, 34, 36, 63.

65. For another perspective on the *Fourth Instruction*, see National Association of Pastoral Musicians, *Pastoral Music*, Volume 19 (1995): 15–73. This issue presents and examination by various authors of the *Fourth Instruction* by sections: Hugh MacMahon, SSC, "The Roman Liturgy and Inculturation, Nos. 1–8: Is the Korean Mass an 'Incarnation of the Gospel in an Autonomous Culture?' ": 19–24; John Gallen, SJ, "The Roman Liturgy and Inculturation, Nos. 9–20: Now It's Time for Artists to Lead the Liturgical Renewal": 25–29; Theresa F. Koernke, IHM, "The Roman Liturgy and Inculturation, Nos. 21–32: Have We Accommodated What We Should Have Inculturated?": 30–34; Mark R. Francis, CSV, "The Roman Liturgy and Inculturation, Nos. 33–37, 46–51: The Dialogue Is Just Getting Started": 35–39; Peter J. Scagnelli, "The Roman Liturgy and Inculturation, Nos. 38–45: 'You Are the Music/While the Music Lasts' ": 40–43; James H. Provost, "The Roman Liturgy and Inculturation, Nos. 52–62: Adapting the Liturgical Books for Our Evolving Ritual": 44–47; Teresita Weind, SND DE N, "The Roman Liturgy and Inculturation, Nos. 63–70: 'I Shall Go to See What the End Shall Be' ": 48–51. The articles are too short in length to present in-depth critiques; however, the opinions expressed by Gallen, Koernke, Francis, and Provost merit attention.

with itself (although here to a lesser degree). This consistency is perhaps due to the overarching influence of the writings of Pope John Paul II that were presented in the genesis of the *Fourth Instruction* earlier in this study. The repeated, methodological insertion of John Paul II's statements from his writings into the present document transfigure the *Fourth Instruction* in such a way that the open, optimistic, and inclusive vocabulary, perspective, and tone reflected in the first half of the instruction appears to disappear about midway through the instruction.[66] The second half of the instruction focuses more on the necessity for regulating the process of adaptation and/or inculturation of the liturgy so that any cultural accommodation of the Roman rite be done with careful examination and according to the procedures spelled out in the *Fourth Instruction*.[67]

Finally, the *Fourth Instruction* advances an understanding of inculturation that is rooted in the living and received liturgical tradition of the Church.[68] Practically speaking, such an understanding necessitates a careful study of both the received tradition and the actual praxis of the Church.[69] Adapting and/or inculturating the liturgical worship of the Roman Catholic Church as it manifests itself as local or particular churches demand a dynamic similar to the double movement that John Paul II identified in the process of inculturation. The Church looks for all that is good within local cultures; local cultures in turn realize that not everything that exists in them is compatible with the Gospel and is

---

66. Cf. Jounel, "Une étape majeure sur le chemin de l'inculturatiion," 271 and 276, respectively: "Après avoir établi une sorte de recueil de textes de Jean-Paul II relatif à l'inculturation. . . .""; "Dans une dernière partie, l'Instruction aborde le domaine des adaptations dans le rite romain (VL 52–69). On remarquera le changement de vocabulaire. Il n'est plus question d'inculturation, mais d'adaptation, car on traite désormais du seul rite romain et no plus de la liturgie dans la multiplicité de ses famille. Les adaptations dont il va être question constituent les premières démarches en vue de l'inculturation. L'objectif est de guider concrètement l'application des articles 37–39 de la Constitution conciliaire, et de l'article 40, c'est-à-dire des adaptations prévues par les livres liturgiques, puis d'une adaptation plus profonde du rite romain souhaitable chez des peuples plus étrangers à notre culture."

67. Bishop Donald Trautman of Erie, PA., then chairman of the Bishops' Committee on the Liturgy of the NCCB, made the following observation regarding the interaction between liturgy and culture: "We must also be on guard against the temptation to accommodate liturgy to the mood of the time, to merge its content into contemporary cultural forms, so that it is subordinated to the culture. An example of this would be the attitudes of time management in American culture that creep into liturgy and hurt it." Donald Trautman, "The Quest for Liturgy Both Catholic and Contemporary," in *Origins* 25 (1996): 484.

68. Chupungco, "Liturgical Inculturation and the Search for Unity," 58.

69. Ibid.

able to be brought into the liturgy or into the life of the Church.[70] The authentic and rich traditions of liturgical rites other than the Roman rite remind us that diversity is not an enemy of unity but a fruit of true *leitourgia*. Hopefully, future theological reflection on the *Fourth Instruction* will reveal that *varietates legitimae*, far from harming the genuine spirit and unity of the liturgy, truly enhance its value.

70. Ibid.

THE FOURTH INSTRUCTION "FOR THE RIGHT APPLICATION OF THE CONSTITUTION ON THE SACRED LITURGY OF THE SECOND VATICAN COUNCIL"

THE FOURTH INSTRUCTION
"FOR THE RIGHT APPLICATION OF THE CONSTITUTION ON THE SACRED LITURGY OF THE SECOND VATICAN COUNCIL"

VARIETATES LEGITIMAE

THE ROMAN LITURGY AND INCULTURATION

*Congregation for Divine Worship and
the Discipline of the Sacraments*

PREAMBLE

1.   Legitimate differences in the Roman Rite were allowed in the past and were foreseen by the Second Vatican Council in the Constitution on the Sacred Liturgy *Sacrosanctum Concilium*, especially in the Missions.[1] "Even in the Liturgy the Church has no wish to impose a rigid uniformity in matters that do not affect the faith or the good of the whole community."[2] It has known and still knows many different forms and liturgical families, and considers that this diversity, far from harming her unity, underlines its value.[3]

2.   In his Apostolic Letter *Vicesimus quintus annus*, the Holy Father Pope John Paul II described the attempt to make the

---

1. Cf. Second Ecumenical Council of the Vatican, Constitution *Sacrosanctum Concilium*, n. 38; also n. 40, 3.

2. Ibid., n. 37.

3. Cf. Vatican Council II, Decree *Orientalium Ecclesiarum*, n. 2; Constitution *Sacrosanctum Concilium*, nn. 3 and 4; *Catéchisme de l'Eglise catholique*, nn. 1200–1206, especially nn. 1204–1206.

Liturgy take root in different cultures as an important task for liturgical renewal.[4] This work was foreseen in earlier Instructions and in the liturgical books, and it must be followed up in the light of experience, welcoming, where necessary, cultural values "which are compatible with the true and authentic spirit of the liturgy, always respecting the substantial unity of the Roman Rite as expressed in the liturgical books."[5]

A) THE NATURE OF THIS INSTRUCTION

3. By order of the Supreme Pontiff, the Congregation for Divine Worship and the Discipline of the Sacraments has prepared this Instruction: the *Norms for the adaptation of the liturgy to the temperament and conditions of different peoples*, which were given in articles 37–40 of the Constitution *Sacrosanctum Concilium*, are here defined; certain principles, expressed in general terms in those articles, are explained more precisely, the directives are further clarified and the norms to be observed in carrying them out are laid down, so that in future these matters may be implemented in accordance with them.

Since the theological principles relating to questions of faith and inculturation have still to be examined in depth, this Congregation wishes to help Bishops and Episcopal Conferences to consider or put into effect, according to the law, such adaptations as are already foreseen in the liturgical books; to re-examine critically arrangements that have already been approved; and if, in certain cultures, pastoral need requires that form of adaptation of the Liturgy which the Constitution calls "more profound" and at the same time considers "more difficult," to make arrangements for putting it into effect in accordance with the law.

B) PRELIMINARY OBSERVATIONS

4. The Constitution *Sacrosanctum Concilium* spoke of the different forms of liturgical adaptation.[6] Subsequently the Magisterium of the Church has used the term "inculturation" to define more precisely "the incarnation of the Gospel in autonomous cultures and at the same time the introduction of these cultures

---

4. Cf. John Paul II, Apostolic Letter *Vicesimus quintus annus*, 4 December 1988, n. 16: AAS 81 (1989), 912.

5. Ibid.

6. Cf. Vatican Council II. Constitution *Sacrosanctum Concilium*, nn. 37–40.

into the life of the Church."[7] Inculturation signifies "an intimate transformation of the authentic cultural values by their integration into Christianity and the implantation of Christianity into different human cultures."[8]

The change of vocabulary is understandable, even in the liturgical sphere. The expression "adaptation," taken from missionary terminology, could lead one to think of modifications of a somewhat transitory and external nature.[9] The term "inculturation" is a better expression to designate a double movement: "by inculturation, the Church makes the Gospel incarnate in different cultures, and at the same time introduces peoples, together with their cultures, into her own community."[10] On the one hand the penetration of the Gospel into a given socio-cultural milieu "gives inner fruitfulness to the spiritual qualities and gifts proper to each people(...), strengthens these qualities, perfects them and restores them in Christ."[11]

On the other hand, the Church assimilates these values, when they are compatible with the Gospel "to deepen understanding of Christ's message and give it more effective expression in the Liturgy and in the many different aspects of the life of the community of believers."[12] This double movement in the work of inculturation thus expresses one of the component elements of the mystery of the Incarnation.[13]

5.   Inculturation thus understood has its place in worship as in other areas of the life of the Church.[14] It constitutes one of the

---

7. John Paul II, Encyclical Letter *Slavorum Apostoli*, 2 June 1985, n. 21: AAS 77 (1985), 802–802; Discourse to the Plenary Assembly of the Pontifical Council for Culture, 17 January 1987, n. 5: AAS 79 (1987), 1204–1205.

8. John Paul II, Encyclical Letter *Redemptoris missio*, 7 December 1990, n. 52: AAS 83 (1991), 300.

9. Cf. ibid. and Synod of Bishops, Final report *Exeunte coetu secundo*, 7 December 1985, D 4.

10. John Paul II, Encyclical Letter *Redemptoris missio*, 7 December 1990, n. 52: AAS 83 (1991), 300.

11. Vatican Council II, Pastoral Constitution *Gaudium et spes*, n. 58.

12. Ibid.

13. Cf. John Paul II, Apostolic Exhortation *Catechesi tradendae*, 16 October 1979, n. 53: AAS 71 (1979), 1319.

14. Cf. *Code of Canon Law of the Oriental Churches*, can. 584 § 2: "Evangelizatio gentium ita fiat, ut servata integritate fidei et morum Evangelium se in cultura singulorum populorum exprimere possit, in catechesi scilicet, in ritibus propriis liturgicis, in arte sacra, in iure particulari ac demum in tota vita ecclesiali."

aspects of the inculturation of the Gospel, which calls for true integration,[15] in the life of faith of each people, of the permanent values of a culture, rather than their transient expressions. It must, then, be in full solidarity with a much greater action, a unified pastoral strategy which takes account of the human situation.[16] As in all forms of the work of evangelisation, this patient and complex undertaking calls for methodical research and ongoing discernment.[17] The inculturation of the Christian life and of liturgical celebrations must be the fruit of a progressive maturity in the faith of the people.[18]

6.   The present Instruction has different situations in view. There are in the first place those countries which do not have a Christian tradition or where the Gospel has been proclaimed in modern times by missionaries who brought the Roman Rite with them. It is now more evident that "coming into contact with different cultures, the Church must welcome all that can be reconciled with the Gospel in the tradition of a people, to bring to it the riches of Christ, and to be enriched in turn by the many different forms of wisdom of the nations of the earth."[19]

---

15. Cf. John Paul II, Apostolic Exhortation *Catechesi tradendae*, 16 October 1979, n. 53: AAS 71 (1979), 1320: ". . .concerning evangelisation in general, we can say that it is a call to bring the strength of the Gospel to the heart of culture and cultures. (...) It is in this way that it can propose to cultures the knowledge of the mystery hidden and help them to make of their own living tradition original expressions of life, celebration and Christian thought."

16. Cf. John Paul II, Encyclical Letter *Redemptoris missio*, 7 December 1990, n. 52: AAS 83 (1991), 300: "Inculturation is a slow process covering the whole of missionary life and involves all who are active in the mission *Ad gentes*, and Christian communities in the measure that they are developing." Discourse to the Plenary Assembly of the Pontifical Council for Culture, 17 January 1987: AAS 79 (1987), 1205: "I strongly reaffirm the need to mobilize the whole Church into a creative effort towards a renewed evangelisation of both people and cultures. It is only by a joint effort that the Church will be able to bring the hope of Christ into the heart of cultures and present-day ways of thinking."

17. Cf. Pontifical Biblical Commission, *Foi et culture à la lumière de la Bible*, 1981; and International Theological Commission, Document on Faith and Inculturation *Commissio theologica*, 3–8 October 1988.

18. Cf. John Paul II, Discourse to the Bishops of Zaïre, 12 April, n. 5: AAS 75 (1983), 620: "How is it that a faith which has truly matured, is deep and firm, does not succeed in expressing itself in a language, in a catechesis, in theological reflection, in prayer, in the Liturgy, in art, in the institutions which are truly related to the African soul of your compatriots? There is the key to the important and complex question of the Liturgy, to mention just one area. Satisfactory progress in this domain can only be the fruit of a progressive growth in faith, linked with spiritual discernment, theological clarity, a sense of the universal Church."

19. John Paul II, Discourse to the Plenary Assembly of the Pontifical Council for Culture, 17 January 1987, n. 5: AAS 79 (1987), 1204: "in coming into contact with the cultures, the Church must welcome all that in the traditions of peoples is compatible with the Gospel, to

7.   The situation is different in the countries with a long-standing Western Christian tradition, where the culture has already been penetrated for a long time by the faith and the liturgy expressed in the Roman Rite. That has helped the welcome given to liturgical reform in these countries, and the measures of adaptation envisaged in the liturgical books were considered, on the whole, sufficient to allow for legitimate local diversity (cf. *below,* nn. 53–61). In some countries, however, where several cultures coexist, especially as a result of immigration, it is necessary to take account of the particular problems which this poses (cf. *below,* n. 49).

8.   It is necessary to be equally attentive to the progressive growth both in countries with a Christian tradition and in others of a culture marked by indifference or disinterest in religion.[20] In the face of this situation, it is not so much a matter of inculturation, which assumes that there are preexistent religious values and evangelizes them; but rather a matter of insisting on liturgical formation[21] and finding the most suitable means to reach spirits and hearts.

I.
The Process of Inculturation throughout
the History of Salvation

9.   Light is shed upon the problems being posed about the inculturation of the Roman Rite in the history of salvation. The process of inculturation was a process which developed in many ways.

The people of Israel throughout its history preserved the certain knowledge that it was the chosen people of God, the witness of his action and love in the midst of the nations. It took from neighboring peoples certain forms of worship, but its faith in the God of Abraham, Isaac and Jacob subjected these borrowings to profound modifications—principally changes of significance, but also often changes in the form—, as it incorporated these elements

---

give all the riches of Christ to them, and to enrich itself of the varied wisdom of the nations of the earth."

20. Cf. John Paul II, Discourse to the Plenary Assembly of the Pontifical Council for Culture, 17 January 1987, n. 5: AAS 79 (1987), 1205; also Apostolic Letter *Vicesimus quintus annus,* 4 December 1988, n. 17: AAS 81 (1989), 913–914.

21. Cf. Vatican Council II, Constitution *Sacrosanctum Concilium,* nn. 19 and 35, 3.

into its religious practice, in order to celebrate the memory of God's wonderful deeds in its history.

The encounter between the Jewish world and Greek wisdom gave rise to a new form of inculturation: the translation of the Bible into Greek introduced the Word of God into a world that had been closed to it and caused, under divine inspiration, an enrichment of the Scriptures.

10.   The law of Moses, the Prophets and the Psalms (cf. Lk 24:27, 44) was a preparation for the coming of the Son of God upon earth. The Old Testament, comprising the life and culture of the people of Israel, is also the history of salvation.

On coming to the earth the Son of God, "born of a woman, born under the law" (Gal 4:4), associated himself with social and cultural conditions of the people of the Covenant with whom he lived and prayed.[22] In becoming a man he became a member of a people, a country and an epoch "and in a certain way, he thereby united himself to the whole human race."[23] For "we are all one in Christ, and the common nature of our humanity takes life in him. It is for this that he was called the 'New Adam'."[24]

11.   Christ, who willed to share our human condition (cf. Heb 2:14), died for all in order to gather into unity the scattered children of God (cf. Jn 11:52). By his death he wanted to break down the wall of separation between mankind, to make Israel and the nations one people. By the power of his resurrection he drew all people to himself and created out of them a single New Man (cf. Eph 2:14–16; Jn 12:32). In him a new world has been born (cf. 2 Cor 5:16–17) and everyone can become a new creature. In him, darkness has given place to light, promise became reality and all the religious aspirations of humanity found their fulfillment. By the offering that he made of his body, once for all (cf. Heb 10:10), Christ Jesus brought about the fullness of worship in spirit and in truth in the renewal which he wished for his disciples (cf. Jn 4:23–24).

12.   "In Christ (...) the fullness of divine worship has come to us."[25] In him we have the High Priest, taken from among men (cf.

---

22. Cf. Vatican Council II, Decree *Ad gentes*, n. 10.

23. Vatican Council II, Pastoral Constitution *Gaudium et spes*, n. 22.

24. St. Cyril of Alexandria, *In Ioannem*, I, 14: PG 73, 162C.

25. Vatican Council II, Constitution *Sacrosanctum Concilium*, n. 5.

Heb 5:15; 10:19–21), put to death in the flesh but brought to life in the spirit (cf. 1 Pt 3:18). As Christ and Lord, he has made out of the new people "a kingdom of priests for God his Father" (cf. Rev 1:6; 5:9–10).[26] But before inaugurating by the shedding of his blood the Paschal Mystery,[27] which constitutes the essential element of Christian worship,[28] Christ willed to institute the Eucharist, the memorial of his death and resurrection, until he comes again. Here is to be found the fundamental principle of Christian Liturgy and the kernel of its ritual expression.

13.   At the moment of his going to his Father, the risen Christ assured his disciples of his presence and sent them to proclaim the Gospel to the whole of creation, to make disciples of all nations and baptize them (cf. Mt 28:15; Mk 16:15; Acts 1:8). On the day of Pentecost, the coming of the Holy Spirit created a new community within the human race, uniting all, in spite of the differences of language, which were a sign of division (cf. Acts 2:1–11). Henceforth the wonders of God will be made known to people of every language and culture (cf. Acts 10:44–48). Those redeemed by the blood of the Lamb and united in fraternal communion (cf. Acts 2:42) are called from "every tribe, language, people and nation" (cf. Rev 5:9).

14.   Faith in Christ offers to all nations the possibility of being beneficiaries of the promise and of sharing in the heritage of the people of the covenant (cf. Eph 3:6), without renouncing their culture. Under the inspiration of the Holy Spirit, following the example of Saint Peter (cf. Acts 10), Saint Paul opened the doors of the Church, not keeping the Gospel within the restrictions of the Mosaic law, but keeping what he himself had received of the tradition which came from the Lord (cf. 1 Cor 11:23). Thus, from the beginning, the Church did not demand of converts who were uncircumcised "anything beyond what was necessary" according to the decision of the apostolic assembly of Jerusalem (cf. Acts 15:28).

15.   In gathering together to break bread on the first day of the week, which became the day of the Lord (cf. Acts 20:7; Rev 1:10),

---

26. Cf. Vatican Council II, Dogmatic Constitution *Lumen gentium,* n. 10.

27. Cf. *Missale Romanum,* Feria VI in Passione Domini, 5: oratio prima: ". . . per suum cruorem instituit paschale mysterium."

28. Cf. Paul VI, Apostolic Constitution *Mysterii paschalis,* 14 February 1969: AAS 61 (1969), 222–226.

the first Christian communities followed the command of Jesus who, in the context of the memorial of the Jewish pasch, instituted the memorial of his Passion. In continuity with the unique history of salvation, they spontaneously took the forms and texts of Jewish worship, and adapted them to express the radical newness of Christian worship.[29] Under the guidance of the Holy Spirit, discernment was exercised between what could be kept and what was to be discarded of the Jewish heritage of worship.

16.   The spread of the Gospel in the world gave rise to other types of ritual in the Churches coming from the Gentiles, under the influence of different cultural traditions. Under the constant guidance of the Holy Spirit, discernment was exercised to distinguish those elements coming from "pagan" cultures which were incompatible with Christianity from those which could be accepted in harmony with Apostolic tradition, and in fidelity to the Gospel of salvation.

17.   The creation and the development of the forms of Christian celebration developed gradually, according to local conditions, in the great cultural areas where the Good News was proclaimed. Thus were born distinct liturgical families of the Churches of the West and of the East. Their rich patrimony preserves faithfully the Christian tradition in its fullness.[30] The Church of the West has sometimes drawn elements of its Liturgy from the patrimony of the liturgical families of the East.[31] The Church of Rome adopted in its Liturgy the living language of the people, first Greek and then Latin and, like other Latin Churches, accepted into its worship important events of social life and gave them a Christian significance. During the course of the centuries, the Roman Rite has known how to integrate texts, chants, gestures and rites from various sources[32] and to adapt itself to local cultures

---

29. Cf. *Catéchisme de l'Eglise catholique*, n. 1096.

30. Ibid., nn. 1200–1203.

31. Cf. Vatican Council II, Decree *Unitatis redintegratio*, nn. 14–15.

32. Texts: cf. the sources of the prayers, the prefaces and the Eucharistic Prayers of the Roman Missal, —Chants: for example the antiphons for 1 January, Baptism of the Lord, 8 September, the Improperia of Good Friday, the hymns of the Liturgy of the Hours, —Gestures: for example the sprinkling of holy water, use of incense, genuflection, hands joined, —Rites: for example Palm Sunday procession, the adoration of the Cross on Good Friday, the rogations.

in mission territories,[33] even if at certain periods a desire for liturgical uniformity obscured this fact.

18.   In our own time, the Second Vatican Council recalled that the Church "fosters and assumes the ability, resources and customs of each people. In assuming them, the Church purifies, strengthens and ennobles them (...). Through the work of the Church whatever good is in the human mind and heart, whatever good lies latent in the religious practices and cultures of diverse peoples, it is not only saved from destruction but it is also cleansed, raised up, and made perfect for the glory of God, the confounding of the devil, and the happiness of mankind."[34] So the Liturgy of the Church must not be foreign to any country, people, or individual, and at the same time it should transcend the particularity of race and nation. It must be capable of expressing itself in every human culture, all the while maintaining its identity, through fidelity to the tradition which comes to it from the Lord.[35]

19.   The Liturgy, like the Gospel, must respect cultures, but at the same time invite them to purify and sanctify themselves.

In adhering to Christ by faith, the Jews remained faithful to the Old Testament, which led to Jesus, the Messiah of Israel; they knew that he had fulfilled the Mosaic Covenant, as the Mediator of the new and eternal Covenant, sealed in his blood on the Cross. They knew that, by his one perfect sacrifice, he is the authentic High Priest and the definitive Temple (cf. Heb 6–10), and the prescriptions of circumcision (cf. Gal 5:1–6), the Sabbath (cf. Mt 12:8 and similar),[36] and the sacrifices of the Temple (cf. Heb 10) became of only relative significance.

---

33. Cf. in the past St. Gregory the Great, *Epistula ad Mellitum:* Reg. XI, 59: CCL 140A, 961–962; John VII, Bull *Industriae tuae,* 26 June 880: PL 126, 904; S. Congregation for the Propagation of the Faith, Instruction to the Apostolic Vicars of China and Indochina (1654): *Collectanea S. C. de Propaganda Fide,* I, 1, Roma, 1907, n. 135; Instruction *Plane compertum,* 8 December 1939: AAS 32 (1940), 24–26.

34. Vatican Council II, Dogmatic Constitution *Lumen gentium* n. 17, also n. 13.

35. Cf. John Paul II, Apostolic Exhortation *Catechesi tradendae,* 16 October 1979, nn. 52–53: AAS 71 (1979), 1319–1321; Encyclical Letter *Redemptoris missio,* 7 December 1990, nn. 53–54: AAS 83 (1991), 300–302; *Catéchisme de l'Eglise catholique,* nn. 1204–1206.

36. Cf. also St. Ignatius of Antioch, *Letter to the Magnesians,* 9: Funk 1, 199: "We have seen how former adherents of the ancient customs have since attained to a new hope; so that they have given up keeping the sabbath, and now order their lives by the Lord's Day instead. . . ."

In a more radical way, Christians coming from paganism had to renounce idols, myths, superstitions (cf. Acts 19:18–19; 1 Cor 10:14–22; Col 2:20–22; 1 Jn 5:21) when they adhered to Christ.

But whatever their ethnic or cultural origin, Christians have to recognize the promise, the prophecy and the history of their salvation in the history of Israel. They must accept as the Word of God the books of the Old Testament as well as those of the New.[37] They welcome the sacramental signs, which can only be understood fully in the context of Holy Scripture, and the life of the Church.[38]

20. The challenge which faced the first Christians, whether they came from the chosen people or from a pagan background, was to reconcile the renunciations demanded by faith in Christ with fidelity to the culture and traditions of the people to which they belonged.

And so it will be for Christians of all times, as the words of St. Paul affirm: "we proclaim Christ crucified, scandal for the Jews, foolishness for the pagans" (1 Cor 1:23).

The discernment exercised during the course of the Church's history remains necessary, so that through the Liturgy the work of salvation accomplished by Christ may continue faithfully in the Church by the power of the Spirit, in different countries and times and in different human cultures.

II.
The Requirements and Preliminary Conditions
for Liturgical Inculturation

A) REQUIREMENTS EMERGING FROM THE NATURE OF THE LITURGY

21. Before any research on inculturation begins, it is necessary to keep in mind the nature of the Liturgy. It "is, in fact the privileged place where Christians meet God and the one whom he has

---

37. Cf. Vatican Council II, Dogmatic Constitution *Dei Verbum*, nn. 14–16; *Ordo Lectionum Missae*, ed. typica altera, Praenotanda, n. 5: "It is the same mystery of Christ that the Church announces, when she proclaims the Old and New Testament in the celebration of the Liturgy. The New Testament is, indeed, hidden in the Old and, in the New the Old is revealed. Because Christ is the center and fullness of all Scripture, as also of the whole liturgical celebration"; *Catéchisme de l'Eglise catholique*, nn. 120–123, 128–130, 1093–1095.

38. Cf. *Catéchisme de l'Eglise catholique*, nn. 1093–1096.

sent, Jesus Christ" (cf. Jn 17:3).[39] It is at once the action of Christ the Priest and the action of the Church which is his Body, because in order to accomplish his work of glorifying God and sanctifying mankind, achieved through visible signs, he always associates with himself the Church, which, through him and in the Holy Sprit, gives the Father the worship which is pleasing to him.[40]

22.   The nature of the Liturgy is intimately linked up with the nature of the Church; indeed, it is above all in the Liturgy that the nature of the Church is manifested.[41] Moreover, the Church has specific characteristics which distinguish it from every other gathering or community.

It is not gathered together by a human decision, but is called by God in the Holy Sprit and responds in faith to his gratuitous call (*ekklesia* derives from *klesis* "call"). This singular characteristic of the Church is revealed by its coming together as a priestly people, especially on the Lord's day, by the word which God addresses to his people and by the ministry of the priest whom the Sacrament of Orders so conforms to Christ that he is enabled to act in the person of Christ the Head.[42]

Because it is catholic, the Church overcomes the barriers which divide humanity: by Baptism all become children of God and form in Christ Jesus one people where "there is neither Jew nor Greek, neither slave nor free, neither male nor female" (Gal 3:28). Thus the Church is called to gather all peoples, to speak all languages, to penetrate all cultures.

Finally, the Church is a pilgrim on the earth far from the Lord (cf. 2 Cor 5:6): she bears the marks of the present time in the sacraments and in her institutions, but is waiting in joyful hope for the coming of Jesus Christ (cf. Tit 2:13).[43] This is expressed in the prayers of petition: it shows that we are citizens of heaven (cf. Phil 3:20), at the same time attentive to the needs of mankind and of society (cf. 1 Tim 2:1–4).

---

39. John Paul II, Apostolic Letter *Vicesimus quintus annus*, 4 December 1988, n. 7: AAS 81 (1989), 903–904.

40. Cf. Vatican Council II, Constitution *Sacrosanctum Concilium*, nn. 5–7.

41. Cf. ibid., n. 2; John Paul II, Apostolic Letter *Vicesimus quintus annus*, 4 December 1988, n. 9: AAS 81 (1989), 905–906.

42. Cf. Vatican Council II, Decree *Presbyterorum ordinis*, n. 2.

43. Cf. Vatican Council II, Dogmatic Constitution *Lumen gentium*, n. 48; Constitution *Sacrosanctum Concilium*, nn. 2 and 8.

23.   The Church is nourished on the word of God as written down in the books of the Old and New Testaments. When the Church proclaims the word in the Liturgy, she welcomes it as a way in which Christ is present: "it is he who speaks when the Sacred Scriptures are read in Church."[44] For this reason the word of God is so important in the celebration of the Liturgy[45] that the Holy Scripture must not be replaced by any other text, no matter how venerable it may be.[46] Likewise the Bible, especially in the Psalms, is the indispensable source of the Sacred Liturgy's language, of its signs, and of its prayers.[47]

24.   Since the Church is the fruit of Christ's sacrifice, the Liturgy is always the celebration of the Paschal Mystery of Christ, the glorification of God the Father and the sanctification of mankind by the power of the Holy Spirit.[48] Christian worship thus finds its most fundamental expression when every Sunday, throughout the whole world, Christians gather around the altar under the leadership of the priest, celebrate the Eucharist, listen to the Word of God and recall the death and resurrection of Christ, while awaiting his coming in glory.[49] Around this focal point, the Paschal Mystery is made present in different ways, in the celebration of each of the sacraments of faith.

25.   The whole of the liturgical life gravitates in the first place around the Eucharistic Sacrifice and the other Sacraments given by Christ to his Church.[50] The Church has the duty to transmit them carefully and faithfully to every generation. In virtue of her pastoral authority the Church can make dispositions to provide for the good of the faithful, according to circumstances, times

---

44. Vatican Council II, Constitution *Sacrosanctum Concilium*, n. 7.

45. Cf. ibid., n. 24.

46. Cf. *Ordo Lectionum Missae*, editio typica altera, Praenotanda, n. 12: "It is not allowed to suppress or reduce either the biblical readings in the celebration of Mass or the chants that are drawn from Sacred Scripture. It is absolutely forbidden to replace these readings by other non-biblical readings. It is through the word of God in the Scriptures that 'God continues to speak to His people' (*Sacrosanctum Concilium*, n. 3), and it is through familiarity with the Holy Scripture that the people of God, made docile by the Holy Spirit in the light of faith, can by their life and way of living witness to Christ before the whole world."

47. Cf. *Catéchisme de l'Eglise catholique*, nn. 2585–2589.

48. Cf. Vatican Council II, Constitution *Sacrosanctum Concilium*, n. 7.

49. Cf. ibid., nn. 6, 47, 56, 102, 106; Cf. *Missale Romanum*, Institutio generalis, nn. 1, 7, 8.

50. Cf. Vatican Council II, Constitution *Sacrosanctum Concilium*, n. 6.

and places.[51] But she has no power over the things which are directly related to the will of Christ and which constitute the unchangeable part of the Liturgy.[52] To break the link that the sacraments have with Christ who instituted them, and with the very beginnings of the Church,[53] would no longer be to inculturate them, but to empty them of their substance.

26. The Church of Christ is made present and signified, in a given place and in a given time, by the local or particular Churches which through the Liturgy manifest the Church in its true nature.[54] That is why every particular Church must be united with the universal Church not only in belief and sacramentals, but also in those practices received throughout the Church as part of the uninterrupted Apostolic tradition.[55] This includes, for example, daily prayer,[56] sanctification of Sunday and the rhythm of the week, the celebration of Easter and the unfolding of the mystery of Christ throughout the liturgical year,[57] the practice of penance and fasting,[58] the sacraments of Christian Initiation, the celebration of the memorial of the Lord and the relationship between the Liturgy of the Word and the Eucharistic Liturgy, the forgiveness of sins, the ordained ministry, Marriage, and the Anointing of the Sick.

27. In the Liturgy the faith of the Church is expressed in a symbolic and communitarian form: this explains the need for a legislative framework for the organization of worship, the preparation

---

51. Cf. Council of Trent, Session 21, cap. 2: *DSchönm.* 1728; Vatican Council II, Constitution *Sacrosanctum Concilium*, nn. 48 ss.; 62 ss.

52. Cf. Vatican Council II, Constitution *Sacrosanctum Concilium*, n. 21.

53. Cf. S. Congregation for the Doctrine of the Faith, Declaration *Inter insigniores*, 15 October 1976: AAS 69 (1977), 107–108.

54. Cf. Vatican Council II, Dogmatic Constitution *Lumen gentium*, n. 28; also n. 26.

55. Cf. St. Irenaeus, *Adversus Haereses* III, 2, 1–3; 3, 1–2: SCh 211, 24–31; St. Augustine, *Epistula ad Ianuarium* 54, I: PL 33, 200: "But regarding those other observances which we keep and all the world keeps, and which do not derive from Scripture but from tradition, we are given to understand that they have been ordained or recommended to be kept by the Apostles themselves, or by the plenary Councils, whose authority is well founded in the Church"; John Paul II, Encyclical Letter *Redemptoris missio,* 7 December 1990, nn. 53–54: AAS 83 (1991), 300–302; Congregation for the Doctrine of the Faith, Letter to Bishops of the Catholic Church on certain aspects of the Church understood as communion, *Communionis notio,* 28 May 1992, n. 7–10: AAS 85 (1983), 842–844.

56. Cf. Vatican Council II, Constitution *Sacrosanctum Concilium*, n. 83.

57. Cf. ibid., nn. 102, 106 and appendix.

58. Cf. Paul VI, Apostolic Constitution *Paenitemini,* 17 February 1966: AAS 58 (1966), 177–198.

of texts, and the celebration of rites.[59] The reason for the preceptive character of this legislation throughout the centuries and still today is to ensure the orthodoxy of worship: that is to say, not only to avoid errors, but also to pass on the faith in its integrity so that the "rule of prayer" (*lex orandi*) of the Church may correspond to "rule of faith" (*lex credendi*).[60]

However deep inculturation may go, the Liturgy cannot do without legislation and vigilance on the part of those who have received this responsibility in the Church: the Apostolic See and, according to the prescriptions of the law, the Episcopal Conference for its territory and the Bishop for his diocese.[61]

B) PRELIMINARY CONDITIONS FOR THE INCULTURATION
OF THE LITURGY

28.   The missionary tradition of the Church has always sought to evangelize people in their own language. Often indeed, it was the first apostles of a country who wrote down languages which up till then had only been oral. And this is right, as it is by the mother language, which conveys the mentality and the culture of a people, that one can reach the soul, mold it in the Christian spirit, and allow to share more deeply in the prayer of the Church.[62]

After the first evangelization, the proclamation of the Word of God in the language of a country remains most useful for the people in their liturgical celebrations. The translation of the Bible, or at least of the biblical texts used in the Liturgy, is the first necessary step in the process of the inculturation of the Liturgy.[63]

So that the Word of God may be received in a right and fruitful way "it is necessary to foster a taste for Holy Scripture, as is witnessed by the ancient traditions of the rites of both East and

59. Cf. Vatican Council II, Constitution *Sacrosanctum Concilium*, nn. 22, 26, 28, 40, 3 and 128; *Code of Canon Law*, can. 2 and *passim*.

60. Cf. *Missale Romanum*, Institutio generalis, Procemium, n. 2; Paul VI, Discourse to the Consilium for the Application of the Constitution on the Liturgy, 13 October 1966: AAS 58 (1966), 1146; 14 October 1968: AAS 60 (1968), 734.

61. Cf. Vatican Council II, Constitution *Sacrosanctum Concilium*, nn. 22; 36 §§ 3 and 4; 40, 1 and 2; 44–46; *Code of Canon Law*, can. 447 ss. and 838.

62. Cf. John Paul II, Encyclical Letter *Redemptoris missio*, 7 December 1990, n. 53: AAS 83 (1991), 300–302.

63. Cf. Vatican Council II, Constitution *Sacrosanctum Concilium*, nn. 36 and 36 §§ 2–3; *Code of Canon Law*, can. 825 § 1.

West."[64] Thus inculturation of the Liturgy presupposes the reception of the Sacred Scripture into a given culture.[65]

29.   The different situations in which the Church finds herself is an important factor in judging the degree of liturgical inculturation that is necessary. The situation of countries that were evangelized centuries ago and where the Christian faith continues to influence the culture, is different from countries which were evangelized more recently or where the Gospel has not penetrated deeply into cultural values.[66] Different again is the situation of a Church where Christians are a minority of the population. A more complex situation is found when the population has different languages and cultures. A precise evaluation of the situation is necessary in order to achieve satisfactory solutions.

30.   To prepare an inculturation of the Liturgy, Episcopal Conferences should call upon people who are competent both in the liturgical tradition of the Roman Rite and in the appreciation of local cultural values. Preliminary studies of an historical, anthropological, exegetical and theological character are necessary. But these need to be examined in the light of the pastoral experience of the local clergy, especially those born in the country.[67] The advice of "wise people" of the country, whose human wisdom is enriched by the light of the Gospel, would also be valuable. Liturgical inculturation should try to satisfy the needs of traditional culture,[68] and at the same time take account of the needs of those affected by an urban and industrial culture.

C) THE RESPONSIBILITY OF THE EPISCOPAL CONFERENCE

31.   Since it is a question of local culture, it is understandable that the Constitution *Sacrosanctum Concilium* assigned special responsibility in this matter to the "various kinds of competent territorial bodies of Bishops legitimately established."[69] In regard

---

64. Vatican Council II, Constitution *Sacrosanctum Concilium*, n. 24.

65. Cf. ibid., John Paul II, Apostolic Exhortation *Catechesi tradendae*, 16 October 1979, n. 55: AAS 71 (1979), 1322–1323.

66. In the Constitution *Sacrosanctum Concilium* attention is drawn to nn. 38 and 40: "above all in the Missions."

67. Cf. Vatican Council II, Decree *Ad gentes*, nn. 16 and 17.

68. Cf. ibid., n. 19.

69. Vatican Council II, Constitution *Sacrosanctum Concilium*, n. 22 § 2; cf. ibid., nn. 39 and 40, 1 and 2; *Code of Canon Law*, can. 447–448 ss.

to this, Episcopal Conferences must consider "carefully and prudently what elements taken from the traditions and cultures of individual peoples may properly be admitted into divine worship."[70] They can sometimes introduce "into the Liturgy such elements as are not bound up with superstition and error (...) provided they are in keeping with the true and authentic spirit of the Liturgy."[71]

32. Conferences may determine, according to the procedure given below (cf. nn. 62 and 65–69) whether the introduction into the Liturgy of elements borrowed from the social and religious rites of a people, and which form a living part of their culture, will enrich their understanding of liturgical actions, without producing negative effects on their faith and piety. They will always be careful to avoid the danger of introducing elements that might appear to the faithful as the return to a period before evangelisation (cf. *below*, n. 47).

In any case, if changes in rites or texts are judged to be necessary, they must be harmonized with the rest of the liturgical life and, before being put into practice, still more before being made mandatory, they should first be presented to the clergy, and then to the faithful, in such a way as to avoid the danger of disturbing them without good reason (cf. *below*, nn. 46, 69).

III.
Principles and Practical Norms for the Inculturation
of the Roman Rite

33. As particular Churches, especially the young Churches, deepen their understanding of the liturgical heritage they have received from the Roman Church which gave them birth, they will be able in turn to find in their own cultural heritage appropriate forms which can be integrated into the Roman Rite, where this is judged useful and necessary.

The liturgical formation of the faithful and the clergy, which is called for by the Constitution *Sacrosanctum Concilium*,[72] ought to help them to understand the meaning of the texts and the rites given in the present liturgical books. Often this will mean that

---

70. Cf. Vatican Council II, Constitution *Sacrosanctum Concilium*, n. 40.

71. Ibid., n. 37.

72. Cf. Vatican Council II, Constitution *Sacrosanctum Concilium*, nn. 14–19.

elements which come from the tradition of the Roman Rite do not have to be changed or suppressed.

A) GENERAL PRINCIPLES

34.   In the planning and execution of the inculturation of the Roman Rite, the following points should be kept in mind: 1. The goal of inculturation; 2. the substantial unity of the Roman Rite; 3. the competent authority.

35.   The goal which should guide the inculturation of the Roman Rite is that laid down by the Second Vatican Council as the basis of the general restoration of the Liturgy: "both texts and rites should be so drawn up that they express more clearly the holy things they signify and so that the Christian people, as far as possible, may be able to understand them with ease and to take part in the celebration fully and actively and as befits a community."[73]

Rites also need "to be adapted to the capacity of the faithful and that there should not be a need for numerous explanations for them to be understood."[74] However, the nature of the Liturgy always has to be borne in mind, as also the biblical and traditional character of its structure and the particular way in which it is expressed (cf. *above*, nn. 21–27).

36.   The process of inculturation should maintain the *substantial unity* of the Roman Rite.[75] This unity is currently expressed in the typical editions of liturgical books published by authority of the Supreme Pontiff, and in the liturgical books approved by the Episcopal Conferences for their areas and confirmed by the Apostolic See.[76] The work of inculturation does not foresee the creation of new families of Rites; inculturation responds to the needs of a particular culture and leads to adaptations which still remain part of the Roman Rite.[77]

---

73. Ibid., n. 21.

74. Cf. ibid., n. 34.

75. Cf. ibid., nn. 37–40.

76. Cf. John Paul II, Apostolic Letter *Vicesimus quintus annus*, 4 December 1988, n. 16: AAS 81 (1989), 912.

77. Cf. John Paul II, Discourse to the Plenary Assembly of the Congregation for Divine Worship and the Discipline of the Sacraments, 26 January 1991, n. 3: ASS 83 (1991), 940: "this is not to suggest to the particular Churches that they have a new task to undertake after the application of the liturgical reform, that is to say, adaptation or inculturation. Nor is it intended to mean inculturation as the creation of alternative rites. (...) It is

37.   Adaptations of the Roman Rite, even in the field of inculturation, depend completely on the *authority* of the Church. This authority belongs to the Apostolic see, which exercises it through the Congregation for Divine Worship and the Discipline of the Sacraments;[78] it also belongs, within the limits fixed by law, to Episcopal Conferences,[79] and to the diocesan Bishop.[80] "No other person, not even if he is a priest, may on his own initiative add, remove, or change anything in the Liturgy."[81] Inculturation is not left to the personal initiative of celebrants or to the collective initiative of a congregation.[82]

Likewise concessions granted to one region cannot be extended to other regions without the necessary authorization, even if an Episcopal Conference considers that there are sufficient reasons for adopting such measures in its own area.

B) ADAPTATIONS WHICH CAN BE MADE

38.   In an analysis of a liturgical action with a view to its inculturation, it is necessary to consider the traditional value of the elements of the action, and in particular their biblical or patristic origin (cf. *above*, nn. 21–26), because it is not sufficient to distinguish between what can be changed and what is unchangeable.

---

a question of collaborating so that the Roman rite, maintaining its own identity, may incorporate suitable adaptations."

78. Cf. Vatican Council II, Constitution *Sacrosanctum Concilium*, n. 22 § 1; *Code of Canon Law*, can. 838 §§ 1 and 2; John Paul II, Apostolic Constitution *Pastor Bonus*, nn. 62; 64 § 3: AAS 80 (1988), 876–877; Apostolic Letter *Vicesimus quintus annus*, 4 December 1988, n. 19: AAS 81 (1989), 914–915.

79. Cf. Vatican Council II, Constitution *Sacrosanctum Concilium*, n. 22 § 2 and *Code of Canon Law*, can. 447 ss. and 838 §§ 1 and 3; John Paul II, Apostolic Letter *Vicesimus quintus annus*, 4 December 1988, n. 20: AAS 81 (1989), 916.

80. Cf. Vatican Council II, Constitution *Sacrosanctum Concilium*, n. 22 § 1 and *Code of Canon Law*, can. 838 §§ 1 and 4; John Paul II, Apostolic Letter *Vicesimus quintus annus*, 4 December 1988, n. 21: AAS 81 (1989), 916–917.

81. Vatican Council II, Constitution *Sacrosanctum Concilium*, n. 22 § 3.

82. The situation is different when, in the liturgical books published after the Constitution, the introductions and the rubrics envisaged adaptations and the possibility of leaving a choice to the pastoral sensitivity of the celebrant or president, for example when it says "if it is opportune," "in these or similar terms," "also," "according to circumstances," "either. . . or," "if convenient," "normally," "the most suitable form can be chosen." In making a choice, the celebrant should seek the good of the assembly, taking into account the spiritual preparation and mentality of the participants, rather than his own preferences or the easiest or quickest form of celebration. In celebrations for particular groups, other possibilities are available. Nonetheless, prudence and discretion are always called for in order to avoid the breaking up of the local Church into little "churches" closed in upon themselves.

39. *Language,* which is the principal means of communication between people, in liturgical celebrations its purpose is to announce to the faithful the good news of salvation[83] and to express the Church's prayer to the Lord. For this reason it must always express, along with the truths of the faith, the grandeur and holiness of the mysteries which are being celebrated.

Careful consideration therefore needs to be given to determine which elements in the language of the people can properly be introduced into liturgical celebrations, and in particular whether it is suitable or not to use expressions from non-Christian religions. It is just as important to take account of the different literary genres used in the Liturgy: biblical texts, presidential prayers, psalmody, acclamations, refrains, responsories, hymns and litanies.

40. *Music* and *singing,* which express the soul of people, have pride of place in the Liturgy. And so singing must be promoted, in the first place singing the liturgical text, so that the voices of the faithful may be heard in the liturgical actions themselves.[84] "In some parts of the world, especially mission lands, there are people who have their own musical traditions and these play a great part in their religious and social life. Due importance is to be attached to their music and a suitable place given to it, not only in forming their attitude toward religion, but also in adapting worship to their native genius."[85]

It is important to note that a text which is sung is more deeply engraved in the memory than when it is read, which means that it is necessary to be demanding about the biblical and liturgical inspiration and the literary quality of texts which are meant to be sung.

Musical forms, melodies and musical instruments could be used in divine worship as long as they "are suitable, or can be made suitable, for sacred use, and provided they are in accord with the

---

83. Cf. *Code of Canon Law,* can. 762–772, especially 769.

84. Cf. Vatican Council II, Constitution *Sacrosanctum Concilium,* n. 118; also n. 54: While allowing that "a suitable place be allotted to the language of the country" in the chants "steps should be taken so that the faithful may also be able to say or sing together in Latin those parts of the Ordinary of the Mass which pertains to them" especially the *Pater noster;* cf. *Missale Romanum,* Institutio generalis, n. 19.

85. Vatican Council II, Constitution *Sacrosanctum Concilium,* n. 119.

dignity of the place of worship, and truly contribute to the uplifting of the faithful."[86]

41.   The Liturgy is an action, and so *gesture* and *posture* are especially important. Those which belong to the essential rites of the Sacraments, and which are required for their validity, must be preserved just as they have been approved or determined by the supreme authority of the Church.[87]

The gestures and postures of the celebrating priest must express his special function: he presides over the assembly in the person of Christ.[88]

The gestures and postures of the congregation are signs of its unity and express its active participation and foster the spiritual attitude of the participants.[89] Each culture will choose those gestures and bodily postures which express the attitude of humanity before God, giving them a Christian significance, having some relationship if possible, with the gestures and postures of the Bible.

42.   Among some peoples, singing is instinctively accompanied by hand-clapping, rhythmic swaying and dance-movements on the part of the participants. Such forms of external expression can have a place in the liturgical actions of these peoples, on condition that they are always the expression of true communal prayer of adoration, praise, offering and supplication, and not simply a performance.

43.   The liturgical celebration is enriched by the presence of *art*, which helps the faithful to celebrate, meet God and pray. Art in the Church, which is made up of all peoples and nations, should enjoy the freedom of expression, as long as it enhances the beauty of the buildings and liturgical rites, investing them with the respect and honour which is their due.[90] The arts should also be truly significant in the life and tradition of the people.

86. Ibid., n. 120.

87. Cf. *Code of Canon Law,* can. 841.

88. Cf. Vatican Council II, Constitution *Sacrosanctum Concilium,* n. 33; *Code of Canon Law,* can. 899 § 2.

89. Cf. Vatican Council II, Constitution *Sacrosanctum Concilium,* n. 30.

90. Cf. ibid., nn. 123–124; *Code of Canon Law,* can. 1216.

The same applies to the shape, location and decoration of the altar,[91] the place for the proclamation of the Word of God,[92] and for Baptism,[93] all the liturgical furnishings, vessels, vestments and colours.[94] Preference should be given to materials, forms and colours which are in use among the different peoples.

44. The Constitution *Sacrosanctum Concilium* has firmly maintained the constant practice of the Church of encouraging the veneration by the faithful of images of Christ, the Virgin Mary and the Saints,[95] because the honor "given to the image is given to its subject."[96] In different cultures, believers can be helped in their prayer and in their spiritual life by seeing works of art which attempt, according to the genius of the people, to express the divine mysteries.

45. Alongside liturgical celebrations and related to them, in some particular Churches there are various manifestations of popular devotion. These were sometimes introduced by missionaries at the time of the initial evangelisation, and they often develop according to local custom.

The introduction of devotional practices into liturgical celebrations under the pretext of inculturation cannot be allowed "because by its nature, (the Liturgy) is superior to them."[97]

It belongs to the local Ordinary[98] to organize such devotions, to encourage them as supports for the life and faith of Christians, and to purify them when necessary, because they need to be constantly permeated by the Gospel.[99] He will take care to ensure

---

91. Cf. *Missale Romanum*, Institutio generalis, nn. 259–270; *Code of Canon Law*, can. 1235–1239, especially 1236.

92. Cf. *Missale Romanum*, Institutio generalis, n. 272.

93. Cf. *De Benedictionibus*, Ordo benedictionis Baptisterii seu Fontis baptismalis, nn. 832–837.

94. Cf. *Missale Romanum*, Institutio generalis, nn. 287–310.

95. Cf. Vatican Council II, Constitution *Sacrosanctum Concilium*, n. 125; Dogmatic Constitution *Lumen gentium*, n. 67; *Code of Canon Law*, can. 1188.

96. Council of Nicea II, *DSchönm.* 601; cf. S. Basil the Great, *De Spiritu Sancto*, XVIII, 45: Sch 17, 194.

97. Vatican Council II, Constitution *Sacrosanctum Concilium*, n. 13.

98. Cf. *Code of Canon Law*, can. 839 § 2.

99. John Paul II, Apostolic Letter *Vicesimus quintus annus*, 4 December 1988, n. 18: AAS 81 (1989), 914.

that they do not replace liturgical celebrations or become mixed up with them.[100]

C) NECESSARY PRUDENCE

46. "Innovations should only be made when the good of the Church genuinely and certainly requires them; care must be taken that any new forms adopted should in some way grow organically from forms already existing."[101] This norm was given in the Constitution *Sacrosanctum Concilium* in relation to the restoration of the Liturgy, and it also applies, in due measure, to the inculturation of the Roman Rite. In this field, changes need to be gradual and adequate explanation given in order to avoid the danger of rejection or simply an artificial grafting on to previous forms.

47. The Liturgy is the expression of faith and Christian life, and so it is necessary to ensure that liturgical inculturation is not marked, even in appearance, by religious syncretism. This would be the case if the places of worship, the liturgical objects and vestments, gestures and postures let it appear as if rites had the same significance in Christian celebrations as they did before evangelisation. The syncretism will be still worse if biblical readings and chants (cf. *above*, n. 26) or prayers were replaced by texts from other religions, even if these contain an undeniable religious and moral value.[102]

48. The Constitution *Sacrosanctum Concilium* envisaged the admission of rites or gestures according to local custom into rituals of Christian Initiation, marriage and funerals.[103] This is a stage of inculturation, but there is also the danger that the truth of the Christian rite and the expression of the Christian faith could be easily diminished in the eyes of the faithful. Fidelity to traditional usages must be accompanied by purification and, if necessary, a break with the past. The same applies, for example, to the

---

100. Cf. ibid.

101. Vatican Council II, Constitution *Sacrosanctum Concilium*, n. 23.

102. These texts can be used profitably in the homily, because it is one of the tasks of the homily "to show the points of convergence between revealed divine wisdom and noble human thought, seeking the truth by various paths": John Paul II, Apostolic Letter *Dominicae cenae*, 24 February 1980, n. 10: AAS 72 (1980), 137.

103. Nn. 65, 77, 81. Cf. *Ordo initiationis christianae adultorum*, Praenotanda, nn. 30–31, 79–81, 88–89; *Ordo celebrandi Matrimonium*, editio typica altera, Praenotanda, nn. 41–44, *Ordo exsequiarum*, Praenotanda, nn. 21–22.

possibility of christianizing pagan festivals or holy places, or to the priest using the signs of authority reserved to the heads of civil society, or for the veneration of ancestors. In every case it is necessary to avoid any ambiguity. Obviously the Christian Liturgy cannot accept magic rites, superstition, spiritism, vengeance or rites with a sexual connotation.

49.   In a number of countries, there are several cultures which coexist, and sometimes influence each other in such a way as to lead gradually to the formation of a new culture, while at times they seek to affirm their proper identity, or even oppose each other, in order to stress their own existence. It can happen that customs may have little more than folkloric interest. The Episcopal Conference will examine each case individually with care: they should respect the riches of each culture and those who defend them, but they should not ignore or neglect a minority culture with which they are not familiar. They should weigh up the risk of a Christian community becoming inward-looking, and also the use of inculturation for political ends. In those countries with a customary culture, account must also be taken of the extent to which modernization has affected the people.

50.   Sometimes there are many languages in use in the one country, even though each one may be spoken only by a small group of persons or a single tribe. In such cases, a balance must be found, which respects the individual rights of these groups or tribes, but without carrying to extremes the localization of the liturgical celebrations. It is also sometimes possible that a country may be moving towards the use of a principal language.

51.   To promote liturgical inculturation in a cultural area greater than one country, the Episcopal Conferences concerned must work together and decide the measures which have to be taken so that "as far as possible, there are not notable ritual differences in regions bordering on one another."[104]

IV.
Areas of Adaptation in the Roman Rite

52.   The Constitution *Sacrosanctum Concilium* had in mind an inculturation of the Roman Rite when it gave Norms for the

---

104. Vatican Council II, Constitution *Sacrosanctum Concilium*, n. 23.

adaptation of the Liturgy to the mentality and needs of different peoples, when it provided for a degree of adaptation in the liturgical books (cf. *below*, nn. 53–61), and also when it envisaged the possibility of a more profound adaptation in some circumstances, especially in mission countries (cf. *below*, nn. 63–64).

A) ADAPTATIONS IN THE LITURGICAL BOOKS

53. The first significant measure of inculturation is the translation of liturgical books into the language of the people.[105] The completion of translations and their revision, where necessary, should be effected according to the directives given by the Holy See on this subject.[106] Different literary genres are to be respected, and the content of the texts of the Latin typical edition is to be preserved, at the same time the translations must be understandable to participants (cf. *above*, n. 39), suitable for proclamation and singing with appropriate responses and acclamations by the assembly.

All peoples, even the most primitive, have a religious language which is suitable for expressing prayer, but liturgical language has its own special characteristics: it is deeply impregnated by the Bible; certain words in current Latin use (*memoria, sacramentum*) took on a new meaning in the Christian faith. Certain Christian expressions can be transmitted from one language to another, as has happened in the past, for example in the case of *ecclesia, evangelium, baptisma, eucharistia*.

Moreover, translators must be attentive to the relationship between the text and the liturgical action, aware of the needs of oral communication and sensitive to the literary qualities of the living language of the people. The qualities needed for liturgical translations are also required in the case of new compositions, when they are envisaged by the liturgical books.

54. For the celebration of the Eucharist, the Roman Missal, "while allowing (...) for legitimate differences and adaptations according to the prescriptions of the Second Vatican Council," must remain "a sign and instrument of unity"[107] of the Roman

---

105. Cf. Vatican Council II, Constitution *Sacrosanctum Concilium*, nn. 36 §§ 2, 3 and 4; 54; 63.

106. Cf. John Paul II, Apostolic Letter *Vicesimus quintus annus*, 4 December 1988, n. 20: AAS 81 (1989), 916.

107. Cf. Paul VI, Apostolic Constitution *Missale Romanum*, 3 April 1969: AAS 61 (1969), 221.

Rite in different languages. The General Instruction of the Missal foresees that "in accordance with the Constitution on the Liturgy, each Conference of Bishops may lay down norms for its own territory that are sited to the traditions and character of peoples; regions and different communities."[108] The same also applies to the gestures and postures of the faithful,[109] the ways in which the altar and the Book of the Gospels are venerated,[110] the texts of the opening chants,[111] the chant at the preparation of the gifts[112] and at the communion,[113] the rite of peace,[114] conditions regulating Communion under both kinds,[115] the materials for the construction of the altar and liturgical furnishings,[116] the material and form of sacred vessels,[117] liturgical vestments.[118] Episcopal Conferences can also determine the manner of distributing Holy Communion.[119]

55. For the other Sacraments and for sacramentals, the Latin typical edition of each ritual indicates the adaptations which pertain to the Episcopal Conferences,[120] or to the individual diocesan Bishop in particular circumstances.[121] These adaptations concern

---

108. *Missale Romanum*, Institutio generalis, n. 6; cf. also *Ordo Lectionum Missae*, editio typica altera, Praenotanda, nn. 111–118.

109. *Missale Romanum*, Institutio generalis, n. 22.

110. Cf. ibid., n. 232.

111. Cf. ibid., n. 26.

112. Cf. ibid., n. 50.

113. Cf. ibid., n. 56 i.

114. Cf. ibid., n. 56 b.

115. Cf. ibid., n. 242.

116. Cf. ibid., nn. 263 and 288.

117. Cf. ibid., n. 290.

118. Cf. ibid., nn. 304, 305, 308.

119. Cf. *De sacra communione et de cultu mysterii eucharistici extra Missam*, Praenotanda, n. 21.

120. Cf. *Ordo initiationis christianae adultorum*, Praenotanda generalia, nn. 30–33; Praenotanda, nn. 12, 20, 47, 64–65; Ordo, n. 312; Appendix, n. 12; *Ordo Baptisms parvulorum*, Praenotanda, nn. 8, 23–25; *Ordo Confirmationis*, Praenotanda, nn. 11–12, 16–17; *De sacra communione et de cultu mysterii eucharistici extra Missam*, Praenotanda, n. 12; *Ordo Paenitentiae*, Praenotanda, nn. 35b, 38; *Ordo Unctionis infirmorum eorumque pastoralis curae*, Praenotanda, nn. 38–39; *Ordo celebrandi Matrimonium*, editio typica altera, Praenotanda, nn. 39–44; *De Ordinatione Episcopi, presbyterorum et diaconorum*, editio typica altera, Praenotanda, n. 11; *De Benedictionibus*, Praenotanda generalia, n. 39.

121. Cf. *Ordo initiationis christianae adultorum*, Praenotanda, n. 66; *Ordo Baptismi parvulorum*, Praenotanda, n. 26; *Ordo Paenitentiae*, Praenotanda, n. 39; *Ordo celebrandi Matromonium*, editio typica altera, Praenotanda, n. 36.

texts, gestures, and sometimes the ordering of the rite. When the typical edition gives alternative formulae, Conferences of Bishops can add other formulae of the same kind.

56. For the rites of Christian Initiation, Episcopal Conferences are "to examine with care and prudence what can properly be admitted from the traditions and character of each people"[122] and "in mission countries to judge whether initiation ceremonies practiced among the people can be adapted into the rite of Christian Initiation, and to decide whether they should be used."[123] It is necessary to remember, however, that the term "initiation" does not have the same meaning or designate the same reality when it is used of social rites of initiation among certain peoples, or when, on the contrary, of the process of Christian Initiation, which leads through the rites of the catechumenate to incorporation into Christ in the Church by means of the Sacraments of Baptism, Confirmation and Eucharist.

57. In many places it is the marriage rite that calls for the greatest degree of adaptation so as not to be foreign to social customs. To adapt it to the customs of different regions and peoples, each Episcopal Conference has the faculty to prepare its own proper marriage rite, which must always conform to the law which requires that the cleric or the layperson assisting,[124] according to the case, must ask for and obtain the consent of the contracting parties and give them the nuptial blessing."[125] This proper rite must, obviously, bring out clearly the Christian meaning of marriage, emphasize the grace of the Sacrament and underline the duties of the spouses.[126]

58. Among all peoples, and in all eras, funerals are surrounded with special rites, often of great expressive value. To answer the needs of different countries, the Roman Ritual offers several forms of funerals.[127] Episcopal Conferences must choose those

---

122. *Ordo initiationis christianae adultorum*, *Ordo Baptismi parvalorum*, Praenotanda generalia, n. 30, 2.

123. Ibid., n. 31; cf. Vatican Council II, Constitution *Sacrosanctum Concilium*, n. 65.

124. Cf. *Code of Canon Law*, can. 1108 and 1112.

125. Cf. Vatican Council II, Constitution *Sacrosanctum Concilium*, n. 77; *Ordo celebrandi Matrimonium*, editio typica altera, Praenotanda, n. 42.

126. Cf. Vatican Council II, Constitution *Sacrosanctum Concilium*, n. 77.

127. Cf. *Ordo exsequiarum*, Praenotanda, n. 4.

which correspond best to local customs.[128] They will wish to preserve all that is good in family traditions and local customs, and ensure that funeral rites manifest the Christian faith in the resurrection and bear witness to the true values of the Gospel.[129] It is in this perspective that funeral rituals can incorporate the customs of different cultures and respond as best they can to the needs and traditions of each region.[130]

59.   The blessings of persons, places or things touches the everyday life of the faithful and answer their immediate needs. They offer many possibilities for adaptation, for maintaining local customs, and admitting popular usages.[131] Episcopal Conferences will be able to avail of what has been decreed on this matter, attentive to the needs of the particular region.

60.   As regards the Liturgical Year, each particular Church and religious family adds its own celebrations to those of the Universal Church, after approval by the Apostolic See.[132] Episcopal Conferences can also, with the prior approval of the Apostolic See, suppress the obligation of certain festive days or transfer them to a Sunday.[133] They also decide the time and manner of celebrating Rogationtide and Ember Days.[134]

61.   The Liturgy of the Hours has as its purpose the praise of God and the sanctification by prayer of the day and all human activity. Episcopal Conferences can make adaptations in the second reading of the Office of Readings, in the hymns and intercessions and in the concluding Marian antiphons.[135]

---

128. Cf. ibid., nn. 9 and 21, 1–3.

129. Cf. ibid., n. 2.

130. Cf. Vatican Council II, Constitution *Sacrosanctum Concilium*, n. 81.

131. Cf. ibid., n. 79; *De Benedictionibus*, Praenotanda generalia, n. 39; *Ordo Professionis religiosae*, Praenotanda, nn. 12–15.

132. Cf. *Normae universales de Anno liturgico et de Calendario*, nn. 49, 55; S. Congregation for Divine Worship, Instruction *Calendaria particularia*, 24 June 1970: AAS 62 (1970), 651–663.

133. Cf. *Code of Canon Law*, can. 1246 § 2.

134. Cf. *Normae universales de Anno liturgico et de Calendario*, n. 46.

135. *Liturgia Horarum*, Institutio generalis, nn. 92, 162, 178, 184.

*Procedure to follow when making the adaptations provided for
in liturgical books*

62. When an Episcopal Conference prepares its own edition of
liturgical books, it decides about the translations and also the
adaptations which are envisaged by the law.[136] The acts of the
Conference, together with the final vote, are signed by the President and Secretary of the Conference and sent to the Congregation
for Divine Worship and the Discipline of the Sacraments, along
with two copies of the approved text.

Moreover, along with the complete dossier should be sent:

a) a succinct and precise explanation of the reasons for the adaptations that have been introduced;

b) indications as to which sections have been taken from other
already approved liturgical books and which are newly composed.

After the *recognitio* of the Apostolic See has been received, according to the law,[137] the Episcopal Conference promulgates the Decree
and determines the date when the new text comes into force.

B) ADAPTATIONS ENVISAGED BY NO. 40 OF THE CONCILIAR
CONSTITUTION ON THE LITURGY

63. Apart from the adaptations provided for in the liturgical
books, it may be that "in some places and circumstances, an
even deeper adaptation of the Liturgy is needed and this entails
greater difficulties."[138] This is more than the sort of adaptations
envisaged by the *General Instructions* and the *Praenotanda* of
the liturgical books.

It presupposes that an Episcopal Conference has exhausted all
the possibilities of adaptation offered by the liturgical books; that
it has made an evaluation of the adaptations already introduced
and perhaps revised them before proceeding to more far-reaching
adaptations.

The usefulness or need for an adaptation of this sort can emerge in
one of the areas mentioned above (cf. 53–61) without the others

---

136. Cf. *Code of Canon Law*, can. 455 § 2 and can. 838 § 3; also for a new edition;
John Paul II, Apostolic Letter *Vicesimus quintus annus*, 4 December 1988, n. 20: AAS 81
(1989), 916.

137. Cf. *Code of Canon Law*, can. 838 § 3.

138. Vatican Council II, Constitution *Sacrosanctum Concilium*, n. 40.

being affected. Moreover, adaptations of this kind do not envisage a transformation of the Roman Rite, but are made within the context of the Roman Rite.

64. In this case when there are still problems about the participation of the faithful, one or more Bishops can propose the questions outstanding to their Brothers in the Episcopal Conference, and examine with them the desirability of introducing more profound adaptations, if the good of souls truly requires it.[139]

It is the function of Episcopal Conferences to propose to the Apostolic See the modifications it wishes to adopt in accordance with the procedure set out below.[140]

The Congregation for Divine Worship and the Discipline of the Sacraments is ready to receive the proposals of Episcopal Conferences and examine them, keeping in mind the good of the local Churches concerned and the common good of the Universal Church, and to assist the process of inculturation where it is desirable or necessary. It will do this in accordance with the principles and considerations laid down in this Instruction (cf. *above*, nn. 33–51), and in a spirit of trustful and ready collaboration and shared responsibility.

Procedure to be followed for the application of n. 40
of the Conciliar Constitution on the Liturgy

65. The Episcopal Conference will examine what has to be modified in liturgical celebrations on account of the traditions and mentality of peoples. It will ask the national or regional liturgical commission to study the matter and examine the different aspects of the elements of local culture and their eventual inclusion in the liturgical celebrations. The Commission is to ensure that it receives the appropriate expert advice. It may be sometimes opportune to ask the advice of members of non-Christian religions about the religious or civil value of this or that element (cf. *above*, nn. 30–32).

If the situation requires it, this preliminary examination will be made in collaboration with the Episcopal Conferences of neighboring territories or those with the same culture (cf. *above*, nn. 33–51).

---

139. Cf. S. Congregation for Bishops, Directory for Bishops in their pastoral ministry *Ecclesiae imago*, 22 February 1973, n. 84.

140. Cf. Vatican Council II, Constitution *Sacrosanctum Concilium*, n. 40, 1.

66. The Episcopal Conference will present the proposal to the Congregation, before any experimentation takes place. The presentation should include a description of the innovations proposed, the reasons for their adoption, the criteria used, the times and places chosen for a preliminary experiment and an indication which groups will make it, and finally the acts of the discussion and the vote of the Conference.

After an examination of the proposal carried out together by the Episcopal Conference and the Congregation, the latter will grant the Episcopal Conference a faculty to make an experiment for a definite period of time, where this is appropriate.[141]

67. The Episcopal Conference will supervise the process of experimentation,[142] normally with the help of the national or regional liturgical commission. The Conference will also take care to ensure that the experimentation does not exceed the limits of time and place that were fixed. It will also ensure pastors and the faithful know about the limited and provisional nature of the experiment, and it will not give it publicity of a sort which could have an effect on the liturgical practice of the country. At the end of the period of experimentation, the Episcopal Conference will decide whether it matches up to the goal that was proposed or whether it needs revision and it will communicate its conclusions to the Congregation, along with full information about the experiment.

68. After examining the dossier, the Congregation can issue a decree giving its consent, possibly with some qualifications, so that the changes can be introduced into the territory subject to the jurisdiction of the Episcopal Conference.

69. The Christian faithful, both clergy and lay people, should be well informed about the changes and prepared for their introduction into the liturgical celebrations. The changes are to be put into effect as circumstances require, with a transition period if this is appropriate (cf. *above*, n. 61).

CONCLUSION

70. The Congregation for Divine Worship and the Discipline of the Sacraments communicates to the Episcopal Conferences

---

141. Cf. ibid., n. 40, 2.

142. Cf. ibid.

these norms by which the work of inculturation of the Roman Rite envisaged by the Second Vatican Council must be governed, and does so as a response to the pastoral needs of the peoples of the differing cultures. Liturgical inculturation should be inserted with real care into a comprehensive pastoral program for the inculturation of the Gospel into the many different human cultural situations. The Congregation is confident that each particular Church, especially the young Churches, will discover that a diversity in certain elements can be a source of great enrichment in liturgical celebration, while respecting the substantial unity of the Roman Rite, the unity of the whole Church, and the integrity of the faith transmitted to the saints once and for all (cf. Jude 3).

The present Instruction was prepared by the Congregation for Divine Worship and the Discipline of the Sacraments by order of His Holiness Pope John Paul II, who approved it and ordered that it be published.

From the Congregation for Divine Worship and the Discipline of the Sacraments, 25 January 1994.

Antonio María Card. Javierre Ortas, Prefect
+ Geraldo M. Agnelo, Archbishop Secretary

WORKS CITED

Sources[1]

Benedicti PP XVI. Summi Pontificis. "Adhortatio Apostolica Postsynodalis, *Sacramentum Caritatis*, Ad Episcopos Sacerdotes Consacratos Consacratasque Necnon Cristifideles Laicos De Eucharistia Missionisque Ecclesiae Fonte et Culmine." Die XXII mensis Februarii, in festo Cathedrae Sancti Petri Apostoli, anno MMVII: http://www.vatican.va/holy_father/benedict_xvi/apost_exhortations/documents/hf_ben-xvi_exh_20070222_sacramentum-caritatis_lt.html.

———. "Post Synodal Apostolic Exhortation, *Sacramentum Caritatis*, Of The Holy Father Benedict XVI To The Bishops, Clergy, Consecrated Persons And The Lay Faithful On The Eucharist As The Source And Summit Of The Church's Life And Mission." 22 February on the feast of The Chair of Saint Peter, Apostle, 2007: http://www.vatican.va/holy_father/benedict_xvi/apost_exhortations/documents/hf_ben-xvi_exh_20070222_sacramentum-caritatis_en.html.

Catholic Bishops' Conference of India. "An Order of the Mass for India." *International Review of Mission* 65 (1976): 168–76.

Codex Iuris Canonici Auctoritate Ioannis Pauli Pp. II Promulgatus. Vatican City: Librería Editrice Vaticana, 1983.

Coetus Generalis extraordinarius habitus, 1985. *Ecclesia sub Verbo Dei Mysteria Christi celebrans pro salute mundi, Relatio finalis.* In *Il sinodo dei vescovi: Seconda assemblea generale straordinaria*, ed. Giovanni Caprille, sj. Roma: Edizioni "La Civiltà Cattolica," 1986.

———. Extraordinary Synod of Bishops, 1985. *A Message to the People of God and the Final Report.* Washington, DC: USCC, 1986.

Commissio Theologica Internationalis. *Fides et inculturatio. Gregorianum* 70 (1989): 625–46.

———. International Theological Commission. *Faith and Inculturation. Origins* 18 (1989): 800–807.

---

1. For the convenience of the reader, when the English translation of a source is cited in the body of this study, the bibliographical references herein will list such translations immediately after the original Latin source.

Congregatio de Cultu Divino et Disciplina Sacramentorum. "Le Missel Romain pour les diocesès du Zaïre." *Notitiae* 24 (1988): 454–72.

———. *De Liturgia Romana et inculturatione: Instructio quarta "Ad exsecutionem Constitutionis Concilii Vaticani Secundi de sacra Liturgia recte ordinandam" (Ad Const. Art. 37–40). Notitiae* 30 (1994): 80–115. Official Latin text in *Acta Apostolicae Sedis* 87 (1995): 288–314.

———. "Instruction (fourth)." *The Roman Liturgy and Inculturation: "Fourth Instruction for the Right Application of the Conciliar Constitution on the Liturgy" (Nos. 37–40).* Vatican English Text. In *Origins* 23 (1994): 745–56.

———. *Liturgiam authenticam.* "*Instructio quinta ad exsecutionem Constitutionis Concilii Vaticani Secundi de sacra Liturgia recte ordinandam (ad. Const. Art. 36)," De usu linguarum popularium in libris lituigiae Romanae edendis.*" Official Latin text available from http://www.vatican.va/roman_curia/congregations/ccdds/documents/ rc_con_ccdds_doc_20010507_liturgiam-authenticam_lt.html.

———. "Instruction (fifth)." *On the Use of Vernacular Languages in The Publication of the Books of the Roman Liturgy." Fifth Instruction for the Right Implementation of the Constitution on the Sacred Liturgy, (Sacrosanctum Concilium, art. 36).* Vatican English text available from http://www.vatican.va/roman_curia/congregations/ ccdds/documents/rc_con_ccdds_doc_20010507_liturgiam-authenticam_en.html.

Ioannis Pauli Pp. II. Summi Pontificis. "Adhortatio Apostolica ad Episcopos, Sacerdotes et Christifideles totius Catholicae Ecclesiae de catechesi nostro tempore tradenda." *Catechesi tradendae.* AAS 71 (1979): 1277–1340.

———. "Apostolic Exhortation *Catechesi tradendae* of His Holiness John Paul II to the Episcopate, the Clergy and the Faithful of the Entire Catholic Church On Catechesis In Our Time." Washington, DC: USCC, 1979.

———. "Allocution à la Commission biblique pontificale: L'insertion culturelle de la Révélation." *Documentation Catholique* 76 (1979): 455–56.

———. "Adhortatio Apostolica ad Episcopos, Sacerdotes et Christifideles totius Catholicae Ecclesiae: de Familiae Christianae Muneribus in mundo huius temporis." *Familaris consortio.* Vatican City: Typis Polyglottis Vaticanis, 1981.

———. "Apostolic Exhortation of His Holiness Pope John Paul II to the Episcopate, to the Clergy, and to the Whole Catholic Church regarding the Role of the Christian Family in the Modern World." *On the Family*. Washington, DC: USCC, 1981.

―――. *Epistula Encyclica ad Episcopos, Sacerdotes, Religiosos Omnesque Christifideles: Memoria Recolitur Undecimo Transacto Saeculo, Operis Evangelici Sanctorum Cyrilli et Methodii. Slavorum apostoli*. Vatican City: Typis Polyglottis Vaticanis, 1985.

―――. *Encyclical Epistle of His Holiness Pope John Paul II to the Bishops, Priests, and Religious Families and to All the Christian Faithful in Commemoration of the Eleventh Centenary of the Evangelizing Work of Saints Cyril and Methodius. Slavorum apostoli*. Boston, MA: The Daughters of St. Paul, 1985.

―――. "Litterae Apostolicae Quinto iam illustro expleto conciliari ab promulgata de Sacra Liturgia Constitutione *Sacrosanctum Concilium*." *Vicesimus quintus annus*. AAS 81 (1989): 897–918.

―――. "Apostolic Letter of His Holiness Pope John Paul II on the Twenty-fifth Anniversary of the Liturgy Constitution." *Vicesimus quintus annus*. Origins 19 (1989): 17–25.

―――. *Litterae Encyclicae Redemptoris missio de perenni vi mandati missionalis*. Vatican City: Librería Editrice Vaticana, 1990.

―――. *Encyclical Letter of the Supreme Pontiff John Paul II On The Permanent Validity of the Church's Missionary Mandate. Redemptoris Missio*. Washington, DC: USCC, 1990.

―――. "Allocutio ad eos qui plenario coetui Congregationis de Cultu Divino et Disciplina Sacramentorum interfuerunt." AAS 83 (1991): 938–43.

―――. "Allocutio ad quosdam Brasiliae episcopos limina Apostolorum visitantes." AAS 88 (1996): 550–59.

―――. "Address to the Bishops from Brazil on the occasion of their *ad limina* visit." [Title of address corrected]. Excerpts in English translation. In Bishops' Committee on the Liturgy, *Newsletter* 32 (April, 1996): 13–15.

Institutio Generalis Missalis Romani. In *Missale Romanum* ex decreto Sacrosancti Oecumenici Concilii Vaticani II instauratum auctoritate Pauli Pp. VI promulgatum. Editio typica. Roma: Typis Polyglottis Vaticanis, 1970.

―――. *General Instruction of the Roman Missal*. Fourth Edition. New York: Catholic Book Publishing Company, 1985. Translated by ICEL.

―――. *Documents on the Liturgy 1963–1979: Conciliar, Papal, and Curial Texts*. Translated by ICEL. Collegeville, MN: The Liturgical Press, 1982.

———. *General Instruction of the Roman Missal.* Translated by ICEL. In *Liturgy Documentary Series* 2. Washington, DC: United States Conference of Catholic Bishops, 2003.

Kaczynski, Reiner, ed. *Enchiridion Documentorum Instaurationis Liturgicae.* Vol. I. Torino, Italy: Casa Editrice Marietti, 1976–1988.

Martínez, Eduardo. Prefectus. Congregationis de Cultu Divino et Disciplina Sacramentorum. *Decretum. De ordinatione Episcopi, presbyterorum et diaconorum.* Editio typica altera. Notitiae 26 (1990): 74–75.

Missale Romanum ex decreto Sacrosancti Oecumenici Concilii Vaticani II instauratum auctoritate Pauli Pp. VI promulgatum. Editio typica. Roma: Typis Polyglottis Vaticanis, 1970.

———. *Roman Missal* revised by Decree of the Second Vatican Council and published by authority of Pope Paul VI. *Sacramentary.* Approved for Use in the Dioceses of the United States of America by the National Conference of Catholic Bishops and confirmed by the Apostolic See. Translated by ICEL. New York: Catholic Book Publishing Co., 1985.

Missale Romanum ex decreto Sacrosancti Oecumenici Concilii Vaticani II instauratum auctoritate Pauli Pp. VI promulgatum Ioannis Paulis Pp. II cura recognitum Editio typical tertia. Città del Vaticano: Typis Vaticanis, 2002.

Paulus VI. Summi Pontificis. *Motu Proprio. Sacram Liturgiam.* AAS 56 (1964): 139–44.

———. *Motu Proprio. Sacram Liturgiam.* On putting into effect some prescriptions of the *Constitution on the Liturgy.* Translated by ICEL. In *Documents on the Liturgy 1963–1979.* Collegeville, MN: The Liturgical Press, 1982: 84–87.

———. "Adhortatio Apostolica ad Episcopos, Sacerdotes et Christifideles totius Catholicae Ecclesiae: de Evangelizatione in mundo huius temporis." *Evangelii nuntiandi.* AAS 68 (1976): 5–76. Translated by the Vatican Press Office. In Austin Flannery, OP, *Vatican Council II: More Postconciliar Documents, "Evangelization in the Modern World,"* Vol. 2. Northport, NY: Costello Publishing Company, 1982: 711–61.

Pontificale Romanum ex decreto Sacrosancti Oecumenici Concilii Vaticani II instauratum auctoritate Paul Pp. VI promulgatum. *De Ordinatione Diaconi, Presbyteri et Episcopi.* Editio typica. Vatican City: Typis Polyglottis Vaticanis, 1968.

———. The *Roman Ritual* and *Pontifical* revised by Decree of the Second Vatican Ecumenical Council and published by authority of Pope Paul VI and Pope John Paul II. *Ordination of Deacons, Priests, and Bishops.* In *The Rites of the Catholic Church.* Vol. 2. Prepared by the International Commission on English in the Liturgy: A Joint Commission of Catholic Bishops' Conferences. Approved for use in the Dioceses of the United States of America by the National Conference of Catholic Bishops and confirmed by the Apostolic See. Study Edition. Translated by ICEL, 1975. Collegeville, MN: The Liturgical Press, 1991.

———. *Pontificale Romanum* ex decreto Sacrosancti Oecumenici Concilii Vaticani II renovatum auctoritate Pauli Pp. VI editum Ioannis Pauli Pp. II cura recognitum. *De Ordinatione Episcopi, presbyterorum et diaconorum.* Editio typica altera. Vatican City: Typis Polyglottis Vaticanis, 1990. The official Latin text appeared in *Notitiae* 26 (1990): 74–95.

———. *The Roman Pontifical as Renewed by Decree of the Second Vatican Ecumenical Council Published by Authority of Pope Paul VI and Further Revised at the Direction of Pope John Paul II, Rites of Ordination of a Bishop, of Priests, and of Deacons.* Second Typical Edition. Trans. by ICEL, 1999. Washington, DC: USCCB, 2003.

Rituale Romanum ex decreto Sacrosancti Oecumenici Concilii Vaticani II instauratum auctoritate Pauli Pp. VI promulgatum. *Ordo celebrandi Matrimonium.* Editio typica. Vatican City: Typis Polyglottis Vaticanis, 1969.

———. *Roman Ritual* revised by Decree of the Second Vatican Ecumenical Council and published by authority of Pope Paul VI. *Rite of Marriage.* English translation approved by the National Conference of Catholic Bishops and confirmed by the Apostolic See. Translated by ICEL, 1969. New York: Catholic Book Publishing Company, 1969.

———. *Rituale Romanum* ex decreto Sacrosancti Oecumenici Concilii Vaticani II instauratum auctoritate Pauli Pp. VI promulgatum. *Ordo Baptismi parvulorum.* Editio typica. Vatican City: Typis Polyglottis Vaticanis, 1969.

———. *Rituale Romanum* ex decreto Sacrosancti Oecumenici Concilii Vaticani II instauratum auctoritate Pauli Pp. VI promulgatum. *Ordo exsequiarum.* Editio typica. Vatican City: Typis Polyglottis Vaticanis, 1969.

———. *Rite of Funerals.* In *The Rites of the Catholic Church* as revised by Decree of the Second Vatican Ecumenical Council and published by authority of Pope Paul VI. Study Edition. Translated by ICEL, 1970. New York: Pueblo Publishing Co., 1983.

———. *Roman Ritual* revised by Decree of the Second Vatican Ecumenical Council and published by authority of Pope Paul VI. *Order of Christian Funerals.* Approved for use in the Dioceses of the United States of America by the National Conference of Catholic Bishops and confirmed by the Apostolic See. Prepared by the International

Commission on English in the Liturgy: A Joint Commission of Catholic Bishops' Conferences. Presider's Edition. Collegeville, MN: The Liturgical Press, 1989.

———. *Rituale Romanum* ex decreto Sacrosancti Oecumenici Concilii Vaticani II instauratum auctoritate Pauli Pp. VI promulgatum. *Ordo initiationis christianae adultorum.* Editio typica. Vatican City: Typis Polyglottis Vaticanis, 1972.

———. *Rituale Romanum* ex decreto Sacrosancti Oecumenici Concilii Vaticani II instauratum auctoritate Pauli Pp. VI promulgatum. *Ordo Unctionis infirmorum eorumque pastoralis curae.* Editio typica. Vatican City: Typis Polyglottis Vaticanis, 1972.

———. *Roman Ritual* revised by Decree of the Second Vatican Ecumenical Council and published by authority of Pope Paul VI. *Pastoral Care of the Sick: Rites of Anointing and Viaticum.* Approved for use in the Dioceses of the United States of America by the National Conference of Catholic Bishops and confirmed by the Apostolic See. Prepared by the International Commission on English in the Liturgy: A Joint Commission of Catholic Bishops' Conferences. New York: Catholic Book Publishing Co., 1983.

———. *Rituale Romanum* ex decreto Sacrosancti Oecumenici Concilii Vaticani II renovatum auctoritate Pauli Pp. VI editum Ioannis Pauli Pp. II cura recognitum. *Ordo celebrandi Matrimonium.* Editio typica altera. Vatican City: Typis Polyglottis Vaticanis, 1991.

———. *Roman Ritual. Order of Christian Marriage.* Provisional Text of the Pastoral Liturgy Committee for use by the Bishops' Conference of England and Wales. Translated by ICEL, September 1993. London: Bishop's Conference of England and Wales, 1993.

———. *Roman Ritual* revised by Decree of the Second Vatican Ecumenical Council and published by authority of Pope Paul VI revised at the direction of Pope John Paul II. *Order of Celebrating Marriage.* Second Typical Edition, approval pending. For Study and Comment by the Bishops of the Member and Associate-Member Conferences of the International Commission of English in the Liturgy. Washington, DC: ICEL, 1996.

Sacra Congregatio pro Cultu Divino. "Instructio tertia." *Liturgiae instaurationes.* AAS 62 (1970): 692–704.

———. "Instruction (third)." *Liturgiae instaurationes. On the Orderly Carrying Out of the Constitution on the Liturgy.* Translated by ICEL. In *Documents on the Liturgy 1963–1979.* Collegeville, MN: The Liturgical Press, 1982: 159–67.

Sacra Rituum Congregatio (Consilium). "Instructio (prima)." *Inter oecumenici.* AAS 56 (1964): 877–900.

―――. "Instruction (first)." *Inter oecumenici. On the Orderly Carrying Out of the Constitution on the Liturgy.* Translated by ICEL. In *Documents on the Liturgy 1963–1979.* Collegeville, MN: The Liturgical Press, 1982: 88–110.

―――. "Instructio altera." *Tres abhinc annos.* AAS 59 (1967): 442–48.

―――. "Instruction (second)." *Tres abhinc annos. On the Orderly Carrying Out of the Constitution on the Liturgy.* Translated by ICEL. In *Documents on the Liturgy 1963–1979.* Collegeville, MN: The Liturgical Press, 1982: 135–40.

―――. *Ordo Missae: Institutio generalis Missalis Romani.* In *Missale Romanum* ex decreto Sacrosancti Oecumenici Concilii Vaticani II instauratum auctoritate Pauli Pp. VI promulgatum. Editio typica. Roma: Typis Polyglottis Vaticanis, 1969.

―――. *General Instruction of the Roman Missal.* In *Documents on the Liturgy 1963–1979: Conciliar, Papal, and Curial Texts.* Translated by ICEL. Collegeville, MN: The Liturgical Press, 1982: 465–533.

―――. "Instructio." *De musica in sacra Liturgia. Musicam sacram.* AAS 59 (1967): 300–20.

―――. "Instruction." Musicam sacram. On Music in the Liturgy. In *Documents on the Liturgy 1963–1979: Conciliar, Papal, and Curial Texts.* Translated by ICEL. Collegeville, MN: The Liturgical Press, 1982: 1293–1306.

Tanner, Norman P., SJ. English ed. *Decrees of the Ecumenical Councils: Vol. II Trent to Vatican II.* Washington, DC: Sheed and Ward and Georgetown University Press, 1990.

Vatican Council II. *Constitutio de sacra liturgia. Sacrosanctum Concilium.* In *Decrees of the Ecumenical Councils: Vol. II Trent to Vatican II,* English ed. Norman P. Tanner, SJ. Washington, DC: Sheed and Ward and Georgetown University Press, 1990: 820–43.

―――. *Constitution on the Liturgy.* In *Decrees of the Ecumenical Councils Vol. II. Trent to Vatican II,* English ed. Norman P. Tanner, SJ. Washington, DC: Sheed and Ward and Georgetown University Press, 1990: 820–43.

―――. *Constitutio dogmatica de ecclesia. Lumen Gentium.* In *Decrees of the Ecumenical Councils: Vol. II Trent to Vatican II.* English ed. Norman P. Tanner, SJ. Washington, DC: Sheed and Ward and Georgetown University Press, 1990: 849–900.

―――. *Dogmatic Constitution on the Church.* In *Decrees of the Ecumenical Councils: Vol. II Trent to Vatican II.* English ed. Norman P. Tanner, SJ. Washington, DC: Sheed and Ward and Georgetown University Press, 1990: 849–900.

———. *Constitutio pastoralis de ecclesia in mundo huius temporis. Gaudium et Spes.* In *Decrees of the Ecumenical Councils: Vol. II Trent to Vatican II.* English ed. Norman P. Tanner, SJ. Washington, DC: Sheed and Ward and Georgetown University Press, 1990: 1069–1135.

———. *Pastoral Constitution on the Church in the World of Today* (i.e., The Church in the Modern World). In *Decrees of the Ecumenical Councils: Vol. II Trent to Vatican II.* English ed. Norman P. Tanner, SJ. Washington, DC: Sheed and Ward and Georgetown University Press, 1990: 1069–1135.

———. *Decretum de ecclesiis orientalibus catholicis. Orientalium ecclesiarum.* In *Decrees of the Ecumenical Councils: Vol. II Trent to Vatican II.* English ed. Norman P. Tanner, SJ Washington, DC: Sheed and Ward and Georgetown University Press, 1990: 900–907.

———. *Decree on the Eastern Catholic Churches.* In *Decrees of the Ecumenical Councils: Vol. II Trent to Vatican II.* English ed. Norman P. Tanner, SJ. Washington, DC: Sheed and Ward and Georgetown University Press, 1990: 900–907.

Literature

Agnelo, Geraldo. "Liturgia Romana e inculturazione." *Notitiae* 30 (1994): 71–77.

Alberigo, Giuseppe, Jean-Pierre Jossua, and Joseph A. Komonchak, eds. *The Reception of Vatican II.* Translated by Matthew J. O'Connell. Washington, DC: The Catholic University of America Press, 1987.

Amaladoss, M. "Inculturation and Tasks of Mission." In *Toward a New Age in Mission: International Congress of Mission.* Manila: IM/ICO, 1981.

Arbuckle, G. A. "Inculturation Not Adaptation: Time to Change Terminology." *Worship* 60 (1986): 511–20.

Azevedo, Marcello de Carvalho, SJ. *Inculturation and the Challenges of Modernity.* Rome: Gregorian University, 1982.

Bevans, Stephen, SVD. *Models of Contextual Theology. Faith and Culture Series.* New York: Orbis Books, 1992.

Botte, Bernard, OSB. *From Silence to Participation: An Insider's View of Liturgical Renewal.* Translated by John Sullivan, OCD. Washington, DC: The Pastoral Press, 1988.

Braga, Charles, CM. "Commentary on the Instruction." In *The Commentary on the Constitution and on the Instruction on the Sacred Liturgy*, ed. A. Bugnini and C. Braga. Translated by Rev. Vincent P. Mallon. New York: Benziger Brothers, 1965: 327–424.

Bugnini, Annibale. "Commentaire," *Documentation Catholique.* 64 (1967): 894–98.

———. *La riforma liturgica 1948–1975.* Roma: Edizioni Liturgiche, 1983.

———. *The Reform of the Liturgy 1948–1975.* Translated by Matthew J. O'Connell. Collegeville, MN: The Liturgical Press, 1990.

Congar, Yves, OP. *The Role of the Church in the Modern World.* In *Commentary on the Documents of Vatican II*, ed. Herbert Vorgrimler. Vol. V: 202–23. New York: Herder and Herder, 1967.

———. "L' 'Ecclesia' ou communauté chrétienne, sujet intégral de l'action liturgique." In *La liturgie après Vatican II: Bilans, études, prospective*, ed. J.-P. Jossua, OP, and Yves Congar, OP. Unam Sanctam 66 Paris: Les Éditions du Cerf, 1967:241–88.

Chupungco, Anscar J., OSB. "An Order of the Mass." In *Towards a Filipino Liturgy.* Manila, 1976.

———. *Cultural Adaptation of the Liturgy.* New York: Paulist Press, 1982.

———. *Liturgies of the Future: The Process and Methods of Inculturation.* New York: Paulist Press, 1989.

———. *Liturgical Inculturation: Sacramentals, Religiosity, and Catechesis.* Collegeville, MN: The Liturgical Press, 1992.

———. "Remarks on 'The Roman Liturgy and Inculturation.'" *Ecclesia Orans* 11 (1994): 269–77.

———. "Liturgical Inculturation and the Search for Unity." In *So We Believe, So We Pray: Towards Koinonia in Worship*, ed. Thomas F. Best and Darmar Heller. Faith and Order Paper No. 171. Geneva: WCC Publications, 1996: 55–64.

Crichton, J. D. *Changes in the Liturgy: Considerations on the Instruction for the Right Ordering and Execution of the "Constitution on the Sacred Liturgy."* Staten Island, NY: Alba House, 1965.

Crollius, Aary A. Roest, SJ. "What Is so New about Inculturation? A Concept and Its Implication." *Gregorianum* 59 (1978): 721–38.

Donovan, Daniel. *What Are They Saying about the Ministerial Priesthood?* New York: Paulist Press, 1992.

Downey, Michael and Richard Fragomeni, eds. *A Promise of Presence: Studies in Honor of David N. Power, OMI.* Washington, DC: The Pastoral Press, 1992.

Egbulem, Nwaka Chris. "An African Interpretation of Liturgical Inculturation: The *Rite Zaïrois.*" In *A Promise of Obedience: Studies in Honor of David N. Power, OMI,* ed. Michael Downey and Richard Fragomeni. Washington, DC: The Pastoral Press, 1992: 227–50.

———. *The Power of Africentric Celebrations: Inspirations from the Zairean Liturgy.* New York: Crossroad, 1996: 141–63.

Falsini, R. "Commento." In *Costituzione conciliare sulla sacra liturgia: Introduzione, testo Latino-Italiano, commento,* ed. F. Antonelli and R. Falsini. *Sussidi Liturgico-pastorali* 7. Roma: Società Editrice "Vita e Pensiero," 1964.

Fischer B. and P.-M. Gy. "De recognitione Ritualis Romani." *Notitiae* 2 (1966): 220–30.

Francis, Mark R., CSV. "The Roman Liturgy and Inculturation, Nos. 33–37, 46–51: The Dialogue Is Just Getting Started." National Association of Pastoral Musicians. *Pastoral Music* 19 (1995): 35–39.

Gallen, John, SJ. "The Roman Liturgy and Inculturation, Nos. 9–20: Now It's Time for Artists to Lead the Liturgical Renewal." National Association of Pastoral Musicians. *Pastoral Music* 19 (1995): 25–29.

Granfield, Patrick, OSB. *The Limits of the Papacy: Authority and Autonomy in the Church.* New York: Crossroad, 1990.

Gy, P-M., OP. "Situation historique de la Constitution." In *La Liturgie après Vatican II: Bilans, etudes, prospective,* ed. J.-P. Jossua, OP, and Yves Congar, OP. Unam Sanctam 66 Paris: Les Éditions du Cerf, 1967: 111–26.

———. "Le nouveau rituel romain du Marriage." *La Maison-Dieu* 99 (1969): 124–43.

———. "La troisième instruction pour une juste application de la Constitution conciliaire sur la liturgie." *La Maison-Dieu* 104 (1970): 167–71.

———. "Le nouveau rituel romain des malades." *La Maison-Dieu* 113 (1973): 29–49.

Jossua, J. P., OP. "La Constitution *Sacrosanctum Concilium* dans l'ensemble de l'oeuvre conciliaire." In *La liturgie après Vatican II: Bilans, études, prospective,* ed. J.-P. Jossua, OP, and Yves Congar, OP. Unam Sanctam 66 Paris: Les Éditions du Cerf, 1967: 127–56.

Jounel, Pierre. "Commentaire: L'Instruction du 26 septembre 1964."
La Maison-Dieu 80 (1964): 51–125.

———. *Les premières étapes de la réforme liturgique: I: L'Instruction
du 26 septembre 1964.* Traduction officielle et commentaire. Paris:
Desclée, 1965.

———. "Les principes directeurs de l'Instruction." *La Maison-Dieu* 90
(1967): 17–43.

———. "Une étape majeure sur le chemin de l'inculturation liturgique."
Notitiae 30 (1994): 260–77.

Jungmann, Josef. "Constitution on the Sacred Liturgy." Translated by
Lalit Adolphus. In *Commentary on the Documents of Vatican II*, ed.
Herbert Vorgrimler. Vol. I: 1–87. New York: Herder and Herder, 1967.

Kain, Anthony. "My Son's Bread": About Culture, Language and
Liturgy." In *A Promise of Presence: Studies in Honor of David N.
Power, OMI*, ed. Michael Downey and Richard Fragomeni. Washington,
DC: The Pastoral Press, 1992: 251–67.

Kilmartin, Edward J. SJ. "Inculturation of the Liturgy." In *Canadian
Studies in Liturgy.* No. 5: "Culture of the Praying Church: The
Particular Liturgy of the Individual Church." Ottawa, Ontario:
Canadian Conference of Catholic Bishops, 1990: 57–67.

Koernke, Theresa F., IHM. "The Roman Liturgy and Inculturation, Nos.
21–32: Have We Accommodated What We Should Have Inculturated?"
National Association of Pastoral Musicians. *Pastoral Music* 19 (1995):
30–34.

Komonchak, Joseph. "The Theology of the Local Church: State of the
Question." In *The Multicultural Church: A New Landscape in U.S.
Theologies*, ed. William Cenkner, OP. New York: Paulist Press, 1996:
35–49.

Lewis, Charlton T. and Charles Short. *A Latin Dictionary Founded on
Andrew's Edition of Freund's Latin Dictionary*, ed. and rev. Charlton T.
Lewis and Charles Short. Oxford: The Clarendon Press, 1879. Reprint,
New York: Oxford University Press, Inc., 1993.

López, Julián. "La segunda edición del ritual del Matrimonio." *Phase*
203 (1994): 403–18.

MacMahon, Hugh, SSC. "The Roman Liturgy and Inculturation,
Nos. 1–8: Is the Korean Mass an 'Incarnation of the Gospel in an
Autonomous Culture?'" National Association of Pastoral Musicians.
Pastoral Music 19 (1995): 19–24.

Martinez, German. "The Newly Revised Roman Rite for Celebrating
Marriage." *Worship* 69 (1995): 127–42.

Mitchell, Nathan. "The Amen Corner: Liturgy Encounters Culture—Again." *Worship* 68 (1994): 369–76.

Phan, Peter C. "Contemporary Theology and Inculturation in the United States." In *The Multicultural Church: A New Landscape in U. S. Theology*, ed. William Cenkner, OP. New York: The Paulist Press, 1995: 109–30.

Power, David N., OMI. "Liturgy and Culture." *East Asian Pastoral Review* 4 (1984): 348–60.

———. *Worship: Culture and Theology*. Washington, DC: The Pastoral Press, 1990.

———. "Liturgy and Culture Revisited." *Worship* 69 (1995): 225–43.

Provost, James H. "The Roman Liturgy and Inculturation, Nos. 52–62: Adapting the Liturgical Books for Our Evolving Ritual." National Association of Pastoral Musicians. *Pastoral Music* 19 (1995): 44–47.

Rahner, Karl. "Towards A Fundamental Theological Interpretation of Vatican II." *Theological Studies* 40 (1979): 716–27.

Rodríguez, José M. "Nueva edición del ritual del Matrimonio: Teología y pastoral." *Phase* 32 (1992): 24–25.

Scagnelli, Peter J. "The Roman Liturgy and Inculturation, Nos. 38–45: 'You Are the Music/While the Music Lasts.' " National Association of Pastoral Musicians. *Pastoral Music* 19 (1995): 40–43.

Schineller, Peter, SJ. *A Handbook on Inculturation*. New York: Paulist Press, 1990.

Shorter, Aylward. *Toward a Theology of Inculturation*. Maryknoll, NY: Orbis Books, 1988.

Standaert, Nicholas, SJ. "L'histoire d'un néologisme: Le terme *inculturation* dans les documents romains." *Nouvelle Revue Théologique* 110 (1988): 555–70.

Synod of Bishops for Africa (April 10–May 8, 1994). *Origins* 24 (1994): 1–13.

Tegels, A. "Chronicle: A Third Instruction." *Worship* 44 (1970): 623–26.

Trautman, Donald. "The Quest for Liturgy Both Catholic and Contemporary." *Origins* 25 (1996): 481–87.

Weind, Teresita, SND DEN. "The Roman Liturgy and Inculturation: 'I Shall Go to See What the End Shall Be.' Nos. 63–70." National Association of Pastoral Musicians. *Pastoral Music*. 19 (1995): 48–51.